MERRY CHRISTMAS - 2005

The Back of Beyond

The Back of Beyond

A SEARCH FOR
THE SOUL OF IRELAND

James Charles Roy

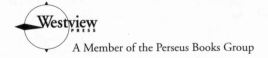

Westview PRESS

A Member of the Perseus Books Group

Credits and Permissions

Extracts from the poetry of W. B. Yeats are from *The Collected Works of W. B. Yeats, Volume 1: The Poems, Revised;* edited by Richard J. Finneran (New York: Scribner, 1997). With the permission of Scribner, a division of Simon & Schuster, Inc. and A. P. Watt Ltd. on behalf of Michael B. Yeats.

Extracts from the poetry of Francis Ledwidge are from *The Complete Poems of Francis Ledwidge,* ed. O'Meara, The Goldsmith Press Ltd. (Ireland, 1997).

Westview Press books are available at special discounts for bulk purchases in the United States by corporations, institutions, and other organizations. For more information, please contact the Special Markets Department at The Perseus Books Group, 11 Cambridge Center, Cambridge MA 02142, or call (617) 252-5298.

Published in 2002 in the United States of America by Westview Press, 5500 Central Avenue, Boulder, Colorado 80301–2877, and in the United Kingdom by Westview Press, 12 Hid's Copse Road, Cumnor Hill, Oxford OX2 9JJ

Find us on the World Wide Web at www.westviewpress.com

Book Design by Heather Hutchison

A Cataloging-in-Publication Data record is available from the Library of Congress.

ISBN 0-8133-3909-X (HC)

The paper used in this publication meets the requirements of the American National Standard for Permanence of Paper for Printed Library Materials Z39.48–1984.

10   9   8   7   6   5   4   3   2   1

For Jan Victoria
First a boat, now a book

And that this place may thoroughly be thought
True Paradise, I have the serpent brought.

—JOHN DONNE

Contents

Illustrations

IRELAND

Atlantic Ocean

Irish Sea

Celtic Sea

Lough Derg
St. Patrick's Purgatory
Inishmurray
Drumcliff
Sligo
Carrowmore
Newgrange
Slane
Boyne R.
Kells
Hill of Tara
Lia Fáil
Trim
Dublin
Ballintubber Abbey
Strokestown
Roscommon
Glinsk
Connemara
Inishbofin
Ross Abbey
Ardoileán
Omey I.
Clifden
MacDara's I.
Woodlawn
Athenry
Clonmacnoise
Galway
Moyode Castle
Roxborough House
Inishmore
Aran Islands
Coole Park
Thoor Ballylee
Bunratty Castle
Shannon
King John's Castle
Limerick Cashel
Cormac's Chapel
Scattery I.
Askeaton
Athassel Priory
Knockgraffon Motte

0   MILES   50
0   KM   50

CORNER DESIGNS:
Grave Markers, Clonmacnoise

Jane Crosen, Mapmaker

You're Welcome to Ireland

 reland is different. Accept that from the start. It's friendlier, easier, warmer, happier, more straightforward, and less threatening to strangers than any other European nation I can think of. It also happens to be, for those who come to know the place, a land foreign, cold, harsh, perverse, uninviting, and devious. Its ability to reconcile such contradictions is but one of many factors that combine to make this country unique. For better or for worse, there is only one Ireland.

In my cramped airline seat, scientifically designed to accommodate in some comfort three-quarters of an average human being, I calculate that this is my twenty-second trip to the Emerald Isle, a conclusion that stuns me. I'm looking forward to my visit—and having paid an astronomical sum for this airline ticket, I'd better be—but in actuality I'm dreading it. "I love the place," I say to myself, adding a split second later the proviso, "I hate it too." This makes me a seasoned traveler.

Cleverly outwitting the Aer Lingus crew, I've brought my own pint bottle of gin aboard. This is one "tourist" who won't be shelling out $4 for a drink. I'm startled instead to be offered complimentary cocktails, a first in my experience with Aer Lingus, whose miserliness was once legendary. Or was it prudence? I recall the danger being explained to me once: You never give free drinks to Irishmen, especially at 35,000 feet.

I settle down to watch the in-flight movie, something called Sgt. Bilko, which I thought was a television show from the discredited 1950s. After a few minutes I turn the sound off and drift into a meditation of sorts on what's going on with my life. In many ways, it's a very happy picture—a great marriage, two enviable children, the semblance of good health, enough money to fill the void come dinnertime. Professionally, however, and too obsessively, I admit, things could be better. Here I am, over fifty, flying to a country that's been a passion all my working life, and yet I'm coming across the great, trackless ocean pretty much a professional vagabond. Four books published on Irish history and travel, a reasonable handful of articles and monographs in print as well—good enough for an academic résumé at any rate—but I've nothing to show for it. My sister, a tenured professor in Baltimore, tells me there's nothing wrong with being an "independent scholar." Lots of weirdos, she says, have been "independent scholars." What I have to do is network, she advises, and I've been networking ever since, for the past decade or so—going to Irish conferences, shaking hands with penniless academics whose knowledge of the arcane astounds me, meeting Irish consuls in various outposts who host the beggarly cocktail parties that keep these functions on track, advising people to forget it when they ask me, as a favor, to help them trace their ancestors. "You don't want to know the details," is what I usually say. I've even had calling cards printed with both my addresses, the one in Massachusetts and the other in Galway, but I've never been called by anyone with a question or a query or a paying job offer. My publisher informs me just before takeoff that my newest book manuscript is "boring." "We can't print this," he tells me. Oh, what a lonely way to die. My wife doesn't even bother to dignify what I do now as work. "Ireland is your hobby" is the way she puts it. In circumstances like these, you go your own way and make the best of it.

The trouble is, I'm not going over to research or write the next great book on Ireland. No, I'm going over to lead a tour. I've been told that is what struggling authors do, and the travel agent who's putting this thing together seems worried. He asks me plaintively before I leave, "You do know Ireland, don't you? You do know what you're talking about?" I assure him I do. I'm an expert.

Most flights to European countries usually land in their elegant capital cities somewhere in the congenial time frame of 8 to 10 A.M. After you emerge from Customs, your hotel room has probably been cleaned after its previous occupant's departure and awaits your arrival, or the friends you've arranged to pick you up . . . well, they've not been unduly put out to be at the airport in time to shake your hand and grab your suitcase. Not so in Ireland. Remember, this is a different sort of place.

Along with my bedraggled fellow passengers, I emerge from the plane at about 5:30 in the morning and lumber a few miles through corridors to pick up my belongings. In the dark I make out a baggage cart roaring in from the tarmac, spewing forth three or four suitcases as it careens around a tight corner before burrowing down into the subterranean fastness of the luggage-pickup system. Some poor travelers from Chicago or New York or Boston are going to find their stuff pretty messed up. The ramp is scattered with belongings: a set of pajamas, a sweater, underwear, a cosmetic bag, all spread about on the unlit pavement. A second baggage car takes the corner and grinds these innocent accoutrements of travel even more into the dirt. I imagine the baggage handler gaily whistling, his hat cocked to the side of his head, a cigarette dangling from his lips. In truth, he's probably hungover from the night before.

I walk into the empty confines of the arrivals hall of Shannon Airport at 5:45 A.M. The panorama is devoid of life. One or two car rental desks are open, hucksters waving to us with brochures. One or two coach tour operators hold up their beckoning signs—"St. Mary's Parish Tour" or "Gather Here, Shamrock Travel"—but other than that, this is a country fast asleep. To make matters worse, my ride is not here. Who can blame him? To get to Shannon from my neighborhood in County Galway, my friend Seamus would have had to be out of bed at 4:00 A.M., a fate worse than death for most Irishmen. I have no choice but to wait.

For three hours I watch Ireland awaken. I observe the bookstore come to life, the newspaper kiosk open for business, the bank people arrive, prepared for another boring day of screwing people on the exchange rate. Most of all, I tally up tourists, and even though it is September, they disgorge in a steady, alarming stream, mostly from the United States.

Many are here on golfing holidays. I myself have never understood people's passion for this sport. I count over fifty golf bags being loaded into huge private coaches, their owners generally of late middle age and overweight. Sports fishermen seem thinner and more athletic, arriving with little tubes containing rod and reel. Little do they know that there aren't any fish left in the west of Ireland, once so famous for its trout- and salmon-choked streams and rivers. Today's *Irish Times* says that more than two hundred trawlers flying the standard of Japan are stretched along a seventy-mile net line just outside the legal limit of territorial sovereignty. With their usual tact, the Japanese appear to be vacuuming the ocean floor. Fish couldn't return to spawn in Ireland even if they wanted to.

A few youngish hippie types float by with backpacks; German and French couples too, many with bicycles they assemble in the lobby. Large pilgrimage tours, led by the parish priest, himself usually doddering and looking somewhat addled, march off in polyester, in all probability head- ing for the Marian shrine at Knock and then the Ring of Killarney, their average stay (according to industry "sources") being six days. I know "polyester" is a cheap shot, but that's what it looks like to this observer. All this is rounded off by a few Down East types, clearly moneyed, who rent their cars in an offhand sort of way and flash off into their future of horseback riding, picnics by the sea, and luxury hotels. And then there's me, the old pro, standing around waiting for his ride.

But Seamus is not coming. As I think about it, and I do have the time to, it occurs to me that I neglected to take into account that you gain a day traveling east and that I gave my poor friend the wrong arrival date. I obviously know what I'm doing after all these trips abroad. I approach the handsome desk of the representative of the public bus line, the logo of which is, aptly as it turns out, an Irish setter, probably the most neurotic, unreliable, and skittish animal ever bred. It is no surprise to me that to get to my place in Galway, as the crow flies a distance of only forty-five miles, will require three bus changes, layover times that total three hours, a cost of nearly £25, and a drop-off point some four miles from home; not to mention the fact that all these buses will be late and will undoubtedly miss their connections. If lucky, I'd walk in my front door by dinnertime. All my arrogance evaporates. I'm stuck.

I hang around the car rentals, approach a sympathetic American with my tale of woe, and ask for a lift. Mistaking me, amazingly, for a wayward youth, he agreeably says yes. His mood turns when, during our drive, he discovers I'm an adult, and his pleasure when he drops me off halfway to my destination is manifest. There I begin a long, miserable day of hitchhiking.

Forget all this talk about "Ireland of the Welcomes" and the friendly, open Celtic spirit, at least when it comes to cadging a ride. If you look like an ax murderer, no matter where you are, no one is going to stop even if you wave money in the air. I lug my ill-assorted gear off the main road to a country lane, thinking I will do better with local traffic than with truckers and businessmen speeding toward Galway City. I comb my hair again and rearrange my attire, but farm wives want nothing to do with me.

At least it isn't raining. Cold and damp, yes, but no actual rain. I stamp my feet to keep warm and start smiling as cars go by, yet time passes slowly. I have to check myself from wallowing in self-pity, because Oliver Goldsmith was right, "Every man has a thousand vicious thoughts, which arise without his power to suppress." The gin I'd been drinking since takeoff gurgles in my stomach, turns my palate. The thought of food is repellent, but after three hours here doing nothing, I eat an airplane roll stowed in my pack to while away a few minutes. I finally get a lift from a farmer, my sleeping and duffel bags tossed into the rusty bucket behind his tractor. He feels so sorry for me that after turning in at his place he tells his wife to get out the car and drive me home. She looks at me suspiciously but agrees. On an Irish farmstead, a man is still the boss.

My grudging chauffeur leaves me off at the Hartys' farm. She is amazed at where I live and eager to leave it. Strange buildings tend to oppress the Irish, and if they're "lonesome" places as well—as this is— you get a look like "ye must be daft" to go along with the blank, uncomprehending astonishment of it all. I offer her a cup of tea, knowing she will refuse. I wave good-bye, and she waves back, which is heartening to me and a relief to her.

My little pied-à-terre in Ireland is a fifty-five-foot-high stone tower, built around 1560 by a mongrelized Norman family known as the Dolphins. This building was pretty much their last throw of the dice, in Irish terms, since everything else this family attempted or aspired to achieve turned sour. Within thirty years of moving into this dank and gloomy fortress they were cast aside into the wet and cold, joining the traditional diaspora of evicted Catholic losers from this benighted land who inevitably ended up in places they never dreamed, even in their worst nightmares, might swallow them up—Canada, Barbados, the hot and dusty climate of Iberia, even Australia. Their string of vicissitudes is just another sad tale in the long, tumultuous saga of what we call Irish history.

The Irish have called my home Moyode Castle for the past four hundred years, Moyode being an Anglicization of the Gaelic *Maigh*

The ruins of Moyode Castle, 1982, before restoration

Fhód, which means the field of the grassy sod. This was famous champaign country, perfect grazing land for herds of cattle, sheep, and horses, the elements of wealth in sixteenth-century Ireland. But if you were to say Moyode to any of the locals around here, it would signify something else: the nucleus of what was once a large estate comprising 3,000 acres, the holding of a Protestant Ascendancy family known as the Persses, whose forebears had come over from Northumberland in the early 1600s, flush with avarice to acquire new lands and wealth.

Originally Protestant ministers, the Persses scrambled up as many "livings" and curacies as they could, and prospered on the backs of the local Catholic populace, who paid for their support via the infamous tithe. The initial family manor lay a few miles south of here, Roxborough House, noteworthy today as the birthplace of Lady Gregory in 1852 and redolent with literary associations. A junior Persse from that line established Moyode in the eighteenth century. Burton de Burgh Persse built a huge and ambitious pseudo-Gothic pile with Tennysonian towers and crenellations in 1823 and named it Moyode House. The call of horn and dog pack echoed about these fields for a century. Hunting foxes was an obsession of the Persses, one they carried out with skill, dedication, recklessness, and financial abandon. It was the only thing in life they really cared about. Ruined by Land Acts initiated by William Gladstone and finally completed in 1903, their great Camelot stood shuttered and empty until 1916, when the Irish Republican Army occupied the place briefly while Dublin burned. During the Troubles in 1922, it was torched to the ground. Its ruins stand next to the Hartys' place. There is hardly a Persse to speak of left in this country.

Alphonsus and Marie Harty are my immediate neighbors, their farm and barns nestling in the shadow of Moyode House. Marie hates the isolation of Moyode, which is about a quarter mile in from the road. She'd much prefer to live where the Taylors do, next to the now-ruined Georgian gate lodge that formerly served as entry to the Persses' estate. Old Frank and Mick Broderick, two bachelors well along in age, complete our mélange. They live in a skeleton of semiderelict buildings at the back of Moyode House, where remains still stand of the dairy, coach house, stables, blacksmith shop, milking parlor, kennel yard, gardener's quarters, and the formal garden itself. The garden remains pungent with the odor of boxwood, even though the sheep that Alphonsus grazes here have nibbled everything down to the roots. Moyode Castle stands three hundred yards east of all this.

The Hartys are not home, but they've left the ponderous "key to the castle" on their windowsill. I trudge across the great field to my noblest possession.

Moyode Castle is situated on the far end of an immense thirty-five-acre pasture. Even today, the agricultural value of this land is amply recognized. When I bought what was then a ruin in 1969 from a local farmer, he had no qualms selling me the building. But acreage—now that was a different matter. I own the tower, a footprint of land in front of it, and a long right of way to the nearest paved road that probably totals in all a few square meters. The sale was contingent on my willingness to forswear ever building a fence or any other barrier that might prevent the nocturnal wanderings of livestock, and that was fine with me. I stand in solitary splendor away from cars, distractions, subdivisions, the hurly-burly of a New Ireland. This is a lonesome spot for sure, just the place to brood and lick your wounds; in Yeats's words, my "emblem of adversity."

2

Cleaning House,
Cleaning Mind

t is never enjoyable returning to Moyode after a long absence. I was last here eighteen months ago and left everything in reasonable shape, but Ireland's miserable weather, featuring in winter a long, continuous wave of dank western winds off the Atlantic, reduces everything to a moldering, oppressive decay. The great outer door, freshly stained by myself before leaving last time over here, looks weathered and denatured, its long iron hinges speckled with rust and almost cemented in place. It takes heaving and cursing for me to push it open. I immediately step into a several inch-deep mound of excrement, the biological inevitability, by the look of it, of having a colony or two of bats living in the castle. The floorboards in the great hall are flecked with large pods of white slime, telltale evidence that the building is springing leaks, the rainwater pooling in various depressions of the wood, and beginning the inexorable slide toward rot. The windows—long narrow slits of glass fitted laboriously into what were formerly embrasures for archers—resemble an Amazonian jungle of spiderwebs, whose makers are now feasting on the autumnal reemergence of tasty butterflies, of which hundreds still flutter in the air to greet me. The plastic wrap over my stove and ice chest glisten with moisture, the kitchen table is heaped with chunks of sixteenth-century mortar that have fallen twenty-two feet from the apex of the hall's

ceiling to land below. Dirt, dirt, dirt, is everywhere, and a few crows' nests clog the great chimney. My coal stoves are a mess, as usual. Foolishly I left the dampers and chute doors closed: They are rusted shut, preventing me from lighting a quick, warming fire.

I am severely depressed, to say nothing of tired. Going up to the top floor, I clear off my sleeping platforms, roll out my down bag, and ignore everything in the sweet balm of utter exhaustion. I haven't really closed my eyes in thirty-two hours. "Sleep is pain's easiest salve," wrote John Donne, "and doth fulfil all offices of death except to kill."

Around midnight I awaken, having no idea at all where I am. My wife often sits bolt upright in bed when we sleep here, in a cold sweat of fear. She's the type of person who sometimes gets nervous in elevators—no way out!—and she feels the same about the dungeonlike claustrophobia of Moyode. "Even if I planned to throw myself through the window to commit suicide, I couldn't do it here," she complains. The tiny window slits particularly grate on her nerves because they bar you from the outside, cut off the view, and turn you inward, even though they admit plenty of light and give these large rooms, especially on sunny days, an airy feel. But she can escape to the roof, our kids tell her. "You can throw yourself over the side up there if you want to."

I climb to the roof myself and walk around the battlements. There is, for a change, no gale-force wind to contend with this evening, so I can go to the bathroom up here without worrying that it will spray back all over my feet. I can hear the stuff trickle to the outside walls via my drainage system of pipes, stone catchments, and gutters. At least something here works as it should.

The night air, though heavy and moisture-laden, is refreshing and clean against my face and bare legs. The night is pitch dark, with not a single light to be seen except in faraway Galway City. When I first bought this place, Galway was pretty much what it had been since the fifteenth century—a downtrodden, dirty, depressed provincial backwater. You could stand up here and not know the place existed. Today, it's the fastest growing metropolitan area in the entire European Union, a progression demonstrably apparent on the western skyline, where a blaze of generalized illumination now marks the city's presence.

Despite this aura of impending urbanity, I feel full of myself and very well, considering all the mishaps of my first few hours here. This is my kingdom that I'm urinating over. I own the place. I rebuilt it. For once, this man's home is his castle . . . the Barony of Moyode. I recall that just a few months ago English auctioneers had a fire sale of hereditary titles, many of them Irish: the Baronies of Conamaragh and Lecale are two that come to mind. My wife and I sat around mocking the poor, status-seeking dodos who would buy such decadent scraps of snobbery for thousands of dollars, but what I didn't dare reveal was that I could be tempted. Baron of Moyode? It has a nice ring to it, and let's face it, a coat of arms would do wonders for my otherwise pedestrian calling cards.

The next day is a blaze of activity. How I love this place! I sweep the castle three times from top to bottom, open every orifice I can to air out the great rooms, wash all the windows, clean the kitchen bric-a-brac, and light two enormous fires in the now-operable stoves. Alphonsus herds in some cattle to my little courtyard (called a bawn) outside the doorway, and these behemoths, although depositing great heaps of manure, also clear away rampaging undergrowth and weeds. By evening of my second day I'm drinking gin the Irish way (with water, no ice), grilling lamb chops by candlelight to the dying wails of Isolde booming out from my revived cassette player, and warming my posterior in front of a blazing fire banked up inside the major fireplace, about twelve feet long and eight high. In the later evening I tramp about the demesne, dropping in on my friends and neighbors, drinking tea and eating fresh soda bread. "Ah, Jim, sit ye by the fire," old Frank Broderick says to me. "We've been lonesome for ye." He brings out a nip of Irish whiskey, which I abhor, and we have a drink together. His toast, "Ye be home again."

My last stop is the Hartys. Marie and Alphonsus are in their midforties and straddle the divide of change that has so altered the face of Ireland. Old enough to respect and honor many traditional attitudes that so governed the rural outback for generations, but young enough to embrace the surge of modernity that has reduced their parents' values to obsolescence, they train a wary eye in both directions. In many ways, they provide me with a useful barometer that either confirms my own jaded impressions or forces me to reconsider what I've thought as overly hasty. This year's report strikes me as gloom filled.

The old ways clearly are under total assault, and by that I do not mean the Ireland of donkey carts or faerie forts. Those were discarded fifteen or twenty years ago, and although an industry of sorts still persists to mine that vein of touristic nostalgia, it has long been buried by the locals of my acquaintance as incidental to their lives. By the old ways I mean family, religion, and cultural respect.

"The family, Jim, it's falling apart even here in the west," says Marie, a woman of firm opinions. She relates to me instances of generational divide in our rural neighborhood here that would have been unheard of in previous years. "The children pay no heed whatever to what their parents say to them," she explains. "The drinking, the wild ways, the brazenness of behavior, it's all beyond containing. Most girls who go to the altar these days, it's the usual thing if they have a baby a year old or even more already. The single mother, I know ye have it in the States, but it's now a fact of life here too. And no one cares. There's no stigma to it at all."

"The amazing thing about that," Alphonsus interrupts, "is that Galway has the highest per capita use of condoms in Ireland. You ask yourself, how could all these girls get pregnant?"

"From the looks of some of those lads, I'm amazed they know which way to put them on." Marie is angry.

Religion? It holds the moral high ground still, though barely, but it enjoys no authority to enforce or back that up. Ireland appears to be five or ten years behind the times in uncovering and then publishing various scandals involving pedophiliac priests, but now everyday's newspaper is full of sordid detail. On tonight's news is the latest mess, the escapades of Roddy Wright, Roman Catholic bishop of Argyll and the Isles in Scotland, who has just eloped with one of his parishioners whom he was counseling after her divorce. The Church might well have covered this one up except for the cumbersome fact that the bishop's paramour of the preceding twelve years, by whom he had a son, was unaware of her female competitor and, rightly or wrongly, felt betrayed and informed the press. "Randy Roddy," as he was then anointed, fled to Ireland with his new woman friend, meanwhile making himself available to London's tabloid press for a fee in the vicinity of six figures.

"We still say the rosary here," says Alphonsus, but he doesn't know anyone else who does. "It isn't even safe anymore to have the electric vigil light on under the Sacred Heart"—a fixture in almost every rural household in the country. "Old Paddy was saying his prayers the other night before bedtime, kneeling in front of the Sacred Heart—now there's a quaint old habit—and there must have been a surge in the current or something because it blew up in his face and almost burned the house down. Ah, the omens are bad enough these days for Holy Ireland."

Cultural erosion is a far more difficult problem to define and admits, by and large, to a variety of impressionistic interpretations. How valid any of them may be is open to question, which I readily admit, though as a professional observer, I'm entitled to my opinion.

Certainly on a coarse level there isn't too much leeway, involving as it does the issue of law and order, the lack of which filled volumes of official correspondence sent to London by hapless officials of the Crown from as long ago as the 1100s. The Irish, according to them, were an incorrigible race of beggarly thieves and night stalkers to whom no outrage was beyond committing. So what's new about the rash of break-ins and muggings that characterize the 1990s in the west of Ireland?

"Ah, Jim, you're too forgiving altogether," says Alphonsus, who remembers the 1950s as a "glorious" period of relative poverty, backwardness, isolation, but oh so quiet nights. Forget the fact that everyone else considers those years a hangover from the austerities of the Eamon De Valera government. For those who were living through them, they were times of at least mental security, where isolation was seen as good for the soul, and who cared anyway that Ireland was regarded (in the words of an eighth-century cleric) "a pimple on the chin of the world?" For Alphonsus, those days come close to being a fond memory.

With some relish, both he and Marie recount a long list of local disasters: enormous drug busts along the largely forlorn coast of Galway, ideal for hundreds of years to smugglers and outlaws; nightly break-ins across the county, many characterized by violence and kidnapping; several sensational murders, one involving a local priest. He recounts the story of a mutual acquaintance, bereaved by the death of her college-aged daughter, who arranged and then attended a novena for the repose of the poor girl's soul. Thieves broke into her house while the service was going on and ransacked the place, discovering our friend's eighty-five-year-old mother ill in bed. They dragged her to a chair, bound her with rope, and threatened to beat her with a metal bar to find out where any money might have been hidden. "Now you know, Jim, those lads were from Dublin, but how did they know which house to go to? And that's the worst of it! Some local people tipped off these lads, and if that isn't the lowest thing you ever heard about. And old people, Jim, they're the targets. It's common for them to be preyed on, because old people often have money in their house, being distrustful of banks and tax people. Some thieves tied up one old man in Oranmore, hit him with a hammer to make him talk, then just left the poor man to die, which he did, of starvation! He wasn't missed for two weeks and starved to death in the chair. Poor Frank here in the demesne, his place was broken into too!"

I register disbelief at that one. "But Frank told me he owns only three things in the world: his watch, a suit of clothes, and his bicycle. He has nothing to steal."

"True enough, Jim, but he had £400 under his mattress, and he did have two old brass candlesticks that his father found in the rubble when Moyode was burned in the Troubles. Everyone in the parish borrowed them when they had the Station in their house, which means everyone knew he had them. So the thieves made off with those. It's terrible, Jim, just terrible. You'd better lock your door now when ye be leaving, if only for a hour or two, which I know you've never done here. The Ireland of Saint Patrick is dead and gone."

In more ways than one, of course. Let's return to a boggier issue, one more open to dispute and less draconian than crime. Back in Saint Patrick's day, for instance, the people spoke Irish. Right up until the Great Famine, sizable numbers of the peasant population still used this ancient language as their primary tongue, particularly in the remoter regions of the west, despite the temptations and pressures to abandon it. But the massive shrinkage in Ireland's nineteenth-century population, whether through emigration or death from starvation and disease, devastated whatever chances Irish might have had to survive. The Catholic church in particular gave up on it, encouraging the popularization of English, seeing it as an inevitable concession to the Empire should Ireland wish to emerge from its cocoon of economic isolation. Within three generations of the famine, Irish had largely disappeared. By 1911, only 17.6 percent of the people in the country were Irish speakers. Attempts to revitalize the language since independence in 1922 have largely met with failure, all this despite reconfiguration of the country's schooling system (which doggedly emphasized Irish), the expenditure of enormous treasure, and the statutory requirement of having to speak the old tongue as a requirement for civil service or governmental employment.

Despite what has been, in effect, an educational fiasco, it has been fashionable these past twenty years to speak of an Irish Renaissance. The Tourist Board would never let us believe that Irish continues to face extinction, nor would the eager college kids who flock to the *Gaeltacht** in summer to practice speaking the language in everyday

---

*Areas, mostly in the west, that feature significant numbers of Irish speakers, who generally receive government grants to encourage their continuing usage of the language in their homes.

Persse family triumphal gateway, Moyode House (to the left, former dairy, now the Broderick cottage)

situations ever let on that the entire exercise is but a symbolic gesture. I recall sharing the speaker's platform at a forum at the University of Wisconsin where a distinguished professor of history assured the audience that Irish was definitely on the rebound. "When I'm in Galway riding the bus, I overhear people conversing in it. Everyday, ordinary people, not college students. The language is alive, colloquial, and growing in usage. Rejoice!" I remember saying in reply that Irish is a university course, not a living language like Hebrew. For better or worse it's a dead horse, window dressing, a wonderful thing to preserve but no gateway to the year 2000 or the handmaiden to European unity. I remember his fury; he wouldn't shake hands with me later. "What are you trying to do, bury Irish?"

Well no, not really. I like the idea of Irish as well as anyone, but as a yardstick it serves to emphasize the cultural deterioration that I see everywhere around me. I ask Alphonsus and Marie the usual questions. Do they know any Irish? A word or two. Do their children? Yes, they take it in grammar school. Will it help their three boys in any way toward sharing in the progress that Ireland appears to want, an integration with continental Europe and the financial plenty that will come with it? They laugh in my face. Irish is something learned today, forgotten tomorrow. It's antique, irrelevant, a nuisance, and waste of time. "There's no return in Irish here," says Alphonsus. Computers and television and jobs abroad in Germany or Italy—what has an old dead language to do with that?

"What about your culture as Irish people?"

"I have no objection to people learning Irish in college if they want to. They can learn Latin too, or any other language; in school these sorts of subjects more or less collide, and no harm done, as they say. But the past is the past, and Ireland has spent altogether too much time thinking about olden times. Farming is humped in Ireland today. My boys, or two of them anyway, will have to learn something else, and the Irish language won't take them there."

Neither will ruins or vestiges of their ancient history. The Earl's Chair, a pre-Norman coronation mound used for almost four centuries, was located just a few miles from Moyode on the banks of a nearby river. The farmer whose land it sat on grew tired of people walking across his fields poking around, and he bulldozed the place into oblivion. An ancient Celtic earthwork, within eyeshot of my tower, was likewise destroyed. The old triumphal gateway leading back to the stables, kennels, and working farm of Moyode House—which still has the Persse coat of arms on it and a memorial plaque reading "Erected by Burton Persse Jun Esq. 1823"—is about to be dismantled and carted off to grace some rich American's driveway in County Meath, and no one seems to care much about that. At least it won't share the melancholy fate of nearby Castle Lambert's seventeenth-century bell cote, demolished ("knocked" in the parlance of our time) as inconvenient to the comings and goings of lorries. The architecturally sublime Church of Ireland edifice in our nearby market town crumbles to ruin, abandoned by an impoverished Protestant hierarchy, and serves now as the haunt of aimless teenagers drinking beer and smoking pot. The great marble plaques erected in memory of various Moyode Persses make ideal targets for empty bottles and cans, and the nave has found a use as an impromptu hearth for winter bonfires. The Irish government spends millions on preserving the obvious, places like the Rock of Cashel, but it lets everything else slide to ruin. If that doesn't smack of a cultural wasteland in the making, I don't know what does.

I go home in darkness across the great field of growing green grass, guided by the light of kerosene lamps shining through the windows of Moyode, a warming sight indeed. I am not unduly upset by all the bad news I've heard, though it blends in with my traditional mind-set as the wandering Jeremiah of Ireland's decay. Having been a visitor here all my life, but more frequently over the past thirty years, clearly, I've seen all this coming for quite some time.

My own reputation here reflects it. I'm the King of the Castle to all my friends and neighbors, the man who looks backward, not forward. Everyone else has a new house, a new car, a new stereo, portable phones by the gross, and a fistful of bank cards with which to forestall the financial day of judgment. Jim still drives his old '69 Citroën, to the amusement of all, says no to electricity, and hates telephones. He's an "eccentric" who asks silly questions about history and famines and old Norman knights and what the Irish words are for such and such, who stops on the road to pick up trash, who can be seen on late afternoons cutting wildflowers or visiting some of the old folk still living in thatched cottages, who curses like a banshee every time a field gets broken off into housing sites. He's the man who claims that Galway City was a wonderful place until the money started pouring in, who claims the Irish were better off in the 1950s—something about poor in pocket, rich in spirit, and isn't that typical of an American? He even says he might join all the Germans and move to Connemara or Donegal, but you can never believe what he says; he's a queer old fellow indeed, he must miss his wife or something, and hasn't he put on the weight, it must be the drink.

3

Heading West

ctually, I rarely miss my wife when I'm in Ireland. It's not that she hasn't a genuine affection for the place or for our friends here, but the building, well, it leaves her cold in more ways than one. She laughs when I talk about our "restoration" of Moyode. "That's in the eye of the beholder," she says. "My idea of a restoration is not a place where you live like a pig."

She's right, of course. People go all wet when they hear we have a castle, so she tells them the truth. If they ever visit us, it will be a real sixteenth-century experience. No hot water, no bathing facilities to speak of, cold and dank, bats buzzing around at night overhead, wretched food, dirty weather, sleeping bags all the time, claustrophobic and Dickensian, especially when the coal stoves down-vent in heavy winds and you get black lung disease from the foul air, rather like London in the old days of pea soup fogs. All matched by the King Jim baloney as we wander about the countryside. This place is just too Jimcentric for her liking. Everyone throws rushes at my feet as we go from place to place, even though she's been coming here for as long as I have.

But worst of all, she sees the ruination of Ireland as the inevitable, unavoidable conclusion of any enterprise having to do with the Irish people. It's in their genes to throw away the paradise they inherited, to grab like a pack of greedy children all the trash that western, industrialized civilization—meaning the United States—has to offer. She respects the Japanese for closing their traditional markets to American business. "Why shouldn't they? Why should they let Kmart or Wal-Mart set up shop in their country, all to peddle the third-rate merchandise that we turn out like hamburger meat." The Irish, in contrast, will take everything they can get.

We've started talking about where we plan to spend our golden years of retirement. I mention a spruced-up Moyode, but she reacts as though bitten by a tarantula. "I'm not going to die in a place that's killing itself at the same time. Forget it."

I'm thinking these thoughts as I lie in bed the next morning, and they gnaw at me and beg the question. Am I seriously considering treason?

I bought Moyode for £1,000, which in 1969 terms came to about U.S.$2,600. I remember Mrs. Uniacke, the widow of the farmer who sold it to me, wringing her hands and saying one day, "Ye'd never think to sell the place, would you?" and I had replied, "Of course not." But I could get a tidy packet for Moyode now, and as I look about me, I have to wonder, in characteristically Irish terms, if it isn't time to emigrate, moving off now before Galway City comes barging out into the countryside, spreading its pall of suburban estates—acre upon acre of tasteless imitations of the Costa Brava, tidal waves of automobiles and trash. Wouldn't it be better to make a trade while the going was good: Moyode Castle for some tidy little cottage in Connemara by the sea, far enough away from everywhere? I've always wanted to live on the ocean.

These are the thoughts of a restless person, a person never satisfied, and I know it. But I wonder whether, for once, I'm not just being practical. My wife dislikes this place, I'm getting too old to lug buckets of coal up fifty-five steps each morning, and a hot shower—well I have to admit it, I get tired of being dirty. Maybe a change would be sensible.

In fact, as I roll over in bed, I'm not quite as shallow as all that. The dissatisfaction runs deeper. If I have any profound feelings for something other than family, it is for Ireland, and my wife's complaints, despite their stridency and their ultimate intention of wounding me, ring true. Ireland, after all these years of my devotion, is betraying me.

Jan (my wife) is right. The Irish don't want to be Irish anymore. They'd rather be American or French or British—maybe even German—but they don't want to be what they've been forever. The most obvious manifestation of this is their materialism, the disease, for such it is, that eats their soul as it empties their pockets, corroding the rich depository of their spiritual heritage faster than sunlight evaporating a morning's dew. No one in Ireland is satisfied anymore. The momentum of the twenty-first century has finally plugged in here, and the pell-mell cascade for all that glitters reminds me of old westerns that I watched as a child, the San Francisco Gold Rush, the Oklahoma land grab, the urge to cheat Indians with a few beads.

There is, beneath all the blarney, a cold and callous side to the Irish temperament. I've seen it many times over, usually when people die, people that other people are glad to see die. I remember old Cathy and Stokes, her brother, lying in their little unheated cottage, both their rooms side by side, in a long lingering drift toward death. Their relations came in twice a day to light a fire and put food on their bedside tables, and then they'd leave. No chat, no love, no care really. One time I found one of the nephews going through Cathy's meager dresser looking for anything valuable. I admonished him; he told me to get out. Cathy and Stokes both died alone.

Marie tells me this is commonplace, and the root of it all is money. A friend of her mother's was dumped in a nursing home after the children took everything she had. Marie went to visit her. "She was crying and carrying on. 'These rosary beads are the only thing I have left,' and I said back to her, 'If they were worth a pound, ye'd not have them at your hand.'"

Frank Broderick, who never had any money, can't believe it. "If you had a few pence in the past, ye were generous with it; it wasn't something you hoarded or cared about. And if you had five shillings, you'd be having a grand time with your friends and all. But now all the money is flowing like water and yet there isn't enough of it. These are queer times, Jim."

If the sale of my books is any indicator, I'm looking in the wrong direction for a remedy. I come to Ireland when home in the United States has exhausted me with its energy, ambition, and bustle, when I long for a good, long, slow rummage through the past. Always interested in the glory years of the Celtic church, when its sanctity, devotion, and asceticism helped preserve the tenets of Christian life through the darkest ages of barbarian disruption, I have repeatedly traveled to remote and often barren monastic sites both here and in Scotland, places like Iona, Inishmurray, Skellig Michael, Inishkea North, the Rough Isles. These have all refreshed the well, so to speak. I have come away renewed and reenergized, ready to tackle, among other things, the banality of having grown up a twentieth-century Catholic.

I've never paid attention to a sermon in my life, for example, having never heard one worth listening to. But the patristic dialogues of the

The Way of the Cross, Skellig Michael, County Kerry

early Fathers, both those of the mainstream such as Cassian, Pelagius, and Augustine, and those from the Celtic tradition, the best known of whom are Columcille, Columbanus, and John Scotus Erigena, have always made sense to me. They spoke of commitment, endurance, hardship, and belief; they smoldered off the page like the burning bush of Moses; they made a connection of seeing and feeling to the scattered remains of crosses, beehive huts, and miniaturized oratories that crowd so many offshore islands in the Celtic world. I'm no born-again Christian, but I could be a born-again monk. It's a temptation.

"Places do not die as people do," William Trevor wrote in one of his novels, and that is the problem. I'm drawn to sites where there are no people, I'm drawn to dead Irishmen, not living ones. And yet my little circle here at Moyode has always dredged deep emotions of kinship, of belonging, from me. These are my friends, yet I seem to have a diminishing tolerance for everyone else. Can the soul of Ireland exist outside the boundaries of everyday contact with everyday people? Is it fair to expect from an entire population the virtue of hermits and holy men who fled from society a millennium ago to inhabit the wastelands of isolated hideaways and islands? Is any of this realistic, and if not, where else am I to turn for the answers? Where else is the heart of this place hidden?

I jumble my various discontents into an urge to get up and get out. My professional failures somehow intermingle with my spiritual failures, folding into a suddenly urgent realization that Ireland has fallen by the wayside too.

I check my calendar. The tour I'm to lead arrives at Shannon Airport in four days. I've time to head off to the west, and I impulsively decide to go, to go and see if salvation—a notion I cannot define—lies there by the sea. I guess I'm just fed up.

◆

Driving across the great field to the old dirt road that passes the Harty place, I notice Marie running down from her farmhouse waving for me to stop. "Your Highness, your publisher called from Dublin with a message. You've been booked on a talk show for today in Galway, they're frantic to get in touch. Now aren't you the famous writer after all!"

Pretending not to be unduly flattered, my heart exults. Finally, these people are coming to their senses! I had written my Irish editor earlier, telling him my travel dates, suggesting that I would readily agree to anything I could do to help move a few copies. This generous offer of several months ago had been cruelly greeted with booming silence. The book, I concluded, must be sinking like a rock in the ocean, and indeed, I had yet to see a copy anywhere, in any bookstore—Irish or American, it made no difference. But now publicity, that golden word, and after that, sales and surely money.

But Marie is grinning mischievously, and I can tell something is suffi-ciently miscued to afford her a joke at my expense. "And what's so funny?" I ask her. "Did you think I was a nobody?"

"Ah, not at all, Milord; here are the details. Here's where you go, here's who you ask for at the studio, and here's the time."

"One o'clock, not bad, the lunch crowd."

"I don't think so, Jim."

"Why not?"

"It says 1 A.M. here. I asked twice, to make sure, and he said 1 A.M. I think you have a word for that in the States—the graveyard shift?"

My elation dips. My wife is right: This is no career. It's a joke.

I arrive at the station at midnight, to an empty car park. I've decided after the show to continue on west into Connemara. I'll sleep in the car and go looking for saints tomorrow.

After I've taken a seat in the lobby, a young production assistant comes out to ask if I want some coffee. I've had four pints of Guinness and my stomach is sloshing back and forth like a half-filled barrel, so I decline. We sit there together uneasily—my usual effect on strangers. She wouldn't have given me a ride from the airport. "You're not nervous, are you?" she asks.

"Not at all. Should I be?"

"Of course not, there's no one listening at this hour." She asks if I'd like to sit in the control booth and hear the guest before me. He's a for-mer priest, and he's babbling on about reclaiming his wounded inner child in order to achieve a purifying catharsis so as to release primal feel-ings of inferiority and repressed pain. "Honest to God, this is bullshit," I say to her and she nods.

"Who else can you get for this time slot?" is her reply.

"Well, you've got me." She actually laughs at that.

I then babble on air myself when it comes time. The fact that my voice is booming out over the airwaves to hundreds, if not thousands of radios, all with their power switches tuned off, emboldens me to higher reaches of eloquence. What the world is missing! The announcer is friendly but tired, and he yawns in my face without embarrassment, only waking up when a red light flashes, which startles me too. Oh my God, a caller!

Since there's no direct hookup, the announcer listens to the call and then asks me the caller's question, producing a certain amount of dead time on air and a certain amount of perspiration on my part.

"Well, Jim, the caller is interested in your theories to be sure, but wonders whether you mean it when you call the saints of Ireland warriors. Where did you discover that they didn't go to island retreats in order to meditate or just pray?"

Thank goodness, an easy one. "I found that out in Seat 88 of the Boston Public Library, as a matter of fact. Seats 87 and 89, by the way, were generally occupied by street people reading phone books, usually upside down, and they gave off the kind of body odor that you'd expect from, let us say, a hermit or anchorite who didn't believe in bathing, which was an eremitic habit, by the way, in direct response to the licentiousness usually associated with the public baths of Alexandria. So in the ethos of desert theology, cleanliness was never considered akin to godliness."

I can tell from the announcer's eyebrows that I'm wandering. Time to get back on track. "Anyway, I got that from books, which I know sounds very old-fashioned, but there you have it. It's in the literature that you find the character of Celtic spirituality most clearly portrayed. Never defined, by the way, but portrayed, and graphically so, I think. The old Saints' Lives, the old legends, the ancient sagas, in all these you find a stance and point of view that is overtly aggressive and pugnacious. These men go out to their island retreats to seek Satan, to reenergize their lives, to find a challenge that goes beyond just remaining celibate. They go fully armed: breastplates of faith, helmets of salvation, spears of bodily mortification. They fight duels, they're eager for more, they have complete confidence in their own ability. Remember the Celts were Pelagians; they did not at first accept the notion of Saint Augustine that we are dependent on God and divine grace. The hermit never needed God's help in anything; in fact, the literature quite often shows the opposite, God asking the hermits for their help. Quite a role reversal, if you think about it."

"How interesting, Jim. Not very orthodox, I must say."

"Exactly so. Think of the Christian epics as a continuation, without a break, of the old pagan epics. Saint Columcille, for example, a Christian druid, a Christian Cú Chulainn."

"My heavens. I hope the bishop's not listening."

"Are you sure that wasn't him on the phone?"

The host assures me as we shake hands good-bye that our segment of twelve minutes was fantastic. "To get a quality call like that, I mean someone who's not drunk, is a real compliment."

"I wonder if he'll buy the book."

"At £30 a crack? That's dear." He ushers in the next guest, an insomnious beekeeper.

4

The Bones of Omey

ince I rarely wear a watch, I have no idea what time it is as I push down the passenger seat and crawl into my sleeping bag for the night. There's only one direct road to Clifden, the major town on Connemara's western ocean shores, and I have pulled off to a rough side road, groggily following a sign for *The Quiet Man* bridge, alongside of which I stop by a rushing bog stream. This locale, evidently, has some significance to the 1952 John Ford film starring John Wayne and Maureen O'Hara. I go to sleep reminding myself that I should rent the video sometime when I'm home. Maureen O'Hara, I think to myself, was one good-looking woman.

It must be late morning when I awaken, unnaturally aware even with my eyes closed that I am no longer alone. A large bus full of Japanese tourists, evidently movie buffs, parks next to the old heap I own, and my first sight of the day is that of several dozen eyeballs staring down at me with undisguised curiosity. In the past this sort of thing would have em-barrassed me, but I guess I'm old enough now and sufficiently indifferent that I couldn't care less, and I roll over for a few more languid moments. However, even here in the wilds of Connaught, this great trackless ocean of bog and wasteland, I cannot ignore the sensation of being a wounded whale, of being surrounded by human predators. Opening my eyes again, I see that my car is now surrounded by Asians, several giggling and taking photographs. See how "western man" lives! I have to hand it to them, when they travel they're going to take in *everything*.

I unzip my bag and roll out—oh, those hairy legs, they seem to say—hop into my pants and emerge to brilliant sunshine and this adoring mob. I shake a few hands spontaneously, which is very effective. I consider this good practice for the dreaded tour that I must lead in a few days time. Then I utter a few bromides to my uncomprehending admirers: May the road rise up to meet you. May the wind be at your back, blah, blah, blah—and off I go. What a way to wake up.

Despite my experience with Ireland, I am more or less a novice when it comes to Connemara. It has always seemed to me the place where tourists go, swarming around the gift stores for Irish sweaters, souvenir boxes of peat, and bottles of sanitized poteen, all the while snapping pictures of the few donkeys still left in Ireland. At parties I always say things like "Donegal is the place for me, connoisseur that I am; now there's the real Ireland." In fact I haven't been north for over a decade. I hate driving and it's a long, long way to go.

So this excursion of mine takes in some relatively new territory for me. I was last here in the early 1970s, and frankly, it looks magnificent. The famous Twelve Bens of Connemara to my right, as majestic an assemblage of craggy mountain peaks as there is to be had in Ireland, and hundreds of acres of bog, lake, and stream to my left. Aside from the inevitable trucks and buses, there is virtually no traffic on the narrow, winding, bump-strewn road, and this is exactly as it should be.

I continue along the little winding rumpled thoroughfare to Clifden, rolling side to side like an ocean liner navigating wave-tossed seas. My kids would get carsick on roads like these, but I'd prefer hearing their complaints and vomits than watch them sit contentedly in the rearview mirror as I speed through Connaught at 80 miles per hour on some sort of Celtic autobahn.

Though I am in a fog of irresolution for the most part—what am I coming here to discover?—I do have the name of an island destination in mind, a place called in the Irish Ardoileán, or High Island. There is supposed to be an almost perfect Celtic sanctuary from the seventh century tucked away somewhere in a little gully there between high ocean crags. I need my spiritual tank filled up, and decide if I can get there, I will.

My ambition slackens a bit as I leave Clifden, taking several almost one-laned boreens onto various outbacks and peninsulas, everywhere surrounded by vistas of unbelievable breadth and beauty. I scold myself for prejudicing this region with foolish, ill-tempered, and perhaps unfounded generalizations about tourists, those vile beings, crawling out of every picturesque cranny imaginable, when in fact this whole place seems to me deserted.

"I am haunted by numberless islands," wrote William Butler Yeats, and this line haunts me. Who knows what he meant by that remark, Yeats being the master of enigma, but I find it resonating as I locate the house of a fisherman who I've been told might take me to Ardoileán. He happens to be out on the sea as I speak with his father in a pasture near Claddaghduff. The old man is sunning himself by the wall as we watch over the boundless ocean together, a vastness speckled with islands, many of which crawled with saints back in the age when darkness and superstition could often make a man happy.

"The last two summers now, they've been the finest in memory." There's no disputing that. I ask how the fishing goes for his son.

"Not so good now, not so good. Lobstering was a fine thing years ago, but it's all gone now. I thought farmers were bad, but fishermen are the worst. They have no thought of tomorrow and they've cleared the ocean floor of every lobster between here and Benwee Head. My son does a bit of farming and he takes the Board of Works people out to some of the islands for repairs and such to the old monasteries, but he won't lay traps anymore; there's no profit to be had." We lapse into silence, overlooking in particular one large and gorgeous island very close to shore. To my amazement I watch a Land Rover plunge into the water from the mainland side and drive right across. It's rather like the Red Sea parting.

"My God, what's he doing?"

"Ah, it's only a foot deep now, the tide's going out. That's Eamon going over for a bit of herding."

"It's a tidal wash?"

"'Tis. Most of the day you can walk across."

"What's the name of the place?"

"Omey Island. I was born on that island, right there at that house. My first wife is buried in the old graveyard, you can see it from here."

"Does anyone live there now?"

"Only an old man, he lives in the old National School, he has a bit of land himself. There are some summer people who have places there, but none of the original people—they've all left. When I was a boy, oh, there were fifteen or sixteen families in the place, but it was lonesome, and even worse now."

"You still live there, then?"

"Not at all, not for years. It was an inconvenient place, to be honest, especially in winter for the schoolchildren. No, no one would want to live there now."

Except me. Full of excitement, I head down for the beach, put on my dung-encrusted Wellingtons, and wade across to Omey.

◆

There are times in this land when the melancholy beauty of a place stumbled over and discovered simply overwhelms your intellect, transforming your mind into a formless stew of incomprehensible joy. I believe firmly that this is the germ of obsession. Some people have it for cars or paintings, others for women or music. For me, it's Ireland, a gene I somehow got stuck with.

Climbing off the shoreline onto Omey, I enter what can only be described as a dreamscape, a panorama devoid of any mechanical distraction, the amphibious Land Rover having disappeared out of view, and seemingly devoid of humanoids as well. I hike up to the central boreen of the island, undoubtedly dignified in the old Gaelic by some place-name akin to "the Great Avenue," and walk into a time warp of centuries ago.

Omey, like most of the minuscule Irish islands I'm familiar with, has a single track that meanders along the course of least resistance, in the nature, not surprisingly, of the beast that first laid it out, some cow from the time of Christ, or well before that, as a matter of fact. If a little hillock lies ahead, the boreen will go around it; should a ridge of stone block the way, it will seek the easier, though undoubtedly longer, perambulation to reach the opposite side. The guiding ethos remains traditionally Irish, that time is of no importance, but that ease of travel is, especially when stone walls are festooned, as they are today, by all manner of wild flowers in bloom, from bushes of fuchsia to the lovely orange blossoms of meadowsweet. I pass cottages in various stages of disrepair, then strike off for the central, brooding, trackless hill that overlooks all of Omey. At its top, I have a complete panorama.

To the east is where I came from, the mountain-strewn backdrop of the Twelve Bens and its many compatriots; to the north, Claddaghduff, at the foot of which is a wide channel of water separating Omey from the mainland. A few battered-looking curraghs ride at anchor there, though it hardly seems a safe anchorage, being open to wind and wave.

To the south, a few other close-to-shore islands like Omey, interspersed among long ocean vistas; and to the west, the great Atlantic, out of whose bowels arise the enormous ocean rollers that pour for miles unimpeded by any obstacle, to pound this coastline every minute of day and night. Perched like a string of pearls, a series of large, mysterious, impregnable islands, all surrounded with silent white froth, stand remote and unapproachable. I pick out Ardoileán from my map, and it gives me a shudder.

◆

It has been a thesis of mine, developed in various books and articles, that the holy land of Christ and his disciples is more alive out here on the outermost fringes of the Celtic purview than almost anywhere else on earth, including, I think, even Palestine. I should adjust that remark to say that what I really mean is the holy land of the disciples' disciples, those men (and a few women) who looked more to John the Baptist than they did to Christ, fleeing "to the desert" beginning in the second and third centuries A.D., rejecting all liaison between themselves and family, society, even organized religion. They did this to purify themselves.

The haunts of the Egyptian desert, the wastelands between Jerusalem and the Dead Sea, the arid backlands of Syria, all found themselves overrun with determined, fanatical, crazed, and generally filthy hermits who daily fought Satan and his variety of deceits and trickeries. Only one snare was truly feared with any conviction, that of *accidie,* described in Psalm 90 as "the destruction that wasteth at noonday," and identified by the saintly monk John Cassian as despair.

In the fourth century this enthusiasm spread to mainland Europe and most particularly to Italy and the province of Gaul, where the energies of Saint Peter's descendants sought to moderate its core of extremism. Most people think of Saint Benedict as the father of monasticism, that most holy, difficult, abstemious way of life. In fact, Benedict compromised almost every ideal of the heroic Egyptian ascetic. Like many contemporaries (particularly the more secular bureaucrats of the early Church—the bishops—who more than anything desired regularity and control), Benedict saw the path of radical self-abnegation as too strict for the ordinary man to even contemplate imitating. The early desert ascetics were to be viewed as "miracles," too beyond the ordinary to even understand. His famous "Rule," basis for nearly all the constitutions that later congregations of monks would write, emphasized work and obedience, not the mystic communion with God that drove men like John the Baptist to the brink of insanity, if not over to the other side. Benedict, again in Cassian's view, prescribed "pabulum" to mortals like myself. If we were lucky, we might enjoy a crumb or two from the master's table, but little more lay within our reach. In Ireland this compromise position did not enjoy universal respect.

The very learned Irish historian Myles Dillon once wrote that only on the periphery of the world does ancient custom find the isolation necessary for its survival. The Church withstood enormous pressures in its early development on the Continent, with doctrine, dogma, and belief flowering, maturing, and evolving through centuries of European persecution and turmoil, to a degree where evangelists of the fourth century would have been aghast at the daily ritual of the tenth. Ireland, to a large extent isolated from mainstream concerns because of its geographical remoteness, took hold of the old ways and refused to let go.

Monastic observance among the Celts was a wayward, idiosyncratic experience. Foreign observers such as the Venerable Bede in the eighth century despaired of Ireland's wild excesses, its determination to ignore restraint, the childish enthusiasm of those who took to the Way of the Cross. "Their ploughs do not run straight," he lamented. Following the example of Saint Antony, the great Egyptian hermit, imbibing the heretic doctrines of the British Celt, Pelagius, which emphasized free will over Saint Augustine's more limited invention of dependence on divine grace, and generally ignoring the pleas of Roman popes and their emissaries, Celts sought "the desert" in their green and bountiful island home. The more dedicated of their numbers left the shores of the mainland and sought the battlefield that places like Ardoileán represented.

That, of course, had been the gist of my talk show response of the evening before, when the solitary midnight caller questioned what can only be described as the traditional depiction of a hermit as "withdrawing" from life. We think of these individuals as retiring types, gentle in nature, inclined to vegetarian diets and nature poetry. Not so, I think. We're talking here of irascible men, argumentative and quarrelsome by nature, who took matters vigorously in hand. In keeping with their Celtic temperament, they went out to places like Ardoileán as warriors. They went to do battle, they invited mortal combat. There is nothing bland about Celtic spirituality. It defied rules, it mixed a potent brew of challenges and rewards, it accepted the notion of bloodthirsty champions in a lifelong duel with Satan.

We should also remember that the whole notion of penance is an Irish specialty, probably the major contribution of the relatively minor Celtic church to the wider corpus of Catholic dogma and tradition. Confession was invented and implemented by Celtic ascetics. In keeping with just about everyone's notion of Ireland as the black hole of anachronistic religious practice, it is interesting to note that confession remains the one final difficult rite that sets Catholicism apart from other religions. It is inconvenient enough, embarrassing enough, and debasing enough to warrant reformation, according to most people. Eating fish on Friday was easy compared to baring your soul in a stifling little box to some complete stranger, or worse, a priest who might know you.

The Tourist Board loves the old myths: the portrayals of monks like the gentle Ciaran, heading off to his monastic church accompanied only by his father's gift, a milk cow ambling down the lane; or even better, the stories of Saint Patrick with his shamrock, explaining the Trinity to his benighted flock. But the genuine literature of ancient Ireland, its tales and sagas, paint a largely different portrait of the early saints. Columcille ignited the entire northern reaches of Donegal into blood feud and battle over his desire for a vellum manuscript. When he refused to follow God's instructions, an angel flogged him into submission. Ruadhán cursed the king of Tara who had offended him, tricking that foolish man with a sly deception. Saint Patrick hurled fire and ice at his druidic foes in gigantic displays of temper, and defied God on more than one occasion. Columbanus screamed incantation in the faces of kings, calling their queens harlots and worse. Kevin of Glendalough pushed women from his hermit cave into the lake below, lest they tempt him. The crosier, or abbatial staff, often doubled as a cudgel or spear with which to drive various points of dogma more painfully home.

These belligerent tendencies do not exist today. Irish religious practice lingered in archaic fashion for centuries after continental churches had conformed to papal demands for obedience. The enormously destructive religious wars of the Elizabethans on down, however, gradually disemboweled not only the Catholic church in Ireland, but all its treasured quirks and abnormalities as well. As British novelist Rose Macaulay wrote, "The Irish Church today, bemeaned and deflowered by the bitter centuries of persecution, has had plucked from it the proud flower of its intellect and breeding, reducing it to a devout provincialism."

But genes are genes. The despised parochialism of Irish Catholicism from the late nineteenth century right up to the 1950s—frigid nuns, rapping of knuckles, the blind sectarianism of rural priests—all disguise the kernel of gold that I think can still be found in the haunts of the dead, or so I pretend to think. Ardoileán glistens in the afternoon sun as a symbol of something lost long ago, difficult to find, but worth the effort.

◆

A fox interrupts my reverie, trotting in a nonchalant sort of way just a few feet in front of me. Moyode Demesne, famous for the hunt, usually sprouts foxes at all times of year, but rarely have I seen such a plump and preening specimen as this. Walking down the hill through bog and ravine to a long fresh water pond, surrounded by pasture, I figure out why. Hundreds, if not thousands of rabbit holes. A free dinner every night for Mr. Fox.

Walking along the shore, I come across the Land Rover and its operator. I yell out a hearty, "Eamon, I haven't seen you in months," which startles the young man out of his wits. I explain how I know his name and he laughs. "Once a day I come over, I drive the beasts to water," he says of the cattle lapping up their late afternoon drink. "Have ye come to see the church?"

"What church is that, Eamon? I know nothing of it." Which leads to this story: The peaks of two stone gables were swept bare of sand by a winter storm, and a priest who happened to be in the neighborhood talked a contractor into coming by with a backhoe to dig it out "and see what might be there." Backhoes, need it be pointed out, are not generally regarded as the archaeological tool of choice, and saner heads intervened after some initial devastation. The result, now sitting in an open amphitheater by the ocean, is a reasonably preserved oratory of moderate size and dating, or so Eamon says, from the 900s. It is certainly impressive as he shows me about, but the story's dénouement is somewhat more somber.

"And here's where they found the bones," he tells me, pointing to a sand dune that erodes directly to the shoreline and its tidal estuary.

"Bones?"

"After another storm a whole avalanche of bones fell out from the dune here, skulls and all, oh, it was a horrible sight. They're still com-

Uncovered oratory, Omey Island

ing." He looks about and pulls some sand from the face of the degrading dune, finds something and pulls it out. "Look at this. I'd say that's a
thigh bone." He shows it to me, then drops it on the ground.

"This must have been a cemetery," I speculate, somewhat abashed at
having this relic of humanity lying at my feet, and surprised it hadn't
turned to dust at impact. "What did they do with what they found?"

"Oh these archaeological lads came down; they put all the bones in plastic garbage bags and dropped them down there in a pile. Then I guess they forgot about them; you know, they were probably looking for chalices and gold, and the next storm took it all away. People were finding bones and things washed up all over here. The older people were pretty unhappy." It's time for Eamon to go. From bones to dinner, all in a day's experience.

Left alone, I pick up the femur. What a sad state of affairs indeed. Whoever buried a father or mother or husband or wife on this sacred spot certainly expected that on the Day of Resurrection these bones would rise again, be girded with flesh, and travel onto heaven in triumph. The idea of a garbage bag, of all things, holding pounds and pounds of bone, the sacred remains of loved ones from centuries ago, being swept out to sea in a sort of mass and common burial, surely ranks as a sacrilege of the first order.

◆

The weather is so abnormally calm that I am confident of a ride to Ardoileán tomorrow. That island has no dock or level sheltered spot anywhere on it, requiring, from what I've read, a vigorous jump onto bare and jagged rock to effect your landing, a scenario that requires calm seas. The fisherman whose father I chatted up this morning deflates me entirely by saying he plans to take advantage of all this Caribbean sunshine to cut and turn his hay. "I'll be doing that for at least the coming week," he tells me, despite my pleading and a hint of overly appropriate recompense. "Make hay while the sun shines," he laughs, an expression that I, an urban being, suddenly take the full meaning of.

I ask him if anyone else will take me. "Thanks be to God, there are several lads who would go, and if it's a drowning ye be wanting, I'll give out the names. But I've been lobstering out here for twenty-five years, and I know the place better than anyone, and if it's going out and coming back alive that's attractive to ye, then you'll wait the week. The Board of Works people had ten laborers they wanted put on just last month, so another lad and his curragh were hired along with me. He's a local too and been in these waters for twenty years, but he didn't know Ardoileán well. So a rogue wave caught him exposed on a calm day and

I watched him tossed into the sea and he had no knowledge of swimming. He says to me later, he'd never go there again. If ye have a free day, take the ferry to Inishbofin, and come by to see me again when the hay's in." This is not what I had in mind.

Later that evening I make a few inquiries at Claddaghduff's single pub, a shabby affair dominated by a grotesque, oversized color television set. At 9 P.M. it's on and showing *Beavis and Butthead* cartoons to the general amusement of several dirty children, all sucking candy and dressed up in Salvation Army attire that somebody scavenged from a dumpster in Chicago—Michael Jordan T-shirts, White Sox sweats, Nike sneakers with their toes worn away, the usual array of baseball and hockey caps worn backward: the Mighty Ducks of Connemara. If John Millington Synge wandered in here of a lonely Tuesday night looking for bits and pieces of old conversation or lore in Irish, my, what a disappointment he would have felt. As for Lady Gregory, who coursed the back roads and lanes of rural Galway on much the same mission, I doubt she'd have crossed the threshold.

The barkeep and assorted locals are indifferent to my inquiries regarding a suitable boatman. They all say Féichín, the one I've been dealing with, is the only man for the job. Clearly, a local conspiracy is at work here.

Finishing my drink, I notice a photograph on the wall. Usually all these places have Mary Robinson, Ireland's attractive and high-profile president, framed and prominently displayed. She's from the west herself and seems to have dropped into every public house in all Connemara to have her picture taken, usually shaking hands with the owner. Whether this ubiquity is public policy or merely politics as usual is an open question. Certainly she doesn't appear to be very thirsty.

But the one I study is that of two men: Charles Haughey, the former prime minister, and, by the look of it, one of the locals, both sharing smiles and drinks. The caption reads, "Two Chieftains."

In the old days of one hundred, fifty, even thirty years ago, when many of the offshore islands were heavily populated by subsistence farmers and fishermen, each community had a "king." Like some holdover from the era of clans and druids and tartan kilts, the "kings" were just that, the leaders of their people. They arbitrated disputes, coordinated harvests and expeditions ashore, oversaw the production of illegal whiskey, and, in the end, negotiated with mainland officials who came out to evict them.

Evict, of course, is a harsh word and probably inaccurate. The one episode with which I am familiar, having interviewed for a previous book the remnants of an island population, involved Inishmurray, a small community off the shore of County Sligo. The king there was one Michael Waters, a man famous among his people for having hood-winked a gullible bureaucrat from Dublin into building—with Inishmurray labor—a totally useless fishing dock. Waters knew the location was hopelessly exposed, but figured once the first was completed, and then proven inadequate, he would finagle a second out of the government, to be built where the first one belonged. This is the sort of sly, devious behavior of which sophisticated people feel islanders are incapable.

The bureaucrats had the last word, of course. When sugar rationing in World War II crippled the poteen industry, and as youngsters drifted off to English jobs never to return, Waters meekly acquiesced when Dublin told him to gather up his people and replant them "out to the country." He managed to cadge a few small cottages, built at public expense, on the shoreline closest to the island, but the moment the islanders touched foot on the mainland, his authority vanished. He had become a king in name only.

Charlie Haughey is frozen in time with the "chief" of Inishshark Island. Shark is good sized, about six hundred acres, and sits due west of Inishbofin, or farther out to sea. It was deserted, I am told, in the early 1960s. The government told the people it was too primitive a way of life, too far away from social amenities and services, and that they should give up the ways of their ancestors. Their chief led them to shore.

Charlie is nattily attired, a big politician's grin wrapped from ear to ear. He's not drinking anything as déclassé as stout, but a nice clean gin and tonic with the obligatory slice of lemon. The chief is wearing the usual beat-up cap of a peasant farmer, an old darned sweater and a ragged jacket, his teeth all yellow and his own smile, though genuine enough, lopsided and uncertain. In his hand, a glass of sloppy Guinness. Here is the old Ireland side by side with the new, the Ireland of donkey carts, curraghs, and wireless sets with the Ireland of Mercedes, teleprompters, and ice cubes in your drink. Given the choice, how many of those people would return to Shark if their chief said he was going back? I figure he'd be on that boat alone.

5

CuLTuRe Shock

oday I'm on the morning ferry to Inishbofin, and the look of the crew reminds me of a disturbing experience from over a century ago. An employee of the nineteenth-century ordnance survey expedition—a project of the British army to chart, and thus demystify, the hidden fastness of rural Ireland—made arrangements in 1832 to visit the island of Inishmurray. He waited by the nearest strand for a while until some of the islanders beached their heavy wooden boat through the surf and ordered him to board. These "wild and rough men" unsettled his composure. He felt, in his heart, that he was in the presence of people outside of civilization.

This morning's crew share the same "wild" demeanor, men from beyond the Pale indeed. Unkempt in appearance, slovenly attired, and remote to the point of rudeness, their hands and faces bright red from the outdoors, as though painted, they remind me of American Indians. The captain lurches to the boat as though in a daze, breakfast remnants all over his coat. No orders are given, no nods or motions that might indicate the nautical necessities of starting the engine or casting off our lines. Nonetheless, all of a sudden, we are under way. Life is simpler here, perhaps.

Inishbofin lies three miles offshore. It is the closest of the larger islands to the western Connemara shores and retains a population of around two hundred people. It is said that tourism keeps the place alive, but aside from a couple of hotels and bars, I wonder how a tourist's cash can make any difference here. My experience with places like this tells me there's nothing to buy except food and drink, and many day trippers, as most of the people on this boat appear to be, seem to have haversacks full of snacks.

Also predictable is my misinterpretation of the weather and seas. It may be a grand day indeed, but the ocean is tumultuous in a way that is hidden from those on shore. No whitecap or foam snarls out here with breaking waves, just enormous bread loaves, huge rollers fifteen feet high by my guess, and around twenty to thirty broad, gently bring the ferry up to a peak, then across the flat reach, before a truly dizzying descent into the trough. Many of these waves are climbed and descended at an angle that is truly unsettling, and already a few passengers are seasick. The captain retains his glazed visage throughout, however. Nothing here he hasn't seen before.

We enter Inishbofin's harbor about thirty minutes later, passing the ominous remains of a Cromwellian fort on a shelf of dirty black rocks to our right. It amazes me that so many of these islands preserve similar ruins from the 1650s, when the economies out here were, if anything, even less prosperous and more primitive than they are today. Why did Cromwell bother?

We tie up to the passenger dock and are met by a few natives trying, in a listless sort of way, to rent out bicycles. A meager shack selling potato chips and candy, the wrappers of which I will find scattered all over the island, is about all I see that smacks of actual commerce. The captain and his men meander off to God knows where. In just a few minutes the place is deserted.

Never judge one of these islands by first impressions, however. Remember that docks are, by necessity, like railroad stations, a no-frills bridge where the outside meets the inside. In Inishbofin's case, a local tragedy reinforces this notion of a meeting ground, for here a local woman had just met her death in what I would call the gray zone, the crossover point of two worlds, two differing sets of values.

The story as outlined in all the local papers surely indicates how times have changed in Ireland. The victim, incredibly it seems to me, was a young single mother native to this island. Leaving the baby in her father's care, she went out to a pub for an evening's drink, continuing on at three in the morning with one of the locals in his car, parked down by the pier. The boy claimed that neither of them was drunk, which does

The state of things, Inishbofin Island

not seem to square with his testimony at the coroner's inquest where he mentioned throwing up, passing out, and thus being deaf to the cries for help that other people, home in bed, claimed to have heard. When he awoke he did not seem to miss his companion, no longer there, and simply drove home. By then the girl was dead and floating in the sea. It is surmised she went to the end of the pier to relieve herself and accidentally fell in. Her screams went unanswered. Two days later the same ferry that brought me out carried her body to the mainland.

This is not the sort of tale, full of Gaelic folklore and native wit, that Maurice O'Sullivan told in *Twenty Years A-Growing*, his marvelous 1933 memoir of growing up on the Great Blasket Island of County Kerry; nor will it remind anyone of Tomás Ó Crohan's *The Islandman* or Peig Sayers's *An Old Woman's Reflections*. This is the currency of our times, however, the antiheroic element that invades our nostalgia for an Ireland where the fisherfolk of the rural outback die in gales and stormy seas as their curraghs are crushed by the elements, not drowned off a dock because they missed their footing during a late night tryst. I hurry off to find the back of beyond, reminding myself not to be so censorious. Dead is dead, after all, and I've been in a few backseats myself. People do not have to die just to satisfy my folkloric expectations.

Consulting a map, I head for the western end of Inishbofin. I pass one or two abandoned cars, a couple of bed and breakfasts with (am I seeing correctly?) "Visa Welcome" signs, and finally come across a boreen that promises to leave all of that behind, as it does. In a few minutes I'm on the ocean side, away from life and its sordid implications, alone with the tumult of ocean waves breaking on shore.

This is, as Synge so often reported about similar spots, a "lonesome prospect" indeed: acres of rough pasture and bog on one side, the ocean that early Celtic saints so little feared on the other. It seems incredible to me that Saint Brendan the Navigator could even think of setting off westward, as he or someone like him did, in animal-skinned vessels that predated in design the birth of Christ. "The Land Beneath the Wave" drew them on, the insatiable curiosity and desire to be ever more dependent on God's whim of wind, wave, and storm allowing them to leave the sight of land with neither fear nor regret. It is an often overlooked fact that when the Vikings, those intrepid sea dogs from Scandinavia, themselves explored the western reaches of the Atlantic, they found Irish hermits there before them in both the Faroes and Iceland. Those they killed, in their typically unreflective way, but who is to say that Greenland and even the American continent might not have witnessed Irish visitors as well. Brendan's connection with Bermuda, for example, long regarded as a quaint little tradition, may well hold a kernel of truth.

With the sun blazing and enormous cloud formations streaming in from the Atlantic, I walk a shoreline of intense beauty. Several cottages line one small bluff, and they must surely bear the undiminished force of wintertime's gales. One old fellow, whose pants are held up with twine, informs me that German and English families own most of what I see. "They enjoy the summer and leave for the worst of it in winter." His immediate neighbors are a lawyer and a doctor. "The perfect couple," he tells me.

I ask him about himself. He's native to the island but spent his entire adult life in England. Both he and his wife are pensioners, and all their children live in either Dublin or the States. "This is no place for young people; they live in the city where life is lively." I find out that by the "city" he does not mean London, Dublin, or New York, but the cluster of cottages down by Inishbofin's pier. And the girl who just died? "She should have stayed out in the country. She'd still be alive if she had."

The boreen peters out after a mile or so. I am now in trackless countryside that eventually culminates in Dún Mór, a huge primeval sea cliff projecting out to the ocean, three hundred feet high and covered with bird life. Shark sits a mile or so farther west against a setting sun, its deserted village and isolated farmsteads clearly visible. Here is the Ireland of picture postcards and calendars, a beauty, as William Thackeray said long ago, "sweet, wild and sad, even in sunshine."

Nietzsche wrote somewhere that a man should build his house at the base of a volcano. On an afternoon as bold as this I would be fool enough to agree. Exposed to all the elements of wind, sea, and sun, in glorious isolation, no one could deny that paradise lies within grasp. But in truth I feel uneasy, the place makes me nervous; it's almost too wild and too tempestuous, the challenge too great. Who's to say a good burst of gale-force bluster wouldn't throw you over the side to rocks below? I restrain my enthusiasm for grandeur. Am I saint enough for this?

6

Martyrdom

ere I am back at Shannon Airport, and this had better be right. My travel specialist (or so he likes to call himself) has not bothered to write me or communicate in any way confirming that the tour is on. Two months ago he told me when and where to show up—September 15, 6:30 A.M.—but that's been it. I think twenty souls are being placed in my care, but as to names, addresses, country of origin, physical disabilities, dietary quirks, or drug interactions, I have no idea.

Seamus and I have been up since four this morning, and he has just dropped me off. If he makes good time for home, he'll catch his usual Sunday mass. I was sincerely tempted to go back with him. Once again, I'm stuck in an airport all alone with nowhere to go.

Ever since my return yesterday from the west, I've been in a sweat. All of a sudden I had too much to do, too many deadlines pressing in, and to my dismay, too much to learn. I'm such an expert on Ireland that I had done no preparatory work for my presentation to this group just commencing, or so I theorize, their final runway approach after passing over the broad reach of the Shannon River, now glistening with the first rays of a rising sun. Even though I dreamed up the itinerary, put all the pieces together, and wrote most of the brochure, I have to admit that I haven't seen many of the places on it in years. As I practiced my introductory remarks last night, intended for presentation at this evening's welcome dinner, I found myself forgetting dates, names, and all manner of detail. "When in doubt, invent!" I told myself, but I'm Catholic enough to feel pangs of guilt even considering such an idea. I sat on the toilet for a solid hour rereading my own books by candlelight. They seemed to me to have been written by a stranger, someone far away and distant, an egomaniac enmeshed in detail who somehow forgot to brush in the larger picture. I jotted down miscellanea on flash cards to keep in my pocket for ready reference. My heart filled with misgiving. Could I do even this job right?

I stand in the arrivals hall and scan the monitors. Boston has arrived, New York and Chicago are right on its tail. Other tour operators, some in special jackets with logos, stand around with placards meant to rally the troops as they pour out from Customs. I ask where to get one of those and scratch my own moniker on it, "Eire Tours." I feel like some pathetic figure from the depression standing on a corner with a sign around my neck selling apples or pencils. As I think about it, the comparison is apt.

I am supposedly being met here by a coach driver, who at the moment is a no-show. The other tour managers, whom I immediately dislike and consider competitors, are now being flocked by energized passengers who I note, in my first experience with the group dynamic, generally exhibit a palpable sense of relief when they realize they've been met by God the Father. So far, I'm alone. My early morning mood, never bright to begin with, starts turning mean.

"Are you with Eire Tours?"

I brighten and turn around, and there's a stewardess before me with the symbol of her trade, a walkie-talkie. I marvel at her youth and freshness, but shudder when I hear the news. "We have one of your people in Customs, she's very elderly, and frankly, we think she's about to collapse. Could you take charge of her for us? She keeps asking for Jim."

I start after her into the baggage area, the old following the new, and there this bright pretty thing full of energy and purpose cheerfully hands over her burden to me. She immediately disappears while I make the acquaintance of Carol. In an instant I feel like a washed-up guy who ought to be "pursuing other options."

Carol is seated in a wheelchair, gasping as though short of breath or perhaps the result of asthma. She has a cane with a golden knob on it, and she's wearing a flowing thin cape. She appears to be an octogenarian, weighs by the look of her about eighty pounds, is pale as a sheet and shaking all over. My immediate thought is that Carol is in the process of dying.

"Are you Jim? Thank goodness! Now get my bags, the dinner on board was awful!" Thoughts as to Carol's demise are premature, it seems. "I feel fine, I'm just tired and I am not doing any more walking. Now let's get out of here." I wheel my charge right past the Customs people, who wave me through and open doors. Clearly, this is the way to smuggle drugs into Ireland.

My coach driver, who arrived while I've been dealing with Carol, has with considerable enterprise gathered up those unfortunate souls who signed on with Eire Tours for this trip of a lifetime, and they await us. These tired, bedraggled people exhibit none of the adrenaline I noted in the other arrivals, nor do they seem particularly pleased (or impressed) with me. I chatter on like a madman introducing myself and asking dumb questions—"Did you have a good trip? No? How surprising!"—all the while immediately forgetting the names that everyone's just told me. I count nine people gathered round our standard. The other operators, with thirty, forty, fifty people, seem to be sneering at us. "Is this it?" I whisper to John, the driver, and he nods. Mortified, I stifle a groan. Small-time to the bitter end.

"Can we go to our hotel now?" an elderly gent asks me. I don't dare tell him that no hotel will take us at this hour, but we have a good two-hour drive to our first lodging, and I tell John on the sly to take it slow. Wheeling Carol out into the morning's gloom, I say to everyone, "Follow me."

I had expected a minivan to trundle us around, but instead John directs us to an enormous coach, painted bright yellow. This behemoth will accommodate over sixty people and will now serve as a perpetual humiliation, signaling to the fact that no one wanted to come here and be entertained by me, no one, that is, except these nine people who obviously had nothing better to do. I review them as they board: four people well into their eighties, three matrons in their seventies, and one youngish couple pushing midsixty. None look fit, one is limping horribly, the result, I later learn, of a dreadful fall sustained in a tunnel of love contraption at Disneyland just a few days before. To round it off, one of the ladies is clearly deaf. John and I must hoist seven of our charges into and out of the bus. And this was billed as a two-week walking tour of Celtic and Norman Ireland!

"Change of plan here, Jim." John hands me over our new itinerary as we pull out in a diesel-belching roar from the airport. We had originally been booked into what my employer had called "a charming village inn," the Dunraven Arms, located in the County Limerick town of Adare. Frankly, I have never heard the word "charming" even once applied to anything in the rural Irish outback. Nevertheless, I was aware that Adare had been prettied up over the past couple of hundred years by the earls of Dunraven, who, being wealthy, had spared no expense transforming a heap of mud-splattered cabins into the replication of some bucolic idyll from Shakespearean England. This was a common Ascendancy desire, to remind oneself of noble, foreign origins (i.e., who would willingly claim to be Irish?), and to provide, as it were, a postcard in mortar and thatch of all that had been left behind in the mother lode of Great Britain.

The second earl went so far as to build, with his wife's money, a colossal mansion for himself in the midnineteenth century, a diversion attributed to his inability to mount a horse or fish anymore because of gout. The impossibly confused and architecturally mangled Adare Manor that he constructed stands as yet another justification for periodic outbursts of Jacobean revolutionary fervor, the judicious use of a guillotine sparing us perhaps from such conspicuous and ostentatious expenditures of treasure. Nowadays, of course, no one knows any better, and this enormous "pile" evokes nothing but admiration. Van Morrison even used the place on a record cover, this famous Irish singer lolling about the lawn with Irish wolfhounds, imagining, I suppose, that it was all high art. Who said rock stars were smart? The Dunravens, typically, could not afford the place and eventually sold out to a hotel chain, with the current earl, or so I've been told, repairing to a gate cottage for his lodging.

This digression is only to highlight my disappointment, as I learn from John that we are not, repeat, not, going to Adare. Adare may be a facade of banality, but at least there are handy things for me to show my tour. Yes, we could see Adare Manor, however contrary to my principles, and yes, the churches, and yes of course, the Franciscan friary, though we would have to evade flying golf balls for that visit, as this fifteenth-century ruin has been surrounded by a nine hole course, and come to think of it, my charges do not seem sprightly enough to dodge anything incoming. No matter, these are things to do. "We're going to Limerick instead," John deflates me, only a fifteen-minute drive away.

That is dreadful news, and I proceed to perspire. How am I to pass the time? Dreary Limerick is the real Ireland, not the Ireland these people want to see. I sit alone up front in the bus, plotting. How many more surprises has Eire Tours in store for me?

The long main avenue into Limerick reminds me of the States, full of gasoline stations and garish shopping malls. Nostalgia for home increases as John turns into the parking lot of our replacement hotel, which might as well be in Des Moines, Iowa. The two-story layout, the plate-glass entry foyer, the reception area with coffee shop, all surely came from the same sort of universal plan that hotel developers, devoid of inspiration, can turn to with a sigh of relief: . . . "This will do!"

Naturally our rooms are not ready and won't be for two hours. We sit in the lobby with all our luggage piled about, the opening hiss of automatic doorways a warning to all that a good long blast of morning chill will now engulf us. This allows me to introduce a few housekeeping details to my flock, the hope that everyone, as forewarned, has waterproof shoes and a good sweater at hand. This is met by blank stares. "We were told to expect weather in the sixties and seventies with plenty of sun."

"By whom?"

"By you. Eire Tours sent us a letter with your name at the bottom saying the weather was great."

"I don't have a sweater," says Carol brightly. I lead her over to the hotel gift shop, not yet open, where the inevitable Aran sweaters, mostly made from Korean yarn, lie stacked. We agree that Carol will purchase one of these immediately. "I don't see a color I like," she complains, but my menacing authority cows her and carries the day.

There's nothing for it but to while away the time here, so I order coffee for everyone (who's going to pay for that?) and start the introductory spiel I had originally planned for this evening, a forty-five minute romp through Irish history, the various phases of which I promise to illustrate at our various stops. Carol immediately falls asleep, and two others slump in their chairs and look out the windows at parked cars. But the rest, to my surprise, snap into it and hang on every word.

Maybe it's the venom in my presentation that startles them into attention. They think of me, after all, as the man who knows everything. My employer, in all his bombastic literature promoting this tour, had bandied me about as the second coming of Christ, the internationally known scholar and writer whose intellectual scribbles are not even wet on the page before they're rushed into print. I disabuse this notion immediately. My publisher, I tell them, thinks Irish history is boring and he doesn't want to publish anything boring. I wave another rejection slip just received a few days ago that implies just the reverse, however. They won't print my material, because, perversely, they don't believe any of it. "This reads too much like a novel," it says, "and a bad novel at that. Who could think that any of this possibly happened?"

This is incredible, I relate, and ask my rhetorical question of the day, quoting my old friend Pontius Pilate: "What is truth?"

A complicated question indeed, the character of Irish history. Let us begin, I say, with talking about what it is not. The story of Ireland is not the story of the universe, is not the story of Western Europe, is not even the story of Great Britain. The story of Ireland is parochial, narrow, and inward, despite all the hyperbole one hears to the contrary. At times, for instance, in the telling or listening or reading of it, one receives the impression that this small island has forever been at the center of great deeds and events from which spectators around the world can only stagger back in awe. In fact, that is utterly false.

Ireland has always been the back page, with most of its recorded history of more import, quite naturally, to the Irish than anyone else. It has never, I assure them, ever affected the greater, wider world in any fashion other than annoyance. The Romans knew the place existed yet found it too poor to bother conquering. Christian missionaries paid it little mind, sending over to Ireland the least of their brethren, ill-used zealots like Saint Patrick, on woefully unsupported missions that were more concerned with stanching bloody raids than with saving souls. Pope Gregory the Great had no knowledge of Ireland; it was Britain he cared for and he knew little enough of that country. The Vikings, fellow outcasts, did make a play for the place, but their interests in the Continent and England, where prosperous societies had produced considerably more attractive pickings to steal and plunder, was far more pronounced.

The First Crusade, a cataclysmic event in European history, contained but a handful of nameless clansmen from Ireland, and was not even mentioned in the Irish monastic chronicles. And no matter what provincial writers from Ireland may say, English kings and queens, be they Plantagenets or Tudors, Stuarts or the House of Orange, never spent more time or attention on Irish details than they had to. No matter what the Irish headache, greater fame or disaster always lay to the east of them, on the Continent, than over their shoulders out in the Atlantic. Rarely was there ever glory to be won in Ireland. The country had potential; it was there to be plucked, harvested, or planted with unwanted populations from Britain, Wales, Scotland, or Flanders, but no one's English heart was ever really in the place.

And so the legendary battles of Ireland, the armies and conquests, with their attendant great threats and parleys and treaties, with magnificent castles, abbeys, and cathedrals as venues, are all really rather mundane when taken in the context of wider European history, as indeed the physical remains testify. The armies in Irish conflicts were never so very large, the battles not nearly so immense, nor the castles ever so grand as all the old sagas relate. Just walking about the countryside will show us that. But this must not disguise what were large and grand: the people, their unbounded desires, the depths of tragedy that often engulfed them.

This is what makes Irish history so attractive and compelling, its utterly human scale. My own Moyode Castle, which Eire Tours induced me into opening for the group, demonstrates this in a very clean way. The many historical artifacts that lie a mile or two in any direction, by their mere inconsequentiality, give substance and authority to the multiple dramas that were played out there. Warriors fought and died around Moyode and its champaign field, not by the hundreds of thousands, not by the thousands or even hundreds, but more likely ten or twenty, fifty or eighty, in any given battle. But the death rattle of one man, with our attention solely on him and his miserable, tortured demise, may grip our hearts more than some anonymous, impersonal conflagration where uncounted souls have fallen. The story of Moyode removes the tissuey myths of Arthurian fantasy, the kind of romantic posturing that I grew up on in reading adventure stories by Robert Louis Stevenson and, later, Tolkien. Those we may properly classify as fantasies rather than history.

The story is thus focused on the few. It is to be seen in small decrepit ruins, in boggy fields and forests, at a crossroads here or a river crossing there. None of it is on a grand historical scale, but the familial dimensions are the stuff of Shakespeare. One wonders at the capacity of the heart for suffering. This is one area where the Irish do not exaggerate.

"Any questions?" I ask. Silence, a few looks between my audience, then, to my surprise, two of them applaud.

"That was incredible," one says, a widow from Ohio. "I had no idea this place was like that. I always thought of Ireland in terms of medieval chivalry and romance. I didn't know it was so sad."

Another says to me, "I don't think I've ever heard a speech like that on a tour like this. I gather we're not going to talk too much about leprechauns or shamrocks."

"Not with me around."

"That's great. When can we see something?" This stirs up the crowd; enthusiasm travels like Saint Elmo's fire from brow to brow. Carol is shocked from slumber. "I'm hungry," she says.

It is with a considerable sense of personal letdown that I suggest our midmorning excursion, a visit to one of Ireland's more abused sights, Bunratty Castle. It will take such and such time to get there, such and such time to tour the place, and by the time we finish, I tell them, they'll want to sleep for four or five hours until dinner. Bunratty fits the bill, so we pile away into the bus and take off.

Bunratty may well be, after Blarney Castle in Cork, Ireland's best-known medieval tower, though its emergence to the limelight of international recognition is of relatively recent origin. An immense creation in Irish terms, and central to many bloody deeds in the history of Connaught generally, and that of County Clare in particular, it was still just another ruin in 1950, one among hundreds. Superbly situated by an old arched bridge that crossed a meandering tidal estuary, it was nevertheless a lonely relic that no one particularly cared about.

That all changed when Lord Gort purchased the place in the mid-fifties and proceeded, in partnership with the government, to restore it in lavish fashion. The great oak roofs and ceilings were meticulously rebuilt, window mullions reinserted, glass restored, and battlements added, the last-named work a largely inauthentic addition that contributed nonetheless to the castle's melodramatic aura. This was considered an acceptable act of mythologizing because Bunratty's intended beneficiaries were judged to know no better: the ever-increasing numbers of visitors, mostly American, who began flooding the place as transatlantic air travel became a commonplace.

Visitors were entertained with that ubiquitous Irish invention, the medieval banquet, for which Bunratty with its Great Hall was superbly suited. Tourists could disembark from Shannon Airport, be bused to Bunratty, hear some harp music, drink some mead, look at a bevy of pretty Irish girls dressed up like Anne Boleyn, eat haunches of Irish beef (presumably free of mad cow disease), be reigned over by a mock "king" and "queen," and then be bused back to the airport and flown off

Bunratty Castle

to whatever congenial European destination they had next in mind. Feast at Bunratty in the evening, take in the Changing of the Guard at Buckingham Palace the next morning. This enterprise represented Ireland's first significant foray into the heady world of international tourism, and it was handled spectacularly well.

Not surprisingly, the novelty has worn off by now. Even though during high season the castle staff manage two sittings per evening, the status of the event has become undeniably déclassé. I haven't seen a full color ad for the place in the *New Yorker* for years, and frankly, I wouldn't be caught dead in the place, bib encircled, beef bone in hand, a tin crown on my head. I disguise these thoughts from the group.

We enter an immense car park. Because it is Sunday morning, the place is pretty well empty, as I had anticipated. We stroll through a hideous folk park that has been built on the castle grounds, an Irish Sturbridge Village, though less successful. There are more thatched cottages scattered here than in all of County Clare, I tell everyone within earshot, and my sarcasm turns some heads. Carol is doddering behind, so I wait for her and send everyone ahead. We will meet in the Great Hall.

Carol is having a fine time. The sun is out, she's warm, we are strolling at what I would call a leisurely pace, her arm through mine, past various examples of ersatz peasant housing with ersatz peasant crops, past donkey carts and ploughs and jaunting cars, through assorted flocks of token chickens, geese, sheep, and cows. The only thing missing from our complete farm package are hogs (too smelly) and a few gypsies to persecute (not dressed in black anymore, thus not picturesque). "This is divine," Carol says.

We enter the Great Hall after surviving a circular staircase. I had decided to follow Carol up the stone steps in case she teetered over, a thoughtfulness that afforded me several opportunities to grab her waist. I am amazed at how light she is.

Everyone is standing in the middle, awestruck. "These people lived like kings," says one.

"Why do you think so?"

"Look at the tapestries and the huge dinner table. Look at those chests!" And indeed, all are lovely pieces. Too bad none of them are Irish. I explain that this entire collection was put together by Lord Gort. One reason he spent so much time and effort on Bunratty was to provide an appropriate, museum-style setting for his various acquisitions, all purchased on the Continent.

"I very much doubt whether the nobility who lived in Bunratty—in Connaught, after all, the back of beyond—were ever surrounded by such splendid furniture as this." They were too poor, too outside the mainstream, too enmeshed in an economic system of simple barter to possess such manifestations of leisured wealth. Anyway, an Irish lord would rather own a hundred head of cattle. I relate the known material effects of the first Lord Clanricard—equally powerful a nobleman as any who held Bunratty—when his widow tried to retrieve his belongings from a pawnshop in 1541: "one ale cup, chalice, and other ecclesiastical jeweles and plate, partly broken."

The huge banqueting table is admired, a centerpiece of the current banqueting tableau. I recount the story of Thomas de Clare, one of the early Norman adventurers, who entered into alliance with a native O'Brien, a stratagem of divide and conquer that most of the French-speaking interlopers relied upon heavily, both because their own numbers were so small and because the peculiarly faction-ridden Irish soci-

ety of the times invited this approach. Infuriated at some lapse in
O'Brien's loyalty, de Clare invited him to dinner at Bunratty, in the
middle of which the by-then inebriated guest was led outside for a
breath of fresh air. There O'Brien was seized, tied to a horse, and
dragged around the castle for several hours until his body was unrecognizable. This improved de Clare's humor, we may presume. Susan, the
widow from Ohio, is horrified. "The cruelty!"

That's nothing. I counter with the even wilder story of Pierce de
Bermingham, who had thirty-two O'Connors at his supper table in
1305. Those were all slaughtered with ax and sword save one: a young
boy and de Bermingham's godchild. The baron dragged him to the top
of his tower and threw the lad over, boasting of the deed until the day of
his death.

Just to demonstrate how the wheel of fortune is so fickle, I describe
the demise in de Clare fortunes that occurred in 1318. Richard de Clare
having been killed in a nearby field, their farms all plundered and razed,
his widow vengefully put the torch to everything she could see, including Bunratty and all the houses around it. She boarded ship for
England and never returned. How many times did this occur in Irish
history, the shattering of dreams, the destruction of effort and invest-
ment, all opportunity and titles turning to ash with a coffin lowered in
the ground? How many widows who said God damn this place because
they couldn't take it anymore? Ireland the desert, best never to have
heard of it, best left behind forever.

We take in the view from the battlements, a view the de Clares
would not have recognized. The new divided highway, now quite busy
with Sunday traffic, skirts the old bridge at our feet. Hotels and guest
houses are scattered all over the place, jets circling to land at Shannon,
and bus tours pulling in at a tourist pub called (and I don't know why)
Durty Nelly's. One of my people asks me why they built the castle so
close to the highway. I have no answer to that.

Back at the hotel we scatter to our rooms. I am so tired that a nap
seems like heaven, but when I awaken, I again have no idea where I am.
At first I think I'm in Minneapolis, where I had given a speech to an
Irish conference last December. Certainly, my quarters look no different:
two double beds, cheap veneered dresser, a huge television set. I am
taken aback that I am in Ireland, an Ireland I have not seen before, since
it dawns on me that I have never, in any visit here, stayed in a hotel. I've
camped in soggy tents and barns full of sweet wet hay; I've slept in any

number of cars and vans; I've been the guest of a few dozen Irish people; I've rented the odd room at a bed and breakfast; and I've spent many a night in Moyode Castle listening to my wife toss and turn and our kids having nightmares. But never a foot set inside a hotel.

Completely programmed by my surroundings, I automatically reach for the remote control and turn on the television. I watch a Croat or Muslim or Serb militiaman—does it matter which?—walk down a road full of bodies, and arbitrarily drop-kick his boot into the head of an old dead woman. The pleasures of victory, I think to myself, and very little different from some of the supposedly primitive goings on that I had blithely described when touring Bunratty. History is one long sordid story. We missed the gore of it in our college textbooks, concentrating as most do on the reigns of kings, the dates of battles, the ever-changing political boundaries. But the reality of it is death, people marching down a street or over a field, gloating over the rotted corpses of their foe.

7

FRONTIER

ur first full day. The thought of food in the morning generally nauseates me, so I avoid the free breakfast and the tour group until 9 A.M., when we meet in the lobby. The first welcome piece of news is that Carol will not be joining us. She evidently overslept and was last seen wandering the hallway in night attire telling the chambermaids that it was too much an ordeal to get dressed. This reminds me, perversely, of the nineteenth-century Lord Wallscourt, whose regal country manse lies in pieces a few miles from Moyode. He used to wander through miles of corridors stark naked, and he too enjoyed accosting the maids to engage them in idle conversation. His wife, not amused, had him carry a cowbell when he took these rambles au naturel as a means of warning all ahead of the catastrophe that was approaching.

Our first stop today is Askeaton, a much ruined town on the southern bank of the Shannon, as that great river broadens into a majestic estuary on its way to the Atlantic. In keeping with my tendency to micromanage the details of this tour, I have John set us down a few blocks from the main attraction here, the Desmond castle, so that everyone will see how shabby this place truly is, as they walk to the site.

My point here is to emphasize the perpetual condition of Ireland as a frontier, the equivalent, in U.S. history, of the west, of civilization left behind, of one's fortunes being gambled on a place wild, dangerous, and strange. I remind them of Conrad's novel *Heart of Darkness*, where European traders despairingly contemplate the mysteries of a primordial continent. For many an adventurer to Ireland, whether Norman or the later English, such foreboding was a commonplace.

The Irish were considered a tempestuous, untrustworthy, barbarian people untouched by civilization, whose work ethic, political inclination, and even language stood impenetrable to those who came to reform and domesticate them. And the ultimate irony, as I point out, is that despite the interminable defeats, catastrophes, and disasters that engulfed the Irish over a period of some twelve hundred years, in the end they remained themselves and were never truly assimilated into the mainstream of whoever it was who sought their conformity (mainly, of course, the English). No one will ever mistake an Irishman for anything other than what he is, and that remains true even today. (I omit from this speech my usual tirade about the homogeneity that membership in the European Union will inevitably produce and other assorted theories thereof. Best left for another time.)

"Now," I say, waving my hands for emphasis, "what does Askeaton look like to you?"

"I think you want me to say the OK Corral," says one of my people.

"In a way I do. How many of you have been to England?" At least half raise their hands. "Does Askeaton remind any of you of an English town?" Heads shake emphatically in dissent. This dirty, run-down, almost squalid place looks more like Vladivostok than Oxford, and that's the point. "Here we have an English climate, an English landscape, an English fertility. Many times in this country's history you also had thousands of English people here who, if they closed their eyes and smelled the air, would swear they were home. And their sole purpose was to husband, farm, milk, and fertilize this place with honest labor and sweat or, to use a phrase of the poet Spenser, 'to buxom' the land. And the point was to produce another England. If all that had worked, Askeaton would be a charming, settled, clean, and prosperous place. But the Irish ruined these schemes. They refused to step aside; they refused to assimilate; they refused to become English."

We approach the castle, stronghold of the Fitzgeralds, direct descendants of the first Norman invaders to come to Ireland in 1169, who turned renegade over the years and adopted Gaelic ways. To distinguish them from their equally famous cousins of the Pale, the Kildare

Fitzgeralds, the former were known by their hereditary title, the earls of Desmond. These warlords, by all accounts a wild collection of rogues, were men grown "insolent" in their obscurity here in the west of Ireland, men who ruled as they wished and paid little heed to the desires of English lord deputies, kings, queens, or any interloper to their territories. They were a proverbial thorn in the side.

Their castle stands on a small island in a narrow stream that runs to the Shannon. It is claustrophobic in feeling, hemmed in by vegetation gone wild amidst several buildings wedged into confining space. The complex is locked up tight behind a gate with a great lock, and I can see why. The enormous central tower, a two-sided shell of precarious structural integrity, soars into the sky. Fireplaces, alcoves, small rooms, a toilet chute, all stand exposed like a skeleton, as though the skin of the building had been ripped off to allow us this enormous view of innards. If it keeled over, heaven forbid, the debris would probably hit us out here on the street.

The tremendous banqueting hall is a separate building altogether, a two-story affair almost ninety feet long that is best viewed from a cattle ramp a few yards away that serves as the local watering hole. I carefully guide my aged crew down this slimy projection to the stream's edge, a turbid body of water choked with weeds and garbage. I describe the merriment this building must have seen, the smoky interior, the loud and raucous feasting, the plaintive wailing of people crowding in to ask a favor of the earl, the strains of music and snarling of dogs as they fought for meat bones thrown on the floor. "All this came to a horrible end for the Desmonds," I say, "ruined in the Elizabethan wars of the late 1500s, done to death by their terrible feud with the Butlers of Ormonde, who were cousins to the queen."

I tell them the story of the fourteenth earl, Gerard, who let himself in 1579 be goaded into open rebellion, an act of folly, to say the least. His forces routed, his friends slain, his earldom devastated by war, famine, and disease, Gerard took to the wastelands of County Kerry in a desperate attempt to avoid arrest. I recount my own visit years ago to the spot where the hounds of war finally dragged him down, a hut (long since gone) in the middle of a wild, overgrown glen. There the exhausted earl was found asleep by marauding clansmen bent on revenge. Some of the earl's ragged followers had reeved a few cattle from a local farmer and stolen clothes from them as well, leaving the man's wife completely naked on a winter's evening. This was a simple man's way of paying the earl back.

Not recognizing Gerard from his wild, frightened demeanor and the filth of his attire, his captors surrounded the poor man yelling and screaming for information—"Where is the earl?"—hitting him with the flat of their swords and breaking his arm.

"I am the earl of Desmond," he finally said, the news of which impelled his captors to strike his head off then and there. Elizabeth I, it is said, spent an entire morning alone, in calm repose, studying the earl's death-tormented face, pulled from a jug of brine and put on her desk. Then she had it stuck on a pike at the Tower of London.

"All these acts of cruelty, it's sickening," says Susan, the widow from Ohio. "Why were all these people so bloodthirsty?" I explain my pet theory. How many of us have sliced the throat, eviscerated, cut into pieces, and then preserved or cooked the flesh of a domestic farm animal? I, for one, have barbecued enough steaks to fill several freezers, but I've never killed anything I ever ate except a fish. Any hunters here? No assenting nods, and I think it proves a point. The idea of putting one's hand in the still warm body of an animal just dispatched, to remove kidneys, liver, and all sorts of other unmentionables, was hardly a reason to vomit in the old preindustrial days of Europe or even America. Cutting the head off a human being, in fact, is less onerous a job than decapitating a bullock, and in Desmond's case, it earned his executioner a thousand pounds of silver. Politics is politics, intrigue is intrigue. Just the form these treacheries take has changed (for the most part, that is). In the halls of power today, the corridors no longer run red with blood. In the old days, when the line between butchering animals and public executions was thin, the niceties of behavior were likewise blurred.

"How many tourists come here?" Alden asks, a retired physician from near Kansas City.

"On a hypothetical scale of a thousand visitors to Ireland, I'd say one or two," is my reply.

"That's great," he says appreciatively. "We're off the beaten track."

Our bus continues along the Shannon, John pointing out the old aerodrome where the first transatlantic flights, amphibious aircraft with great pontoons, landed in the river. It is remembered now as the birthplace of Irish coffee, the inspired creation of a local chef who got tired of delivering two glasses to groggy passengers, one full of Irish whiskey, the other with coffee. This perks everyone up and I promise we'll have some for lunch. Right now we have to hurry and catch the 11:30 ferry to the other side of the river.

The boat ride had been my idea of a scenic way to see the Shannon, a remembrance, as it were, of the atmospherics that John Keane put in his otherwise dreadful play *The Man from Clare*, which tells the story of competing football clubs from Clare and Limerick being rowed across the river for their annual match. Again, that kind of quaint aura from the old-fashioned 1950s, that time frame so regularly skewered in the fiction of Edna O'Brien and William Trevor, but that I find attractive. I had forgotten, however, that most of the river's ambience at this crossing is dominated on the Limerick side by a huge plant that generates electricity, and the scene, evidently, of a recent drug bust when a sizable cache was discovered on a ship of foreign registry delivering fuel. As we approach the Clare side, that view is replicated by yet another set of belching smokestacks that anchors yet another collection of gigantic turbines. All those television sets in all those hotel rooms must take a lot of juice. I'm the only one who seems upset by this industrial plenty, so I leave it alone. One of my little touches that didn't work.

The high point of today is meant to be Scattery Island, my problem being that I haven't taken lunch into account. The crew, who I imagine had probably gorged themselves at breakfast on Irish bacon and bread, is now clamoring for lunch, a part of daily ritual that I really had not much considered, being a snack person myself until dinnertime when I get serious. Still, they are not to be denied.

We pull into Kilrush, a backwater town from whence a launch can be hired for Scattery. Well, Kilrush is not so "backwater" anymore, but a bustling, spruced-up, clean, and prosperous-looking little place. I pick a pub from among several attractive possibilities and call my people in.

The season being largely over, the young proprietors are overjoyed at the business and stop at nothing to please. Soup, sandwiches, Irish coffees are pulled from a hat; it's an hour and a half before I can get everyone out. "Well, they had fun," the pretty owner says to me as I pay, "but I don't think you did."

"Well, I'm a married man and you flirted with all the old guys here terribly. That's not good for the heartbeat and I don't like being tempted."

"Just because you're on a diet doesn't mean you can't look at the menu."

"But did they learn anything here from all the jokes and the patter and the talk?"

"Certainly they did. They learned we're a friendly people and that we don't hold them a grudge because they're rich and have everything in the world. And I hope they come back to Kilrush when next they're over."

"To this pub in particular, of course."

"We have traditional music every Tuesday and Thursday, and wouldn't they love it? Have a good day!"

I have a written copy of our launch reservation, but of course the dock is deserted with no one in sight. I am glad to see that some things in Ireland will never change. John goes off in search of someone, anyone, who will take us out, and eventually he shows up with a teenager who promises not to lose us at sea. In a few minutes we are out in open waters, engulfed in a haze of diesel fumes. But the scenery is magnificent.

Scattery is a small island that lies in an exposed portion of the Shannon estuary. It takes about twenty minutes to reach it in this ancient sea dog of a boat. The sun is really blazing now, and refreshing Atlantic winds push billows of huge foamy white clouds across the sky. This is snapshot paradise, and everyone is oohing over the ancient round tower as it comes within camera range. I am asked to pose for my first photo.

Since the theme of our trip is Celtic and Norman Ireland, I thought it desirable to see at least one example of a remote and insular Celtic monastery, something along the lines of Ardoileán (which would have been logistically impossible for this group). The problem is, of course, that most of the good sites really are difficult of access, but Scattery is an exception. There is a dock on the island; there's a regular boat to it; the trip is short and thus seasickness is of no concern. Best of all, Scattery is obscure. Not too many people come here and that's fine by me.

They don't come, I suppose, because there really isn't much to see except the round tower, one of Ireland's tallest, as a matter of fact. No beehive *clocháns* (huts), no high crosses, no high corbeled chapels, no collection of grave slabs from the eighth century, no museum, gift shop, or rest room. Naturally, this is all nonsense. There's plenty to see.

We begin with the old Gaelic village, long abandoned. It consists, as so many of these island communities did, of a single lane lined with old cottages, their thatched or tin roofs fallen in, their whitewashed facades stained with bird droppings and the assorted airborne flotsam slammed hither and yon by winter gales. An old green post office box, once red, with Edward VII stamped on it, still remains. I mention that mail boxes, or drops, were invented by the British novelist Anthony Trollope, who spent many of his earlier years in the employ of the postal service. "Oh, I love Trollope," exclaims Julie, who so far has said nothing to me, "and I hate it when they make movies from his novels." She proceeds to launch into a tirade about films of Austen's novels and Shakespeare's plays, things like *Sense and Sensibility*, *Much Ado About Nothing*, so on and so forth "ad nauseam," in her words. "People just can't read anymore, so they go to the movie instead, sit there on their bottoms for two hours, then come out thinking that, yes indeed, I read that book and it wasn't too bad. *Masterpiece Theatre* is the worst thing that ever happened to us!"

We are all momentarily stunned, but then dribbles of assent start rolling in. "Thank goodness we're here and not there," someone says. I don't exactly get the literal meaning of this remark, but it's safer to nod and agree.

The village, I continue, probably had a portentous name, as most of them did. "The City," perhaps, or "The Great City on the Hill"; and the overgrown path that we're standing on was also, I am sure, equally ennobled with some gaudy catchphrase—"The Great Road" or "The King's Avenue." Irish is a hyperbolic language given to rhetorical excess, as Elizabeth I learned when Shane the Proud came to London in 1562 to pledge obeisance. The English court had never seen such a performance, the torrent of language, the unleashing of tears, the pulling out of hair, the groveling on the floor, and so on, all to profess an allegiance that, in Shane's case, evaporated about as quickly as it took him to ride out of London. As the old cliché has it, Gaelic is best suited for love and hate.

I recommend Maurice O'Sullivan's *Twenty Years A-Growing*, written in 1933, which describes what living on such precarious places was like. To me, it sounds like heaven on earth, and I say so. In reality, the life was probably harsh and exceedingly difficult. Romantics among us would argue that the richness of the people's cultural identity—stories around the hearth, the songs and dirges known to all, the poteen and simple outdoor life, the certainty of religious belief—more than made up for it, but even I question that. If I lived out here, I'd probably want electricity. How can you listen to opera without it?

Round tower, Scattery Island

I'm not certain when Scattery was deserted, but I say 1963. I suppose it matters, but not to these people. They are engulfed in the mystery that always attaches itself, in the words of Brian Moore, to "islands abandoned by man."

Wandering inland, we pass various remnants of the old Celtic monastery. Thankfully, the island has a caretaker in season, some old buck who hangs around the tourists as they get off the boat, lending the place some local color and giving tours full of blarney and cadging for tips. He is responsible, evidently, for scything a path through the heavy undergrowth; otherwise, my charges would never be able to penetrate the weedy morass to take in the sights. They do not strike me as a group who, like the monks of old, would tear their bloody way through nettled brambles to touch the hem of Christ's cloak. Still they are, collectively, deeply moved by the old tower, the altars, the plain and primitive chapels.

I am talking now about the essence of monasticism—not the variety espoused by Saint Benedict, but that of the Desert Fathers—and how the Irish maintained the old traditions of John the Baptist and Saint Antony longer than anyone else. I emphasize the metaphorical imagery of Scattery as wilderness, as the back of beyond, as the place where men came, physically and conceptually, to escape the frivolous world of "women and druids." And then I disabuse them of the notion that these patristic Irish saints, those who first accepted the challenge of a white (or bloodless) martyrdom in the sixth century, were in any way pallid, tame, or timid men. I repeat what I said the day before: We tend to think of monkish people as shy, retiring, gentle, withdrawn. But in fact the Irish came to Scattery and the other bleak and remote western isles as warriors. They wanted to test their mettle against the worthiest foe to be found, the Prince of Darkness, just as knights-errant left the safety of their castles to seek out the metaphorical dragon. Their armor, as an old prayer put it, was faith; their buckler, the Psalter; their sword, prayer. Scattery was not the scene of a withdrawal, but the object of an invasion.

In a totally infantile remark I mention how attractive all this is to me personally. I can be very much into penance at times, a phase I slip into three or four times a year, much to my wife's annoyance. I go to confession in Boston; I go to church; I take communion; I put Gregorian chants on the stereo; I talk about fish on Friday and fasting. Usually I've had a glass or two of Chardonnay when I start these harangues, which lessens my wife's belief that I'm serious. I'm too brash a personality to affect such humility for long, she says. But the monks, the monks, I feel temperamentally attracted to those eccentrics, and I say so. The bond is, I know, superficial and frivolous, my complaints about modernity and its gross excesses somehow juxtaposed and confused with the hermits' more profound denial. Who am I kidding?

Evidently, these people. As my diatribe continues, I can tell the group is really into this. They want this island and its few scraggly remains to have a meaning for them; they want to feel there's something significant here to take away, and my inarticulate meandering about waging war with Satan is having an effect. They have, momentarily at least, forgotten about postcards and souvenirs and their next meal. All of a sudden, they're hungry for truth, whatever that is. I can see it in their eyes, and I respect it.

Our attention is called for by Ted, a retired something (not quite sure what) from Pennsylvania. Off in some underbrush he's found a grave slab, evidently old, and we troop over. It turns out to be a fine example of

Celtic stone carving, a raised cross in cord motif, where the lines curl and intertwine in curious, seemingly random fashion, much as in a Celtic manuscript or, for that matter, an Aran sweater or Celtic reel. I figure it dates from the eighth or ninth century and point out triumphantly that here we have Ireland at its best. Did any of us tramping about this shabby, overgrown island, full of detritus from a variety of historical eras, ever expect to see such a jewel of craftsmanship—indeed, art—hidden away in the bracken, ignored and almost lost to sight? Ireland rewards the patient visitor in many unexpected ways. If this were England or the States, this whole place would be manicured, sign posted, chained off, and open to guided tours only. Here, we're in the wild.

The beauty of this rough piece of stone mesmerizes all of us. Ted is particularly proud of himself. Henceforth I refer to him as the Heinrich Schliemann of our group. If only he could find a golden chalice, we would all be rich.

Our day ends, after two or three more stops on the mainland at castles and abbeys, on a single-lane boreen in the backlands of County Clare. John is an excellent driver and he skillfully maneuvers our bloated yellow tub down excruciatingly twisted byways until we reach our goal. "I've never been on this road, Jim, and I know the reason why," he says to me.

"Why?"

"There's nothing here." Everyone peers out the windows and agrees. Nothing here. I step out of the bus and stroll over to a fine stone wall. I lean on it and look out into a field. "There, ladies and gentlemen, is the coronation mound of Thomond. As you can see, it's not Camelot. But think for a moment about your own desires and ambitions, the daydreams you had as a child, and then look at this. In the days before Christ was born, to be crowned on this mound was probably the most thrilling event of a young man's life. It was also likely to be a short-lived moment of joy. Most of these warriors rarely made it to middle age, and I doubt few if any died in bed of natural causes."

We are viewing a rough and much eroded man-made hillock. Oscar Wilde's father, as noted an antiquarian as he was a surgeon, wrote eloquently about the ceremonies that gave such places meaning, the white wand of sovereignty being placed in your hand, the cheers of hundreds as a wreath was crowned on your head, the feasting and poetry that followed. Not so Edmund Spenser, who waxed scathingly on such heathen rites. They were not kings but "captaines," and the rabble who gathered at these dung-littered mounds were no better than illiterate thieves and murderers. The truth, as usual, lies somewhere in between.

The Celtic notion of kingship was essentially that of a marriage. As with any beautiful woman, various suitors would circle the prize and vie for her favors. In Celtic terms this meant slaughtering, maiming, or "blemishing" your rivals, and the countryside could, as a direct result, be full of young men wandering about with empty eye sockets or minus their hands. With competitors eliminated, a king would then take his bride, the "sovereignty" of his petty kingdom (called in Irish a *tuath*), and the ceremony itself would involve an appropriately sexual finale, formalized by the mating of king with sovereignty, the surrogate usually being a horse. This unfortunate creature would be sacrificed after intercourse, then cooked and distributed to the people as a sign of union. "It's a funny thing about life," I say, "the ability to combine in one event the sublime with the tawdry, and we see it here in this otherwise ordinary pile of dirt. It's nothing really, and yet the stuff of dreams."

"I've heard the Irish are not very strong on feminism, but this is misogynist in the extreme," says Ted's wife.

"Perhaps," I agree, "but that was long ago and the whole tradition grew more gentlemanly as time went by. After the disastrous Battle of the Boyne in 1690, Ireland was no longer depicted as a beautiful woman but rather as the poor peasant crone with her harp smashed to pieces, always looking for a gallant savior, usually James Stuart. After Stuart deserted the island, any Stuart would do, as long as he came to the rescue."

"That's still misogynist. Women don't need men to be free." She returns to the bus.

"This is great," says Alden. "How many people come here to see this?"

John answers for me. "Not a soul, Alden, not a soul. Jim here, he's the only one, believe me."

8

"Princes Do But Play Us"

he gods continue smiling. Another lovely day in store, or so it seems. At least the sunshine will show an otherwise gloom-filled Limerick City to good effect, and frankly, this place can use all the help it can get. I have always liked Limerick, especially in the rain. It has an aura of despair that can almost be touched, especially when a thin sheen of moisture turns the whole place gray. It's a mood I wouldn't wish on my worst enemy, least of all the tour, so I agree with all the mumbled praise of our weather.

The Vikings were the first to break ground here, on a defensible island overlooking a set of shallow falls that mark the first obstruction to navigating Ireland's interior. It was an ideal base for their depredations. They hauled their longships upriver over the rapids and plundered all the monasteries they could find, or they sailed downriver straight from here to the ocean when they sought targets or trade farther afield. The nucleus of their settlement became known as English Town after the Normans came in the twelfth century, building one of Ireland's largest medieval castles in the process.

Like all Ireland's cities, Limerick was a bastion for strangers. When colonizing efforts stalled or the Gaels went on one of their periodic rampages out in the country, hordes of refugees flooded the place, pulled up the drawbridge after them, and cowered behind its walls. When the contretemps of the moment subsided, they would emerge, return to the charred remains of home and hearth, and try once more to settle the land. It was either that or go down to the wharves for that inevitable ship going home to wherever.

Irish entrepreneurs were eventually drawn into the orbit of Limerick's activity, and they mostly settled across the Shannon's watery divide on an adjacent spit of land. This came to be known as Irish Town, a segregated quarter that was to be found in all the urban centers then springing up in Ireland. Kilkenney had one, Dublin too, even Athenry with its English Street and Irish Street. At night all the Irish theoretically were to leave English Town and have the gates closed behind them. They could eat and sleep with their own, and besides, they couldn't be trusted. Over time, these distinctions were often moot, depending on how mongrelized the original settlers had become.

King John's Castle, when I first saw it as a child of seven, was an almost complete derelict, the center of English Town's maze of slums and council housing. What gentry there were in Limerick City had long since decamped to the more fashionable quarter of Georgian construction known as Newtown Pery, which itself was speedily losing the battle with decay. The castle courtyard, I recall, full of apartments, army barracks, and pig sties, had a Dickensian air of putrefaction about it, what I have since imagined a debtor's prison might look like. I continue to associate the place with fond memories of my parents, however, who indulged my interest in old places and old things whenever they could. I remember my mother sidestepping mounds of manure as we negotiated the filthy, rutted streets.

Tourism had largely passed this quarter of the city by. Too far gone or too dangerous for the unwary to enter was the semiofficial attitude. Nowadays nothing is considered too far gone, and the castle, or what was left of it, has been tidied up and put in order, all the derelictions bulldozed, the yard scraped flat and clean, a visitors' center built between two ancient curtain walls. The Irish usually do these things in impeccable taste, but the visitors' center here is very strange, a two-story metal cargo container that appears to have been airlifted to the site. The approximation of what is presumably a drawbridge connects this enterprise with the outside world. I can only infer that the oddity of this particular touch is meant to symbolize how alien a presence these Normans were to the native Gael, who at first had no fathom as to what these "heroes dressed in gray" were all about. In that respect, it probably works.

There are several "King John" castles in Ireland. Carlingford, Athenry, Dungarvan are three that come to mind, but Limerick is the most graphically linked with that wretched man. I say wretched because little good to say about him has ever been recorded. In movies he is generally portrayed as a sniveling, treacherous, devious man of slight build and a good two feet shorter than his valorous brother, Richard the Lion-Heart, who enters the script, usually at the end, to undo all the villainies that John has initiated.

In fact, though he deserves some of this dreadful odor, John was no more venal than most medieval monarchs and is given credit by historians for having some idea as to how to run a kingdom. He mastered the bureaucratic aspects of ruling and developed some measure of insight into the intricacies of raising money and spending it. But his political decisions were generally poor, his success on the battlefield was slight, and of course the Magna Carta situation irretrievably ruined his reputation. To top everything off, he had a temper more violent and vindictive than most.

Limerick Castle was a royal castle, which meant that it belonged to the king and not the man to whose care he entrusted it, whether justiciar or lord deputy. One of the first of these, William de Braose, failed miserably to perform for John. William never succeeded in pacifying the countryside and planting it with productive manor farms, which meant he never paid John any rents or percentages from income, which he alleged to be nonexistent. John, by nature grasping and prone to think the worst, did not accept the notion that de Braose was a poor warrior and a worse businessman. He concluded instead that de Braose was a thief and a liar, and he proceeded to dismiss, harry, pursue, and otherwise destroy the man and everything he owned in a truly titanic display of royal wrath. De Braose died a penniless fugitive in Normandy; his wife and infant son were chased through the entire Angevin domain, then thrown into the dungeon of Windsor Castle and starved to death. We may presume that the king visited them on occasion to enjoy the spectacle of their lingering demise.

I tell this story in the shadows cast by the castle's two enormous drum towers, which have the royal coat of arms prominently displayed. Everyone is disgusted with John's cruelty. They haven't seen anything yet.

We enter the visitors' center. I included it on our itinerary in order for the tour to spend some time in the small museum here. The castle has featured in so many sieges and battles that in order for any of them to make sense, a chronological display is helpful to sort out the various phases in Ireland's long story. The exhibit here is particularly fine. Gaels, Normans, Elizabethans, Catholics, Protestants, Jacobites, Cromwellians, Williamites, Ascendancy types, and the IRA will all fly by in chronological order and in far more detail than I can offer. Moreover, they can watch an audiovisual presentation (good for twenty minutes, no slight advantage for me) and then visit a genealogy booth for a computer printout of their family's origin, no doubt inaccurate but certainly colorful. I leave everyone to start these various activities and go off to the toilets. Free at last. Standing at the urinal I already feel a little talked out, and the day has only just begun. In a split second of awareness, however, I realize I have company, and glancing over my shoulder I find Carol, weaving side to side like a reed in the wind, alone with me in the men's room.

"What is this, Jim?"

"It's a toilet, Carol. Men only, I believe."

"This isn't on the tour?"

"No, not really, Carol. Nothing much to see here."

"Oh, darling, how silly. I thought I was supposed to follow you!" With that, her cane taps out of the room.

I reenter the exhibit area, but most of my group has sped right through. I assume they're at the more exciting slide show. I read over the placards and look at the models. The only fault I can find is in the medieval section, where a large projection screen on the wall replays the battle sequence in Laurence Olivier's 1944 film *Henry V.* This footage is full of galloping knights in gorgeous attire, their horses and shields emblazoned with lions rampant, their helmet plumes waving in the breeze, not a drop of blood anywhere. A great movie, but this is absurd.

The battles for Limerick Castle, the battles these Normans fought in the pastures around us, were never glamorous affairs. More often than not they consisted of mounted men running people down in fields like rabbits, which usually resulted in Norman victories and piles of Irish heads collected as battle trophies. When the Gaels won an engagement, it was usually even more squalid, treacherous ambuscades along forest pathways where kerns ran out from the cover of trees to hack a man's leg off or cripple his mount, never standing firm to fight longer than necessary but running off again into the undergrowth where a horseman could not follow. These forays did much to drain the morale of Norman settlers, generating an attrition that could hardly do anything else.

◆

Whether they like it or not, I force the group to walk a little bit through English Town. Across the way from King John's Castle is an interesting remnant of Protestantism, a nineteenth-century retirement community for Church of Ireland clergymen and their widows. These were row houses built in the same distinctively handsome Gothic style that so enriched this country in the many Protestant parish churches that still stand, however empty and ruinous they may now be. These small residences run stacked one by one in a line to the old parish church with its distinctive bell tower, topped by crenellations and high pointed decorative stonework on each corner. I prefer the single slender spire that is also characteristic of this period, but nonetheless my group agrees as to the gracefulness of the overall design.

This particular church now houses a theater group, or so a crudely painted sign proclaims. If anyone were here, I'd recommend to them replacing the roof, repairing the enormous belfry shutters, reguttering the drains, and fixing the myriad of broken windows. While they were at it, the cemetery grounds could be attended some care and the wrought-iron fences and gateway sandblasted and painted. But of course, no one is here, and I doubt any budding thespians have been seen or heard practicing their lines or projecting their oratory for many a season. This place is dead.

The Protestant hierarchy would like to sell every one of these churches to just about anyone with some ready cash to offer, a commodity desperately needed to maintain the prestigious behemoths they still must preserve in places like Dublin, which boasts not one but two Church of Ireland cathedrals, an absurd pretension, to say the least. The last statistics I saw indicated that barely 4 percent of the population here in the Republic claims to be Protestant. In Limerick I'd guess there may be a hundred or so.

But even if you hadn't money in hand, these buildings can be had. Need a local library, a place for the boy scouts to meet, a "heritage center"? Please apply to the local bishop. Even an old rock star from the 1960s, Donovan Leitch, better known simply as Donovan, picked one up for a song. It can make a charming summer home and a wonderfully atmospheric place for incense.

The tour is demonstrably moved and amazed at this sadly dimin-

The Treaty Stone, Limerick City

ished building. "If this was in Ohio," offers Susan, "it would be the finest place in town."

We now walk over the gloomy Thomond Bridge, which crosses the river right at King John's Castle. The breeze is up and the air is chilly, but I want them to study the Shannon, look at its rapids, examine its strategic value, get a feel for the cold, black water running at our feet, the "river that kills" in the phrase of Frank McCourt, the Irish-American who has written so memorably of growing up in Limerick during the miserable 1930s and 1940s. I hold on tightly to Carol, making certain a sudden gust doesn't throw her over the side into the frigid tumult below.

Gathering at the infamous Treaty Stone of 1691, the reputed site where Patrick Sarsfield signed the last capitulation of the Williamite wars, I run through the litany of battles that led to this disaster for Catholic Ireland—the Boyne, Athlone, Aughrim, the second siege of Limerick. This is a dirge with which the entire group can sympathize, aside from Carol, who is oblivious, and they dutifully photograph the old stone from every conceivable angle. But it is the Thomond Bridge that I really want to talk about.

By 1691, as I explain, James II had long since fled to France, and one look at his contemporaneous profile by an unknown artist in London's National Portrait Gallery will tell you why. Disdain is written all over his face, a slight lip curl that transcends arrogance, that transcends the simplistic dogma that men like James routinely clung to as their justification, best known to us today as the divine right of kings. No, I emphasize, James's demeanor says more than that; it reeks of divine indifference.

Though a brave man personally, James did not possess the kind of resolute personality that could suffer the infidelity of wavering fortunes. He was too often given to disgust at any given situation that required for its success more spark and grit. He had walked away from his throne in London with barely a struggle, for example, and at the Boyne two years before the siege of Limerick, he had been the first to leave the field of battle as a beaten man. This is not to say that James would not have willingly died on the spot in combat if called on by circumstances to do so. His difficulty lay in always missing the right opportunity and being then confronted with a situation that did not merit such a sacrifice. The Boyne was lost, or James considered it so, before he had the chance to determine its outcome, as befitted a king. He left it for other men to die in his stead, which he considered perfectly proper, and decamped for France, much to the amazement of his patron Louis XIV, who had expected him to win or perish in the attempt.

Like the Stuarts who came before him (particularly Charles I), James simply viewed the Irish as a necessary evil, or the court of last appeal. They were the metaphorical dice to be rolled and rolled again in a final, desperate attempt to turn a winning score, and if victory never came, shoulders were shrugged and players walked away. The Irish never truly mattered. As John Donne succinctly put it, "Princes do but play us."

At Limerick, a group of about eight hundred Irish foot soldiers abandoned an outwork and withdrew in some disorder for the Thomond Bridge during the city's last siege in 1691. Essentially of medieval construction, the Thomond was barely a lane wide, and about a third of the way over the Shannon, it featured a tower and drawbridge. As the soldiery broke into a run, the Williamite besiegers charged the straggling column, and a French officer in charge of the drawbridge gave in to a wave of panic himself and ordered it raised. I point out to the group how narrow the Shannon really is, how intimate the death zone then created by that officer in fact was, how the Irish garrison holed up in Limerick, women and children as well as men, could witness in minute detail from its walls the slaughter that was to come.

As the fleeing Irish surged onto the bridge, what faced them? The uplifted drawbridge. Turning if they could, they found the Williamites in hot pursuit, pouring fire into their congested mass. Men close to the drawbridge found themselves inexorably pushed into the river by the pack of men behind them pushing forward, there to drown. Others could not bring weapons to bear on their pursuers and were shot in the back or slashed with sabers. All soon raised their hands in surrender or waved handkerchiefs but no quarter was given; they were stabbed, hacked, blasted with shot as they stood. Over six hundred men died in a horrible orgy of bloodletting. Women from the walls watched their menfolk stumble and fall like a herd of cornered cattle.

This single ghastly episode sucked the heart right out of the Irish army. Ginkel, the Williamite commander, did not consider this a signal victory, just a skirmish, and he despaired of taking the city by assault. He was astonished the next day when the Irish treated for surrender. Their men had been sacrificed by everyone: the French, Louis XIV, James II. They just gave up.

Later in the bus, Susan sits next to me. There is so much room in our conveyance that the group spreads apart as they wish, so for someone to choose the seat adjoining mine takes on psychic significance, as though people are coming to me for confession. Susan is perhaps the most serious individual on the tour, and she wants answers. She wants to know, Why?

"What are you trying to tell us, Jim? This just isn't like other tours I've taken. You seem to be going out of your way to point out the horrors, to emphasize all the gloomy things in Ireland, to purge us all of our silly ideas."

"And here we are, only on our third day," I reply.

"Exactly!" She laughs. "Come on, tell me, what's your philosophy about all this?"

"I think people are forgetting the past. Do you realize that most of the stuff I dredge up, even the Irish don't remember?"

"That's exactly right, and for good reason," says John, who's been eavesdropping. "When all you do is lose, who wants to remember all that? I'll tell you something, Susan, I've been driving tours for sixteen years, and I've never heard half the things he's talking about. But I can drive the Ring of Killarney with my eyes closed, and that's what most people want to see."

"I don't want to see that kind of stuff," she responds emphatically. "I like the stories we've been getting, but it's kind of unrelenting. Massacres here, massacres there, massacres everywhere. Does it ever end?"

"Ask the Indians of North America," I say piously. "But really, there are several issues at play here on many different levels. I can take you to the usual places and give you the usual patter, but I'd go crazy. I need the money I'm being paid to do this, but I have a few principles, and if I bore myself, I'm going to bore you too and then everyone loses. I look at this as a trial by combat. If you can stand it, I can too." I blather on for a good ten minutes more as we rumble down the road for our next stop, the Rock of Cashel. And although I cannot recall, as I sit here writing this, my exact words, the gist went something like this.

The word "ancient" was invented to describe Ireland. Over the course of four millennia, the people here have been squabbling, fighting, and tearing out each other's throats for both glory and profit, much to the disdain of those who may have happened, by mistake or on purpose, to pass the place by. I recall a remark by Benjamin Disraeli when taunted by Daniel O'Connor in the House of Commons, "Yes, I am a Jew. And when the ancestors of the Right Honorable Gentleman were wearing animal skins and clubbing each other to death, mine were conversing together in the Temple of Solomon." Or words to that effect. Actually, I think Disraeli got it wrong. The Jews were snipping off the foreskins of slain Philistines as war spoils, in much the same manner as the Celts were lopping off heads. It's the human condition.

But once you sprinkled into the fire bits of gunpowder—and by that I mean religion—the nature of this mayhem changed. It elevated several notches, it became a matter, to some degree, of character. In Irish terms, the struggle evolved into race war, and over time the inequality of resources to which the warring camps could repair for supply and sustenance tipped the balance sheet in favor of the "foreigners." The Irish people, faced with wars for which the goal was their extinction, found themselves worn and worn and worn away: their lands gone, their religion proscribed, their status as helots confirmed by law, their very numbers evaporated by famine.

Through all of this, the Irish tried. They tried militarily to the best of their haphazard abilities. They tried spiritually with the uniqueness of their religious outlook and their inner vitality. And they tried culturally, with the wisdom of a long memory. Only the memory is still left, and apparently most in danger now.

As Julius Caesar noted, memory is a fragile thing. He was commenting on the Celtic Gauls, their propensity for selecting as their wise men those who could rattle off the deeds and genealogies of kings and warriors long, long dead to the amazement of clansmen who sat round the campfires listening. Caesar insisted that the Gauls, being "quick of mind and with good natural ability for learning," be taught the rudiments of reading and writing. "It is normal experience," he wrote, "that the help of the written word causes a loss of diligence in memorizing by heart." Yet such was not the case for the Irish.

True, they took to the basics of literacy; they became known for their scholarship, however idiosyncratic, but at the same time they kept the old ways alive as well. The dreams and glories of the past lived on in the panegyrics and annals of tribal bards and poets, historians and genealogists, scribes and storytellers, right on through centuries of chaos. The final repository was the blind harpists, the peasant raconteurs, the hunted priests and rogue hedge scholars of Penal times, all despised, mocked, and murdered by the new masters of Ireland. From their meager rememberings—all that was left—famous scholars of the nineteenth and twentieth centuries managed to reassemble a portrait of the Old Ireland that served as a spiritual nucleus for a country finally freed in 1922. That is far too precious an inheritance to fritter away.

I go the old ways and tell the forgotten stories because someone has to. And I'm not even Irish! The demands of mass tourism, the pressures of time and money, the general amnesia of the population as a whole, all conspire to obliterate the tremendous saga of remembrance that is Ireland's unique preserve as a tormented and Catholic place. Half-baked clichés and a stew of blarney do little justice to what happened on the Thomond Bridge two hundred years ago. I'd be willing to wager that 90 percent of the people who walk that bridge daily have no idea as to the sacred blood that washed over its side and flowed on down to the great ocean beyond.

That's about what I said to Susan.

9

The Rock And The Palace

y early evening the skies have blackened and rain clouds scud in from the Atlantic. The Rock of Cashel looms before us in heavy melodrama, perhaps the most famous image in all the country, a multifaceted array of ancient buildings crowded together on a great protrusion of stone that overlooks miles of plain and pasture. There's nothing "back road" about this place, and it compares favorably with some of the heavyweight attractions that countries like England, France, and Italy so abundantly provide.

That is curious, really, because when its components are analyzed separately, Cashel doesn't amount to much. The roofless cathedral is not distinguished, its round tower hardly unique, the free-standing cross too weather-beaten to elicit much more than curiosity, and the cemetery lacks outstanding monuments or stones. But when viewed as a whole, this complex exudes enormous power. It is one of the few sites in Ireland that give kingship the aura of nobility and grandeur that we commonly associate with royalty. Most Celtic kings lived in earthen enclosures called raths with their cattle and pigs. Cashel is the exception. From here you truly sense the allure of power, the desire for it propelling untold generations of greedy young men to acts that in the plain light of day would seem repulsive or degrading. Cashel reeks of ambition.

The exception to this overall architectural plainness is Cormac's Chapel, a strange little building much obscured by the larger and later medieval cathedral, and the purest expression of a design style labeled by scholars as Irish Romanesque.

Beginning in the eleventh century, the Irish church began a long and tortuous procedure to conform with the usage of continental religious practice. This long-delayed accommodation would see its fullest expression with the coming to Ireland of religious orders, principally the Benedictines, Dominicans, Augustinians, and Cistercians, who would build some of the island's loveliest abbeys and monasteries. Erected largely along standardized European designs, these would replace in taste the distinctly local constructions of beehive *clocháns*, oratories, and round towers that outsiders came to identify with Irish religious irregularities. During the interim period before these changes dominated the thinking of ecclesiastical builders, a distinctly Celtic innovation would make a last bid for architectural supremacy, and that would be the Romanesque phase that Cormac's Chapel so embodies.

One can see this Romanesque implosion—for such it was, a final gasp of defiance, a turning inward for sustenance, not outward—in all manner of ancient churches here. Usually the efforts were confined to doorways, where older, plainer formats were eliminated and replaced with elaborately carved and ornate archways. They were emblazoned with all manner of grotesqueries, replicas in stone of the famous intricacies of the illuminated manuscripts, the *Books of Kells* and *Durrow*. "Gargolian" heads, weird animal shapes and visages, creatures too strange for identification, suddenly glared at churchgoers as they entered for service. And unlike the massive entryway to cathedrals such as Chartres and Notre Dame, equally festooned with figure sculpture, the Irish variations, being smaller in scale, were generally at eye level and thus uncomfortably close in a squirmy kind of way. Bizarre is really a rather apt description.

Cormac's Chapel, however, is not just a doorway or a window built into the older fabric of a structure. Unique to Ireland, the entire building is Romanesque, a one-of-a-kind creation, built oddly askew and featuring twin towers of differing form. The outer walls are covered with decorative twists and turns, all seemingly different and yet harmonizing in a dance of the devil's maelstrom. The whole effect is breathtaking.

That is my excuse for bringing the tour here. I plan to indulge their enthusiasm for Cashel, which will overwhelm their sensory capacity, but then I will pull them aside and deflate all these extravagant feelings by telling them that Cormac's Chapel is the only thing worth studying here, all the rest being ordinary. That is malicious on my part. They'll look at their cameras and estimate how many snaps they've wasted on stuff that their guide has just judged mediocre. But it will be worth it. I genuinely want them to realize how the little things in Ireland are often what should command our greatest attention. If they bring anything home from this trip, that will be it.

Mr. Know It All gets his comeuppance in the first thirty seconds. Pushing Carol up the hill in a borrowed wheelchair, I notice that Cormac's Chapel is engulfed in scaffolding and a green, impenetrable mesh. The tour guide's nightmare. What we came here to see is bundled like a package.

I cannot conceal my disgust. To come all this way for nothing! I fulminate about Irish incompetence. They could have told me yesterday when I had telephoned to reserve this wretched wheelchair that Cormac was suddenly out of bounds. How dare they trample my itinerary. I demand to speak to whomever is in charge, and even Carol, seldom at a loss for words, however disjointed, seems awestruck at my unseemly anger. An innocent little girl emerges from an office and I berate her.

"Why didn't you tell me about Cormac's Chapel?"

"What was there to say, Sir?"

"That you had it all wrapped up for Christmas, by God, that it can't be seen, isn't open to the public, is impenetrable, locked away, and for all intents and purposes, invisible! That's enough for you to have said!" I can feel spittle on my beard, my hands are sweaty. I want to do something outrageous, vent my anger, push Carol over the side, wheelchair and all.

"I'm sorry, Sir, but I guess I thought you'd have known."

"Known? How could I have known? I'm not a mind reader."

"The chapel has been like that for six years, Sir. Surely you'd be aware of that, being a tour guide and all."

Alden twerps in, "Six years, Jim, that's a long time. How could they know that you wouldn't be quite up to date? There, there, Jim, take it easy, blood pressure and all, take it easy."

"No one's blaming you," says Susan. "Don't take it so seriously. It's not important to us; we're going to love it anyway."

I'm led away like a wounded soldier just blinded by tear gas, my troops consoling and taking me away arm in arm. I hear Carol behind me. "Exactly. Don't be so ridiculous, darling, it's only a building."

Cormac's Chapel, Rock of Cashel

We troop into the little auditorium and watch a film or a slide show, I forget which. I'm in a total stew and try to get a grip on myself. Rain thunders on the roof, tourists flee the rock amid heavy gusts of wind. During an interval in the showers I lash my group up the hill.

The view is remarkably fresh and vital, and I feel somewhat restored.

The gorgeous blend of gray skies and sodden green meadows, the under-appreciated ruins of Hore Abbey in the fields below us, and a gypsy campfire by the stone wall at the edge of a copse of trees bring wisps of music to my mind—bagpipes, a snippet of Van Morrison, some half-forgotten reels. We seek refuge in the cavernous cathedral, open to the furious sky. Everyone is suddenly cold and wet, the women wrap plastic rain hats over their heads. I'm getting soaked too, Carol is shivering, but no one wants to leave as I go into my spiel. I get a big appreciative laugh from what was, in fact, a pretty funny story regarding one of the earls of Kildare, scolded by his English master, Henry VII, for burning all this to the ground in 1495. "Your Highness, the fault is mine to be sure, but I thought the archbishop was inside." He, like me, was forgiven. "That was great," Alden exclaims, as we dash for the bus. Carol loves the wheelchair and regrets that we must leave it behind.

Our lodgings tonight are unexpectedly sumptuous, and I try to feign indifference as we enter the luxurious Palace Hotel, located at the foot of the rock just off the main street of town. This Georgian masterpiece was the work of Sir Edward Lovet Pearce, the architect responsible for the Houses of Parliament in Dublin. It was completed in 1732 for the Protestant archbishops of Cashel, who had tired of the damp, dark, windy, archaic, and cramped quarters traditionally available to their office up on the hill. One of these noble gentlemen, traditionally identified as Archbishop Price, who held the post from 1744 to 1752, took this domestic inconvenience one drastic step forward by abandoning the cathedral as well, being either too fat or too lazy (possibly both) to hazard walking up the hill twice a day for service. The roof was then unceremoniously stripped from the old medieval building, and Cashel's decline to a ruinous state commenced.

We are led to our various quarters and I am gratified as the door swings shut behind me. Peace . . . and what a room! Floor-to-ceiling windows look over the charming driveway, lined on either side by trees. Genuine antique furniture is all over for me to sit in, write on, and hang all my odds and ends of clothing. The bed is dwarfed by an enormous canopy of ruffled, expensive-looking fabric (surely an inauthentic touch), and the bathroom has a tub the size of John's bus. I greedily collect all the freebies in sight: shampoo, conditioner, soap, shoe polish, postcards, and tuck them away. This certainly beats camping.

However, one of the tour telephones me to complain about a lack of heat in her room. I suggest she talk to the hotel people and not me.

Rather than subject myself to further such harassment, I decide to go out for a walk. The receptionist says I should visit the local Catholic church. "It's finally been redone, and it's gorgeous." I get directions and tramp off in the rain.

◆

Being a Roman Catholic entitles me, I think, to the freedom of saying what I wish when it comes to my own religion, or at least its "physical" properties. Entering most churches in this country is a depressing experience and personally makes me wonder how the severance between a Cormac's Chapel and what passes for a decent place of worship can be so complete. Whatever happened to taste? According to my wife, of course, the answer is simple: The Irish never had any to begin with. Walking with (or without) her at places like Clonmacnoise and Devenish and Kilmacduagh disposes of that argument pretty quickly, as does a stroll through any of the museums in Dublin that features works of art by the ancient Celts. But there is no denying the fact today that taste is a feature in short supply, at least in the domain of modern ecclesiastical architecture. The newest of these churches resemble little more than drive-in banks for the most part, claptrap that postures as groundbreaking advances in the science of design, but that in truth reveals a fundamental ignorance of just about every notion regarding form, balance, and appropriate reserve. On the other end of the spectrum is this one in Cashel, nineteenth-century ersatz Gothic with lavishly decorated multicolored slabs of polished marble, gleaming and prolific applications of brass, brightly illuminated murals with layer upon layer of gold leaf application—an overwrought blizzard of Victoriana. As I sit in a pew I am reminded of the equally garish church I went to as a child in Boston, the many hours spent gazing at the Virgin Mary as she ascended into heaven through an orgiastic rainbow of paint, the pathetic sermons, my mother pushing me out in the aisle to be a server when the priest came out alone for mass. I knew more Latin than he did.

Four elderly parishioners recite the rosary aloud off in a corner, confirming my loathing of the Mariolatry I endured growing up. The famous Irish historian William Lecky had it right. Catholicism is a woman's religion—sentimental, superstitious, soft, and weak—which makes me wonder why I believe. Lecky, need it be said, was a Protestant, and that irritates me. How would he know what it's like to be Catholic?

Back at the Palace I have an enormously hot bath, then get into my finest attire and head for the bar. It is full of Americans, though no one from my crew, who evince little weakness for alcohol. On my third gin I take stock of the place. Its walls are covered with the autographs of famous guests, the peripatetic Richard Burtons and Elizabeth Taylors of the world who have probably never spent a night in their own beds. Surprising to me, though, is the number of rock stars who have come to Cashel: Peter Townsend, Marianne Faithful, Van Morrison, Mick Jagger, and even Bob Dylan, of all people. As I think biographically, it seems to me that most of these characters came from rough-and-ready backgrounds, the backstreets (and even slums in some cases) of urban decay. Now, probably, being millionaires, they take all this luxury as a right and a commonplace. They would never deign to notice enormous bathtubs and free shampoo—it's all of a day's pleasure for them. I meditate on the moral advantages of spending nights in hay barns or off the side of a road in a cramped car, sleeping bag fetid or full of crumbs from a late-night sandwich. Smelly socks, dirty underwear, blue jeans stiff with three weeks straight out in the backcountry. I begin to feel uneasy. This place really isn't for me.

One of the obviously rich Americans here is engaged in a conspiratorial conversation with the barkeep. "When can we go?"

"Ah, tomorrow, Sir, we'll have success tomorrow, you can count on it."

"Are you sure? How much will it cost?"

"Ah, if it's cost you're considering, Sir, we needn't bother to go at all."

"No, no, no, don't worry, MNO, MNO."

"Sir?"

"Money's No Object, so long as we get it."

"And we will, Sir, we will."

The American goes off. "What was that all about," I inquire. "Drugs?"

"Not at all, Sir, not at all. It's Michael Collins, Sir, the gentleman would have something of Michael Collins."

"What's your connection to Michael Collins?"

"Well now, a cousin of a cousin of a cousin, if you get my meaning. The gentleman wants something that Michael Collins might have been in contact with, again if you get my meaning."

"You mean a toothbrush?"

"Well I was thinking of something else, a picture frame, I'd say, that his mother owned. That'll do it for sure." Add Michael Collins to the celebrity list. He would have loved the Rolling Stones.

The group gathers at the dining room door promptly at 6:30. I assume promptly only because they're all there whenever I show up, usually late. I had originally been told by my employer that the tour would eat separately, in other words, that we could all eat dinner when we wished and sit alone if we wished, but the group dynamic has decreed otherwise. Strange as it seems to me, the tour members want to take their meals en masse. This evidently makes everyone feel secure, part of the mainstream, one for all and all for one. It also ruins my evenings.

It has inevitably led me to drink more than I customarily do. I'm the last to arrive, "one for dinner" in hand. That means I also always sit next to Carol because once I'm viewed tottering along a sort of musical chairs ensues and we two end up together. God knows, no one else wants to be her dining partner and I certainly understand why. This woman is, well, tiring.

Tonight, as we eat in the archbishops' magisterial dining room, the ambience is cruelly distorted by Carol's recitation of her life's story, which appears, if any of this is to be believed, risqué. Titillation, however, resembles pornography and inevitably becomes boring after an hour or so. Drink service is slow, so I have to listen as Carol announces that she's a famous actress. "I did *The Great Man's Lady* with Barbara Stanwyck. Oh she was divine, my dear, simply divine. And *In Our Time*, Warner Brothers did that one. And my most famous movie was *Juke Girl*, with Ron . . . you know, darling, Ron Reagan. He was a dream. I played Jane, she was a saucy little thing but unstable." Carol passes around her photo ID card for the Actors' Guild or the Screen Guild or whatever, in which her smile is the widest this side of the Atlantic Ocean, all teeth. Why are actors and actresses so much bigger than life, I think to myself in annoyance. Big smiles, big laughs, big expressions, and all wrapped up in capes and gold-headed canes and enormous rings, the jewels of which are most certainly fake—the theatricality of it all, for want of a better word. I begin to think I'd have enormously disliked Yeats. Carol keeps churning away. "Surely you remember Jane, darling, my most difficult role. I was losing my mind the entire film, and that's not an easy thing for an actress to do." What a thin line there is between art and life.

I walk through the bishops' garden after dinner and through a gate in the wall up to the hill, all illuminated in a yellow glare of spotlights. The gypsy fire is still burning. This would seem romantic to me if I didn't know how squalid their little trailers indeed are.

I recall an old peasant story about the Rock of Cashel, that it was a loose tooth spat out by Satan, and happened to land here in the middle of this Vale of Tipperary. It is said that a cavity in the crest of a hill south of here known as the Devilsbit mimics exactly the proportions of Cashel itself, an intriguing coincidence, if true. I wonder whether to tell this old wives' tale to my group as we drive to Clonmacnoise tomorrow, despite my promise to spare them the usual malarkey. I had never expected this job to present me with such a wealth of moral dilemma.

"With Head Held High, I Will Touch the Stars"

I go to mass this morning with Ted, a born-again Catholic, who attributes his recovery from kidney disease to God Above. I hate to disabuse him with my own serious reservations as to the likelihood of such a divine intervention. Ted is, after all, on vacation and paying my salary, as it were, so why should I convey a doubt about anything so serious? This insight makes me feel like a personal chaplain, indulging my patron with whatever whims he might need to get through the day. We light votive candles together after the service. He notes when we're outside that my offering was woefully insufficient, and he's right; I was emptying my pockets of ha'penny pieces. He actually seems miffed with me, so I go back inside and put a pound in the poor box.

Our first stop this morning once again challenges John's skill as we twist and turn along a series of boreens that seemingly go nowhere. If we didn't have my ordnance survey maps to guide us, we'd never find anything, because John's never been here and wouldn't know a motte from a bailey anyway. I can tell I'm beginning to open his eyes at least. When he says to me, under his breath, "Do you think they really want to see *this?*" I know I'm doing the right thing.

When the Normans first laid claim to a piece of the countryside, they generally built a motte, and there are few artifacts of their occupation so essentially mundane as these. A motte, quite simply, is a mound of dirt surrounded by a dry ditch. Many of the more hastily constructed mottes are not very imposing—the one I see from the top of Moyode, for instance, is only twenty feet high—but others are often immense, such as the one in front of us, called Knockgraffon, which rises to a steeply pitched eighty feet or so and dominates all of us staring up at it. On top of these artificial hills the Normans built for themselves one or two wooden shacks with thatched roofs, and surrounded them with a palisade, usually logs driven into the earth. As time, resources, and settled conditions allowed, a smaller and larger mound called a bailey was then built at the base of the motte. It too was encircled by a rough wall of timber and then another ditch and usually contained an assortment of outbuildings for retainers and the usual collection of livestock, mostly stolen. Generally a crude, elevated walkway connected the lower bailey with its higher motte, which featured a ten-to-fifteen-foot gap about two-thirds of the way up. During daylight this gap was traversed by rough boards, which were drawn up each night as a security precaution, hence the sobriquet "drawbridge."

When I played with toy soldiers and castles as a child, the drawbridge had special appeal, the huge gate with its creaking chains lowering and raising some cumbrous contraption for armored knights to pass to and fro. The simple progenitor of such a grand edifice—just a few slabs of wood used at Knockgraffon and hundreds of places like it—mocks the illusions we all have of medieval life, mostly gleaned from movies totally removed from reality, and I try to explain to the group how both simple and tawdry life must have been here. One story I relate is of a motte under siege by Celtic raiders who had succeeded in breaching the bailey's defenses. The Normans holed up in the motte were soon to be inundated by fresh hordes of attackers, but they held a certain advantage in one respect: They had hostages of the clan in their keeping. Rather than bargain for their lives with these captives, they threw them over the walls with ropes around their necks and hung them all, a grisly necklace of writhing bodies that could do nothing but inflame the passion of their enemies. No one ever accused the Normans of either subtlety or cowardice.

Knockgraffon impresses the tour, but no one wants to climb up to the summit for its fine view. I go myself. I cannot imagine coming here without going to the top. Even if I were eighty, I'd crawl to get there.

Knockgraffon Motte, County Tipperary

A couple of miles down the road we stop at Athassel Priory, founded by one of the famous Norman invaders in 1193, one William de Burgo, about whom the tour will have an earful later on. This is a charming spot, a fortified monastic settlement once surrounded by a moat supplied from the nearby river. I blithely climb over the stile and start for the ruins, but John calls me back. Rebellion at the wall.

"What about them?" Cynthia asks.

"I'm sorry, what about what?" I reply, missing the point.

"Them," she points out, as a herd of thirty to forty cows ambles in our direction. These cattle are admittedly huge animals, but their collectively dumbstruck demeanor is a pretty accurate barometer as to the behavior that can be expected from them, and I say so.

"I don't know," says Cynthia. "Are you sure they won't hurt us?"

"What about bulls?" asks Alden helpfully.

"Right, Jim," John joins in, winking maliciously, "I just saw some footage from Spain that would make your stomach churn, nasty stuff, a young girl gored and stomped." He means this as a joke, but the group isn't taking it that way. Meanwhile, one of the animals in question deposits an enormous plod of fresh manure at my feet, followed by the sound of Niagara Falls as she urinates a couple of gallons of waste.

"Oh, how disgusting," Carol cries, and back she totters to the bus, a sequence of events I know I'll want replicated in the next few days. This cow is my friend.

But anyway, to the task at hand. "Harke then, ye jolly shepheards, to my song," says I.

"John Donne," laughs Susan.

"No, Susan, we're in Ireland! Spenser . . . "

> With that they all gan throng about him neare,
> With hungrie eares to heare his harmonie:
> The whiles their flocks, devoid of dangeres feare,
> Did round about them feed at libertie.

In this merry poetic mood, I wave my hands and herd these offending animals a safe distance away, then return to urge my timid travelers onward. They walk to the priory in gingerly little steps, aghast at the organic mess these cattle have left in their wake. Almost on purpose I step into a fresh cow pod. "See, still alive!" I cry. Cynthia later asks me if I'm going to leave my boots out for the hotel people to clean. "Not in my lifetime," I reply.

This brush with reality has exhausted the troops, so we stop for an early lunch. Carol has started ordering hot toddies as her noontime beverage of choice, which is fine by me. She usually nods off for the afternoon and doesn't cause any trouble. The others, I am glad to observe, are loosening up as well, orders for Irish coffee coming in a rush. Everyone is curious about the Guinness I perpetually drink: What's it made of? What's it taste like? and so on, though never venturing to try it themselves. I order a pint and nine glasses, pouring a sample for everyone. This staff of Irish life receives uniformly low marks. "That is really revolting," says Cynthia, who orders a whopping Canadian Club and ginger to get the taste out of her mouth. "Canadian and ginger," says the bar girl, aged thirteen, "what's that?"

◆

This afternoon's highlight is my idea entirely. We have driven two hours north to Banagher, a small village on the Shannon, there to board our rental boat for the trip upriver to Clonmacnoise, one of Ireland's premier monastic sites. I want the group to feel just how lucky the Vikings were.

Camped at Limerick City, the first Viking raiders probably had no idea as to the reach of this enormous watery highway that lay before them. The Shannon wanders into the very heart of Ireland, a two hundred–mile stretch of navigable river that left exposed to those ruthless despoilers an array of both domestic and ecclesiastical treasure, the former in agricultural bounty and female slaves, the latter in gold and jewels. The monastery at Clonmacnoise was plundered thirteen times between 722 and 1205, more than half of these raids undertaken by pagan Vikings and the rest by their Irish and English imitators, who saw no reason not to join in such profitable enterprise. The propensity of Celtic monks to establish their settlements in remoter areas of the countryside contributed to their vulnerability. That was especially true for Clonmacnoise, which sits in plump display along the river's edge, no more than a thirty-second jog for a Viking whose ship had just run up on the river's edge.

I sought to recreate this aura for the tour in my usual innovative fashion. We would glide up the river in one of the new and gleaming cruise boats I had often seen from the shore as I drove about here in the past. We would pass through acres of unspoiled countryside, watery flood plains full of wild swans and other bird life, gaze at meadows with contented herds of livestock in a tableau little changed from eighth-century Ireland, and we'd dock at the foot of MacCarthy's round tower and enter the monastic precinct on foot, like true pilgrims. In other words, just another day on a first-class tour.

We arrive at Banagher on time and are met by a smiling friendly teenaged representative of the boat company, who leads us to, and then past, several expensive-looking river launches with open, outdoor seating that would take full advantage of the glorious sunny afternoon before us. Why does my heart sink with premonition, why do I know that this deal has been botched? This is Ireland, my friend, remember that.

We finally reach our craft, a derelict relic, I would guess, from De Valera's navy (if he had one), a diesel-spewing, noisy, totally enclosed, and claustrophobic death trap whose greatest achievement, to my mind, is that it somehow remains afloat. I go on board first and note that all the windows, being Plexiglas, are permanently fogged from years of abuse and thus impenetrable. So much for the view. Our captain is a ragged-looking youth with his nose stuck in a newspaper, the public address system is blaring with rock, and the only thing going on here in a shipshape sort of way is a bar set up in the back. Totally unacceptable.

"This is not what I had in mind," I tell the girl. "I want a boat that lets us sit outside. I'm not going in this thing." I sense a tremor pass through the group, a sort of thermal charge streaking from body to body. I see Alden turn to his wife, an eyebrow arched, as though in warning, "Oh, Oh, here he goes again."

The girl's smile evaporates and her face turns steely. "And what's the matter then? Here's what you ordered."

"No, I ordered a nice quiet open boat, not a stinkpot like this. We're going up the beautiful, serene Shannon, and you're going to poison us with fumes and drown away our thoughts with engine noise." Pearl Jam is blasting away behind me. "And tell him to turn off that music!"

"Tommy, cut off the music," she barks. "Shall we discuss this in the office?" I follow her, ready for mortal combat. As though spitting in my direction, she hisses something along the lines of "I've lived here all my life, and you take the cake. The Shannon serene? Ha!"

"And what is it you want then?" This from behind her desk, which reminds me of a convenience store for some reason. Has she a gun underneath the counter?

"A different boat."

"I don't understand this. No one has ever complained before."

"There's always a first in life."

"Thirty Germans took that boat yesterday and they had a grand time."

"How much beer did you sell?"

"Quite a bit actually, they really enjoyed themselves. If you loosened up a bit yourself, you'd enjoy it too." That's it, I leave the office to get John, just in time to see him pull out of the car park on his way to Clonmacnoise to meet us. I run after him waving my arms, but he doesn't see me in the cloud of exhaust. The group, however, does see me. They're old enough to note some similarities here between their guide and some farce with Peter Sellers or Terry-Thomas in the starring role. Even I'm aware that my dignity factor is slipping.

I return to the office, where the girl and three cohorts are arguing behind closed doors. I can see some vigorous gesticulating through the
plate glass window, then all eyes turn to me. If looks could kill, I'd be up
dangling from the light pole outside.

"No other boat is available, Mr. Roy."

"Why not?"

"Insurance regulations."

"That's ridiculous. I'll take that boat there," pointing to a bright new
Chris Craft.

"Out of the question."

"Why?"

"We don't own it."

"Show me one you do own."

"You've seen it already."

Silence. A long silence. "That's your only boat?"

"It's the only boat currently in service. The others are undergoing
maintenance."

"How many others would that be?"

"Oh, there must be twenty in our fleet."

"All undergoing maintenance."

"Just so. You could, of course, continue running after your driver.
Your guests would enjoy the exercise, I'm sure, particularly the two
women with the canes. In which case you'll forfeit your deposit, as I'm
sure you realize." Not bad for a kid, I say to myself. Now I understand
why the Irish love the chase, how they thirst for the kill, the final death
throes of the poor, outgunned fox.

I count out $250 in Irish money and hand it over. What I'd like to do
is pull out a flamethrower and incinerate the stuff right in her hand, but
instead I give out a smile, a "let bygones be bygones" sort of gesture. She
is by now so torqued that nothing I can do will alter her petty hatred of
me, so I refrain from offering congratulations, that all of them should
be very pleased, they've just screwed a famous author and sent yet another tubload of dumb American tourists up the sunny river. I walk out
a defeated man.

The group regards my approach with both relief and some degree of
apprehension. They remind me of children who hate to watch their
parents fighting. Susan points to our maritime disaster, smiles, and signals thumbs up. Carol cries out in shrill, theatrical tones, "Anchors
aweigh!"

The trip is a disaster. The barmaid, yet another girl of sixteen or so, has a microphone in hand encouraging us all to get drunk as quickly as we can because Clonmacnoise is *only* two hours away. Then she launches into what promises to be a long, garbled, incoherent, disheveled, and utterly ridiculous rendition of ancient Irish history that might have impressed the Germans of yesterday, particularly those who understood no English, but that I simply am in no mood to tolerate. I'll do the talking here, I suggest to her in pointed fashion, and she returns to the bar in a pout. Everyone looks out the windows in embarrassed silence, but because you can't see anything out the windows, they look at me instead. Ted takes pity on the bar girl and buys a Coke. Carol goes to sleep, as do one or two others, and we motor noisily upriver in a kind of mindless oblivion.

Clonmacnoise had long been my favorite place in Ireland, though for many reasons unrelated to anything very special there. The monastery, for instance, is simple and unpresupposing, despite its two round towers, a plethora shared with only one other ecclesiastical settlement on the island. Its high crosses are famous, though many similarly fine examples can easily be found. The Romanesque doorway of the Nuns' Chapel, commissioned by the famously wayward Dervorgilla O'Melaghlin in 1167, is fine, but not the best you can see. And the location, superb though it may be, is not unique in the desolation and splendor that nature provides here. But for me the place has always been special, tinged as it is with my own quite elevated sense of personal worth as a writer and gifted observer of this special land. Over the years, however, it has descended into the netherworld of Golgotha. It is thus personal to me in ways that I often find difficult to explain.

Many travelers, when they stumble across something special or out of the way, think of themselves as discoverers and subconsciously plant a flag of sovereignty and declare it under God as their own private preserve. In Irish terms that is, of course, absurd, because there isn't an inch of ground in this parochial land that someone hasn't rummaged through hundreds of years before and probably claimed with far more right than some idle tourist. Even so, I've been coming to Clonmacnoise for over thirty years, in every season of the year and in all types of weather, and I know every inch of it.

I know every inch because I've tramped it all so many times, and I did that because I could never get anything I wrote into print. My first book of Celtic history, for instance, took over thirteen years to see the light of day, the only benefit thereof being the opportunity to revise the manuscript many times. As Clonmacnoise was a featured chapter, it gave me the excuse to always came back to get more insight and that perfect photograph, the one that always got away. In summer I'd camp in the ruins or on the top of a long esker ridge that overlooks the entire site; in winter, I'd sleep in the car. Before dawn I'd get up and wander about trying to get shots of Clonmacnoise by moonlight or Clonmacnoise by the dawn's first glimmering in the east. I'd wade through boggy pasture, slip into mud holes in the predawn ink of night, startle bullocks into terrified shrieks of wonderment as to who this stranger could be, to no avail. In all that time I never got a photograph that really pleased me, but in some ways it didn't matter, at least I was out there trying. And the wonderful memories! The flocks of swans battering down or up the river, the heavy beat of their wings like muffled drums; the ponderous procession of cattle wading into the quiet river for their first drink of the day; the lovers I disturbed among the tombstones, the thief I nearly scared to death as he tried to pry an ancient grave slab from a wall; the schoolkids who laughed at me brushing my teeth at the old hand pump by the National School. I remember one time when a teacher came to work early and silently, on foot, and caught me with my pants down washing up. She laughed in a merry sort of way, "If Saint Ciaran was here, he'd surely cry, Now hurry up like a good lad." But most of all I recall the serenity of this place, its detachment from everything that was busy, distracting, and venal in the real world just a few hours away by plane. I rather felt like Galahad.

As the years passed, my enthusiasm became turgid with morose defiance. Galahad wasn't the role model here, but Modred, that dark, depressed, crudely ambitious man. The pink slips were adding up, the literary world wasn't much interested in my particular take on the old Emerald Isle. In a childish confusion of metaphor, I saw Clonmacnoise as the symbol of my own personal epic, a place of literary martyrdom. It wasn't Christ I was dying for, but my work, my poor neglected work. Everyone in New York was going out on expense account luncheons, eating pâté, drinking gin, but here I was slogging about, growing older by the day and a good deal more crotchety, susceptible now to pneumonia and broken bones, blasting my lungs with an atomizer to choke down the asthma this wretched climate engendered, shaking my fist at an indifferent world. I'd think to myself in self-pitying, semidrunken moods, who else would be here, doing this, to thine own self be true.

(For ages I thought Donne had written that. I was only just reminded it was Shakespeare, another comic blot on my puffed-up reputation.)

After a decade I gave up the bitterness, turned it in for resignation, which more befits a noble character. The book finally came out and then disappeared. I retracted my ambition and grew up. Clonmacnoise may be unique, but I'm not. I pretty much stopped coming. And so, getting off the boat with my groggy crew, I feel like the hack I have become, a degenerative state I realize that Clonmacnoise has slipped into as well.

The years of my absence have not been kind to this place, or so I have read and been told. This process arguably began in 1979 when John Paul II visited Clonmacnoise to immense crowds. A specially built papal helicopter pad was poured just for the occasion alongside Mac-Carthy's round tower from the twelfth century, a juxtaposition that no one at the time thought peculiar. Since then the Church regrettably proclaimed Clonmacnoise a fully sanctioned pilgrimage destination, with all the usual inducements of plenary indulgences kicking in, a new and elaborate visitors' center was built, and an enormous parking lot added on to the complex. Paddy Burke, who helped me restore Moyode Castle, got a contract to build the first set of lavatories seen here in several centuries. Fit for kings, he said to me, extorting a promise that I'd try them out when I came with the tour. I know Alden will want to head for the *Fir* room immediately, being eighty-five and finding it hard now to hold things in between stops. "I never saw a bathroom I didn't like," he tells me cheerily.

We assemble after leaving the boat in the new car park, waiting for Alden to take care of business, then board our bus. In keeping with my authoritarian tendencies, I want to enter Clonmacnoise from the north, not by the main entrance with its ticket kiosks and "interpretive" displays. This is a quirk on my part, I know it and admit it, and everyone indulges me. God knows, they want me happy after that boat ride. John drops us off at the Nuns' Chapel after a five-minute drive, turns around, and goes back to the lot. I wait for the yellow tub to disappear before turning to the group.

I can tell they appreciate these special touches. I decide not to say anything and just lean on a wall. They so expect to be herded and lectured to that at first they can't figure out what's up. I say look around, take in the silence, get a feel for the place, and they do just that. For twenty minutes they walk about on the narrow lane, ponder the tiny, elegant chapel, spot the inevitable swans moving here and there on the Shannon below, and generally marvel at the pastoral perfection of the place. Then we wander onto the monastic precincts along the ancient pilgrims' way, a raised avenue of stones along which generations of ancient travelers once approached Clonmacnoise.

I tell them what I consider the most charming story of its founder's hagiography, the day Saint Ciaran told his parents that he planned to join a monastery. Taking his young son by the hand into nearby fields, his father gave him a present, any dun cow he saw that pleased him, to provide the beloved boy with a drink of milk each morning and evening for the journey ahead. Ciaran left hearth the next day with a staff and a cow, his progress determined each day by the leisured gait of his father's bequest.

We pass through the old graveyard and examine a tiny stone sanctuary known as Ciaran's Church, which allegedly marks the site of the founder's grave, who died of the plague at only thirty-three years of age in 555. Two magnificent crosiers were found here during excavations, and those of course were taken away to Dublin. As we approach the cathedral, a larger than usual Celtic building, though hardly as regal as one might expect from being so characterized, trouble brews. Multiple tours, many as large as sixty people by the look of them, are lined up to approach the principal high cross of Clonmacnoise. I have to take a number, as it were, and put my pathetic assemblage of nine in queue. The other tour guides view us contemptuously.

I use the thirty or so minutes it takes to reach our goal with a few chosen words on Celtic monasticism and its special affection for abstinence and penance. Susan is all ears. "I find this repugnant yet fascinating," she says. "This assault on the body! We're not angels inserted into flesh, we're just poor human beings. Why did these monks always concentrate on the flesh? Isn't the development of the intellect and will what's important?"

I remind her of the age-old maxim of the Desert Fathers, "When the body is weak, the spirit is powerful."

"That is not a modern point of view," Julie pipes in. "It's fine to come here and look at the past, but that's all there is here, the past, and let's face it, it has no message for us today. When the pope came here, what did he preach about? Old monks or new problems?"

"There's no such thing as a new problem."

"Birth control, abortion? Saint Ciaran didn't bother himself with these things."

"Those are just variations on themes as old as time," I reply. "I think what we're talking about are values, and many that some of us grew up with, and usually with difficulty—resisting temptation, not giving in to sensual desire, turning the other way when an easier path invites us to safety or pleasure—these are just as relevant today as yesterday."

"I'll agree with that!" Susan stamps her feet. "What a world we live in!"

"Eire Tours? Your turn," a young girl interrupts. I ascend the pulpit, and address myself to the Cross of the Scriptures.

Irish high crosses are unique, enigmatic, and deeply moving. Often immense—some are over fifteen feet high—and bulky (they can weigh two tons or more), these richly carved and ornate sculptures have enthralled both atheistic antiquarians and peasant believers for untold generations. And the secrets they continue to hide from us! No one knows the origin or meaning of the mysterious halo that usually surrounds the upper shaft, and no one can decipher with complete assurance the identity of various scenes or biblical figures that fill up every available inch of these behemoths. Those are matters that the passage of centuries and the calamities of war, devastation, famine, emigration, and the death of Irish have obscured from us forevermore. There are no answers.

The wonderful contradiction of these pillars is typically Celtic, and thus typically perverse. Like the round tower, high crosses were the inspired response to what many contemporary clerics regarded as the end of the world, the plague of Viking heathens that descended on Ireland beginning in 795. These rapacious dogs of war were connoisseurs of plunder: jeweled miters and crosses, gold chalices and heavy gospel books adorned with covers sprinkled with precious stones, all those they considered well worth the splattered blood of monks, abbots, and workmen who lived in and about the ancient monasteries, many of which were already entering their third century of holy habitation.

What soon became needful to all Irish patrons of ecclesiastical art was some artifact of sanctity and holiness that, in fact, would fetch nothing in the marketplace of gold and silver. Viking burials and hordes in Scandinavia of the eighth through twelfth centuries routinely offer up the brooches and cups and crosiers of monastic Ireland, but no worthless chunks of ordinary stone. A high cross, as the Vikings would discover to their rage, could not be hauled away, broken up, and sold for its precious essence. However valuable in an ethereal, spiritual fashion, there was nothing about it that gave the Viking any profit for body or soul. Even worse, the cross provided none of the vicarious thrills to which Vikings had grown accustomed, the smearing cloud of destructive fire and the happy sound of crumbling rafters. It could not be put to the torch; it could not be vandalized in any meaningful fashion; it was too difficult to even drag away and throw into the river. All one could do was push it over to the ground, a dull thud or squish the only reward for all the heaving and grunting required. Very anticlimactic.

For the modern visitor, however, just the opposite. Here's a priceless fine art treasure that is accessible, free of restraint, not hidden away in some museum in Dublin, London, or New York, guarded by security people and a myriad of barometric devices intended to monitor climatic change in a vault. The high cross is Ireland's Rosetta Stone, Ireland's Michelangelo, Ireland's version of *The Night Watch*, open to the air in its natural environs. "This is the real thing," I say emphatically, giving the cross a good, resounding whack with my hand. Everyone is in awe. Everyone is dumbstruck. Everyone knows something's wrong.

Ted speaks right up. "That was a hollow sound, Jim; that didn't sound right." I pat the cross again. Definitely not right. It looks like stone, it feels like stone, but it isn't stone. Truly bewildered, I look about me, but my mind isn't working. I find one of my compatriots in the group tour business giving me a very sour look, one of open exasperation. What's the matter with her, I recall thinking to myself, is she in a hurry?

This young arrogant upstart approaches, and I half expect her to ask me for my union card. She takes me by the elbow. "Have you been doing this for long?"

"For years, dear, for years. Why?"

"The cross is a replica, a casting. The real thing is over there in the visitors' center. The same for the North and South Crosses over there. Honestly, where have you been?"

"Here and there, mostly there I guess. Well, no point in getting mad about it."

"And another thing. We know perfectly well what all the panels mean. We're all agreed on that around here. The one you said might be Daniel in the Den? It's Christ Entering Jerusalem. You really could do with an update. They sell guidebooks in the visitors' center. I suggest you buy one and read it."

My cheeks are burning, her triumph is complete. In front of forty or fifty people this half-baked provincial Yahoo has humiliated me in public,

raised blisters on my face the way ancient Celtic poets did when they sat-
irized their foe around the open fire or in a banqueting hall. What's more,
she's enjoying herself.

I feel a stirring behind me, however, and sense of movement among
my troops. Susan pipes up, "So you've decided that that's Christ Entering
Jerusalem?"

"Of course not," my antagonist replies. "The archaeologists decided
that."

"They certainly have not. The latest issue of [and here Susan dredges
up, from God knows where, an Irish journal noted for its sleep-inducing
propensities] just reviewed the entire iconography of these crosses, and
noted how controversial many of these readings are. The archaeologists
don't know, and I dare say you don't either. Are you a professional?"

"A professional what?"

"A professional academic, of course, an historian or an archaeologist or
whatever."

"No, I'm a professional guide."

"I thought so," says Susan scornfully.

"And your book, Madame, is it for sale near here so that I may purchase a copy?" Alden asks helpfully.

"I never said I wrote any book," replies the enemy, getting nervous.

"Oh dear," says Alden. "Have you read . . . ," and here he name-drops
my three no-doubt-remaindered books.

"I'm quite familiar with those titles," the guide replies. "I pride myself
on being quite up to date on all the current literature."

"Well then, meet Mr. Roy, their author." The tides are turning. I feel
it in my bones.

"Oh my God, I just bought your book in the gift shop," blurts out a
young American woman in my antagonist's group. She brings it over
and I autograph it. I am on fire with delight. "Have we finished here?" I
ask my followers, and we retire in triumph to our various cubicles in
Paddy Burke's lavatory, as excited as any band of Fianna returning from
battle, the tumults and shouts of victory still fresh in our ears. "That was
divine," says Carol. "Just like in the movies."

That night, feeling mellow, I buy everyone an Irish coffee. As Hor-
ace said, "Sublimi feriam sidera vertice"—with head held high, I will
touch the stars.

II

Ashtown

oscommon Town is not a destination most casual tourists place on their Irish itineraries, though it is often crowded with Americans, many of whom come here to unravel their roots, particularly if their last names happen to be O'Connor. The O'Connors are generally appreciated as the closest thing there is to royalty in Connaught, and until recently there was still alive a direct male descendant of the last "high king" of Ireland, known as the O'Conor Don. The royal seat remains, as it has for over a hundred years, a nearby nineteenth-century country house, called Clonalis, which houses a library of fairly rare manuscripts from as long ago as the sixteenth century. The current blood of this line is female, however, and has resorted to hiring the place out for luncheons and teas, mostly to the aforementioned American trade of Irish extraction and appropriate O'Connor pedigree.

I am familiar with Clonalis mostly because the old coronation stone of Connaught lies in pieces on its lawn. It formerly stood on a hill known as Carnfree, which dominates the ancient Iron Age settlement of Cruachain, where many raths and earthworks lie scattered over several miles, and is the scene of an enormously important collection of saga tales known as the *Táin Bó Cuailgne* (Cattle Raid of Cooley). You can still make out the chiseled imprint of two feet on the royal stone, where the king, or "captaine," stood when he received the wand of sovereignty. Most of the young bucks so crowned probably died some miserable, bloody death well before they turned thirty.

The O'Connors were primary antagonists of people like the Norman de Burgos, those rapacious barons who never seemed content with their lot in life. William de Burgo, whom I introduced to the tour at Athassel Priory near Cashel, left those environs soon after his victories there and headed north into Connaught. The O'Connors and other Gaelic clans resisted stoutly, but the relentlessness of Norman ambition wore them down. In 1175 Rory O'Connor admitted defeat, sending envoys to far-away London to plead with Henry II that he protect the Irish from further encroachment. Henry granted O'Connor the five *cantred*s of Roscommon in perpetuity, but afterward unleashed his vassals for further spoil. In 1278 the "foreigners" built their first castle in Roscommon Town. Though burned repeatedly by the O'Connors, this edifice gradually evolved into one of the largest castles ever built in either England or Ireland.

The center square of Roscommon is handsome and busy. The beautiful Georgian courthouse, now a bank, from whence those condemned were inevitably led to the nearby prison and its execution yard, is locally famous for the deeds of one Lady Betty. This dreadful creature had murdered her own son, mistaking him for one of her lodgers who had been sporting a heavy purse. On the day of her punishment the executioner failed to appear, and the energetic Betty volunteered her services in exchange for a pardon. It is said she hanged hundreds of her luckless countrymen over the course of a long, thirty-year career, ghoulishly drawing their portraits in charcoal before applying the noose. The tour group loves this story as we drive on up to the castle, outside of the town center, and park amidst a crew of shabby gypsy vans, out of which emerge the usual motley collection of dirty children and beseeching mothers.* I remark to the group that if Lady Betty were alive today, a lot of people in Roscommon would love to see her busy out here by the castle. "Just like the Nazis," says Marguerite. "They murdered gypsies too. What is it with gypsies?* Why do people hate them so?"

"Well first of all, no one murders gypsies here, let's get that straight, but they are disliked in a culturally distinct way. Aside from being perceived as tramps and thieves and hustlers, I think they suffer from the

---

*Now referred to in Ireland as Itinerants, Travellers, or Tinkers.

same sorts of black magic suspicions that so haunted the Jews in Eastern Europe, sparking off pogroms there of complete irrationality.
They're just automatically blamed when things go wrong." My unexpected sympathy for this underclass produces a completely unexpected
bonanza for the fifteen or so itinerants who are following us around. I
estimate that about £20 in coin and notes is pressed into their grasping
little hands by members of the group. The only person who doesn't give
a farthing, besides me, is John. When our backs are turned, I see him
shooing them away. The tone of his body language is not friendly.

A few miles later, guided by my maps and memory, we pull into a
crossroads called Glinsk, and drive up to an old ruined chapel. John
gives me a look of incredulity, which has become his trademark, so the
group licks its chops in anticipation, another buried treasure in the off-
ing. Alden asks me again, on a scale of one to a thousand, how many
tourists would come here in a year. Zero, is my reply.

People often look to gunpowder as the decisive ingredient that
changed the course of medieval warfare, and in parochial Irish terms
such is certainly the case. Without it, and the primitive trains of artillery
that could, over time, batter down the walls of castles like Roscommon,
the Elizabethans would never have subdued Ireland, however tenuously,
as they had by the year 1600. But the first recorded use of a firearm in
this country is revealingly crude, I think, and dates to 1504 and the Battle of Knockdoe in Galway. There a combatant killed his opponent with
a pistol, but not by shooting him. Instead, the soldier in question found
the gun stock more efficient as a club, battering the man to death with
repeated blows to the head.

Which leads me to Glinsk. Probably the most horrific and wasting
introduction of something innovative to the custom of Irish warfare in
the Middle Ages was not gunpowder or the introduction of some mechanical wizardry like da Vinci's tank, but the gallowglass.

Originally the term "gallowglass" applied to a Scottish mercenary, clad
in helmet and chain mail, the wielder of an incredibly lethal broadsword
that carved a windmill swath through any assemblage of lightly armored
Irishmen who stood against him. These ruthless warriors first appeared
ca. 1250, and though the resort to professional soldiery was nothing new
in the annals of Irish warfare, the savagery of these particular practition-
ers was. "These are men who byde the brunt of death but lightly," wrote
one observer, more used as he was to seeing the Gael cut and run rather
than fight to the very end. When hordes of gallowglass swept through a

countryside in the course of any number of petty feuds for which their hire was required, it is said that nothing lived thereafter. The badge of importance for any chieftain worthy of the name became the number of gallowglass he could afford for his retinue. Some had one or two, others ten or twenty. The greatest lords often mustered hundreds. According to the annalists, they made the land shake in trepidation.

In this despoiled and ruined chancel lies the effigy of a gallowglass, reputedly a Burke, helmet on his head, draped in chain mail, his right hand clutching a sword grip, his left a scabbard, as though ready in an instant of fury to draw this instrument of death. The figure is close to life-sized and striking in its realism. In any other Western European country the sculpture would be a commonplace, unremarked and unremarkable, but in Ireland you can count the number of such memorials on one hand. People do not realize the scale of physical destruction that this country has endured, nor do they understand that when an annalist recorded something along the lines of "the province was wasted," he meant just that. Sometimes I marvel that anything is left.

I had worried that the group would find this stop anticlimactic, but it's pretty clear instead that our visit here is a triumph. Cameras are whirring, clicking away, and I have a hard time dragging people off to the bus to keep on our schedule. "That was more moving to me than Westminster Abbey," Cynthia says to me. "When you have so much to see in a single place or building, it kind of loses the individual touch, you just get overwhelmed by mass. But when you travel so far to see just one thing, one thing alone in an old broken-down shell of a building covered in weeds, it just sings to you."

"It doesn't sing to me," says John, "it yells. That lad looks like my boss in Dublin, and he's a Scot too. A terrible people, if you ask me, altogether too hard."

◆

Driving through pretty countryside en route to the town of Athenry, we detour for Woodlawn, not a village or even a hamlet, but a geographic entity named solely for its grandest ingredient, a ubiquitous Irish Big House.

I had guessed the situation might arise where a degree of surfeit in the realm of abbeys, castles, and medievalism in general might manifest itself within the group, and that a dash of more recent decline would be in order. Woodlawn, one of the largest derelict houses in the west of Ireland, now comes in handy. The problem was arranging our visit.

I had walked the enormous property solo one afternoon before the tour had arrived. A winding avenue leads past a huge gothic gateway "folly" into parkland long ravaged by neglect. Gone are the lovely oaks and beeches, the manicured lawn and finely maintained iron fences. Instead the mighty trees lie uprooted and bulldozed, the valuable wood ignored, roots lying heavenward. Heavy chains tie the rusted gates shut, the noble bridge once built over an artificial lagoon lies festooned with ornamental stonework—Georgian vases, plinths, and quoins—all pushed over or cast aside into weeds as though so much trash. The great house, with hand-painted signs daubed roughly on the huge entry doors warning of nonexistent attack dogs, reeks of dry rot, decay, and terminal abandonment. Out back, the enormous semifeudal assemblage of kitchen gardens, horse and livestock stables, garden sheds, and cottier homes, lies in picturesque and suitably melancholic ruin. This vanished life, not gone for so very long now, seems hung in the balance. A man with deep pockets could pull this place back together, but the window for opportunity is closer to shutting with each passing, destructive year.

On leaving the property, I came across a farmer, who gave me a rueful look. "Today's your lucky day, Sir, your lucky day indeed."

"Oh my God," I replied anxiously, "is there a bull in there I didn't see?"

"No, no, but the owner, praise be to God, he didn't see you. If he had, he'd have pulled his shotgun on you, and that wouldn't have been pretty. He's a terrible temper on him."

As a lifelong trespasser in Ireland, I can hardly believe this and say so, but my informant shrugs his shoulders as though to say warned once, warned enough. I decide to pay the owner a visit and ask my man for directions. "Up the road and past the train station and past the mausoleum and on to the pub, that's where he be."

"The mausoleum?" my ears perking.

"Yes, in the woods to the right past the ornamental gate, if you look carefully, you'll see it. That's where the Trenches all be buried."

Since Ascendancy graveyards hold a special interest for me, I stop there first. The mausoleum sits a quarter mile or so off the country road. Mature trees now obscure its profile, which in the old days must have been prodigious. The central round tower, almost the height of Moyode, sits in the center of a curved burial yard, itself surrounded by a fifteen-foot-high stone wall with ersatz Gothic crenellations, each adorned with the usual cross slits for medieval archers, the sort of Crusader-style decoration the Ascendancy set admired. This exceedingly ambitious memorial was probably thrown up in the midnineteenth century.

The tower is actually a cylindrical shell, open at the top. I hike over the pointed iron gateway, no mean feat, before discovering that the padlock is rusted away and need only have been given a pull to initiate its self-destruction into a pile of corroded debris. Oh well, I needed the exercise.

Inside the tower a huge grave slab covers the mortal remains, presumably, of Frederick Trench, first Baron Ashtown. I say presumably, because the inscription, being open to the weather, wore away years ago. Given its primacy of place and the magnitude of the funerary arrangement, however, it is clear that this noble edifice was meant to recognize the founder of a line.

One's hopes, naturally enough, circulate round the premise that this long-dead individual was worthy of such ostentation, that his sword stroke won the day at some great battle, or that his oration during parliamentary debate on some essential question helped turn the tide. In truth, of course, the exact opposite is true. These memorials honor the power of vanity. What they really commemorate is the successful bribe.

Frederick Trench, like so many other grasping landlords, wanted more out of life than wealth. This is an ambition that people usually reach when money problems have long since receded into the background, as was certainly the case with Frederick Trench. His family's holdings would eventually reach 43,600 acres, delivering an income of £34,700 yearly, a fortune in those days. But Trench was dissatisfied. He wanted a noble title, and in 1800 a title could be had for your vote in the Irish parliament.

In that fateful year William Pitt, English prime minister, sought to dissolve the Irish parliament and to merge it with Westminster, his reasons for doing so being perfectly practical from Great Britain's point of view. Ireland was too wavering a neighbor, too perverse, opinionated, and riotous to provide the kind of security that Pitt felt England required for its western flank, especially in an age of discord and revolution. His solution was to bind Ireland ever more closely, in every way, to English control. It would require the end of Ireland's nominal independence, a merger into the union, as was the case with Wales and Scotland, and Irish nationalists recognized that implicitly. So did people like Trench, and when Pitt began his canvass to procure the necessary votes for Dublin's parliament to, in essence, legislate itself out of existence, he found easy men, easily bribed. "Mr. Trench's venality excited indignation in every friend of Ireland," wrote one disgusted observer, who presumably listened to the future lord's speech in the House, wherein Trench remarked that he "had, *since the night before*, been fully convinced of the advantages of an Union, and would certainly support it." Trench chose Baron Ashtown as his title.

The first, second, and third barons lived well and comfortably at Woodlawn, periodically enlarging the property, building a private railroad station convenient to the mansion (from which the third baron was often rolled out, dead drunk, after parties in Dublin), adding a ballroom to one wing of Woodlawn, and periodically burying their mothers, brothers, sisters, and the usual array of poor-mouthed appendages to Big House society—far-removed cousins—whose only handout in life was a grave plot. The Ashtowns went to the trough of sorrow and hard times as well, however. The fourth baron, heir apparent, does not lie here, but in Mailly Wood in France, where he was shot to pieces in 1916. And Woodlawn survived the Troubles only because the detested Black and Tans used the place as their local headquarters and vigorously defended the baron's interests. Today's Woodlawn does not bespeak of wealth and fortune, only bitter ruination.

The public house to which I was directed, like many a lonely country place, is strictly utilitarian; its mission in life to serve up porter and beer and whatever happens to be showing on TV. I wonder if an air raid drill is in progress when I enter, not a soul in sight, but the warmth of a human presence so palpable that you can almost feel it, hangs over the room. Dozens of soiled, reeking, grim-looking beer glasses, many half full, lie strewn about the place, cigarette stubs overflow what ashtrays there may be, otherwise are scattered, still smoldering, on the concrete floor. The vertical hold on the television is askew, so Jack Nicholson goes through the ceiling, as it were, every four seconds or so in endless cycle, ghoulishly leering in whatever foolish role he happens to be playing. The volume, of course, is at decibel level, the cash register is blinking " £26, 10 pence." The Tourist Board will not be featuring this place anytime soon.

I shout about, "Anyone here?" No reply. I turn down the TV and pour myself a glass of port. Not the usual half gill, but a nice good wallop. After ten minutes or so, I pour another. In about twenty I hear the crunch of gravel and go outside to meet the present lord of Woodlawn.

The apparition before me is probably Ascendancy Ireland's worst-case scenario, the sort of renegade emerging from the night that would cause dainty little girls to wake up screaming as though from a bad dream. A huge man emerges from his new—though filthy—Land Rover, hooked up to a trailer with a couple of miserable-looking heifers penned inside. A several-day's growth sprouts unevenly over his craggy face, topped by a shaggy head of hair that hasn't seen a comb in a couple of years. Uneven teeth, ragged work clothes, Wellington boots covered in mire, complete a scene of utter wildness. I am reminded of cartoons from the rebellion years of 1798 satirizing the ruthless pikemen of Wexford, riding around on enormous donkeys and shouting, "Erin Go Bray."

The cattle bellow like a couple of foghorns. "They're off to the factory," he says to no one in particular in a voice like a shout, followed by "and what's your business, eh?"

"I'd like your permission to take a small group of Americans to see Woodlawn."

"You'll not be taking anyone on any property of mine!"

That sounds pretty final, but I persist. "They're academics, won't harm a thing, I promise to keep them on the path and we won't be there for more than thirty minutes. I'd be happy to pay you £5 a head."

He looks at me carefully for a moment. "We'll have no talk of money." A pause. "And what interest could they possibly have in the place?"

"It's a magnificent building. They're all students of Irish architecture and very eager to see it."

"And have you seen it?"

"Not for years and years," I lie, "and as a matter of fact that's one reason I'd like to bring the tour here. I'd love to visit the place again."

"Do ye think any of them would be willing to buy the place?"

"You can never tell. They all have money, I know that much. You know Americans."

"Ah, 'twould take three or four million to put it right, 'twould indeed, and 'tis an awful shame. I have vandals there all the time, the damage they do and the cost of insurance that I have for liability, it would turn your head in shock."

"I'm sure it would." I cannot resist this question: "Why on earth did you ever buy the place?"

"The value of the land, to be honest, but I'll tell you something, I always had a respect for the great house, if you get my meaning. The last owner, now, he had no respect. He set a fire in the ballroom to burn it down to collect the insurance money, and that was a low thing to do. I'd like to see a rich American take it over, I would."

"What about a rich Trench or Ashtown?"

"That's a different thing ye be saying now, a different thing altogether."

"Well look, I'll give these Americans the tour, and we'll see what happens."

"You will and all, you're welcome to show it. Keep to the paths, whatever you do."

"I owe you for a couple of drinks, by the way."

"We'll not fall out over that. You're a good lad and off with ye." The two sad cattle are hauled to their fate in a cloud of dirt.

The tour is eager for some easy exercise, so we start walking in along the main avenue. The upended trunks of enormous trees and the shaggy condition of what was once, quite obviously, a magnificent park, reminds Bill of some ruinous nineteenth-century battlefield a few months after the carnage has been swept away. Bull Run, Antietam, Shiloh, come out of his mouth. Everyone feels the heavy air of neglect, desertion, decay, particularly as the huge edifice of Woodlawn comes into view. "This is creepy," says Susan.

"I could move right in," says Carol.

We cross the formal bridge, the gardeners among us drooling over the ornamental stonework that lies strewn about. "That would look magnificent in my goldfish pond," Julie, who lives in Flushing, notes ruefully. In case anyone thinks I'm a snob, I admit to having given the same notion considerable thought on my own, to the point of seeing if I could lift one. Not a chance, they won't budge. "You'd need a tractor to move one of those," I confess.

At the mansion we peer through windows, see long rooms full of ornamental plasterwork, then amble out back to the endless stables, milking parlors, an enormous and ruined greenhouse, a cottage for the estate manager and his family, and finally what was once the formal garden. The odor of boxwood is almost overwhelming, even though the immense enclosure is daily trampled by cows. Ted finds an ornate stone pillar. "A sundial," he announces authoritatively, "minus the sundial," which was of course pried off and stolen years ago. We come to a solid stone cattle trough where John has parked to meet us. These are in some demand these days for bathtubs, I'm told, even though this

Woodlawn

particular specimen would fit our entire party. "This place reminds me of Tara," observes Cynthia, which I don't register at all, thinking of the storied Tara Hill in County Meath, which we will visit. My look is so obviously vacant that she clues me in. "You know, Tara in *Gone with the Wind*. It has that same sad feeling."

"Wait until you see Moyode."

The afternoon passes pleasantly enough. After Woodlawn, we motored south for an hour or so to my old stomping grounds, the decrepit town of Athenry. Moyode, on tomorrow's agenda, is just three miles beyond Athenry's crumbling walls.

Disembarking from the coach, the tour is expecting a Carcassonne or a Neuschwanstein, something resonant with culture, rich, textured, restored, evocative. Both John and I, of course, know better, and frankly, so should they by this point in our saga. I repeat for the benefit of all how threadbare and meager so many of these Irish artifacts can be, the result, as I tediously repeat, of the dreadful history this country has endured. The Elizabethan wars of the 1500s, for example, devastated Athenry repeatedly, so much so that everything here that I've brought them to see looks even today as though a disaster of fire and rapine has just swirled down its filthy streets. As a result, a few of my flock are unimpressed with just about everything that I, of course, find fascinating.

The old town walls, I admit it, are spindly and ragged. The Dominican abbey, "knocked" by Oliver Cromwell, isn't much to see either, despite its many tombs and some fine tracery in the windows. The Collegiate Church was pretty well ruined when Protestants built their parish hall inside the nave a hundred years ago. As that too has been deserted, the whole forlorn assemblage is now one pile of crumbing masonry. The sole remaining gate is admittedly an unimpressive example of medieval architecture, but at least I have its old legend to fall back on, that it will collapse when the handsomest man in Ireland passes through it. Susan grins at that. "You're in no danger," she says.

We tour the castle. It was built by a Norman family, the de Berminghams, in 1270. They were vassals of the powerful de Burgo barons, like the Dolphins who threw up Moyode, and they clearly designed this market town with great expectations in mind, expectations never realized, as any visitor here can figure out for himself.

The Berminghams had begun their job as colonizers on a high note. They subdued the natives, O'Kellys and O'Connors for the most part, afterward building their castle as a time-honored symbol of authority and might. Then they sent runners to the Continent, what we might call modern-day travel agents, who spread the word of the new settlement, offering generous terms from the Berminghams to all those merchants and craftsmen who would venture to try their hand in faraway Connaught. They finagled the right to hold fairs from King John and later kings, and then invited to Athenry the Dominicans, a new order of preaching friars who specialized in urban ministries. Athenry was never intended to be a village, after all, but a city large and prosperous. Meyler de Bermingham went as far as to give the Dominicans land and money to start their church, and when the monks had finished, he happily rolled over a hogshead of wine and a merry drunken feast ensued. But his joy was premature.

Athenry never made it; its fortress—a modest little two-story keep—did not exponentially grow, as did Windsor Castle for William the Conqueror in London, spewing out in time new walls, new towers, new gates, new moats. The savage wars between Gael and Norman, then between Gael and Gael, and finally between Gael and English, never afforded the tranquillity that would allow commerce to develop or wealth to accumulate. Athenry stagnated, as marauding freebooters spoiled the countryside, ruining crops and reeving cattle, occasionally breaching the very town walls to burn and plunder inside as well. Athenry was a frontier marcher town that never outgrew the insecurity of its earliest years. Cynthia, expecting Devonshire or the Cotswolds or maybe even York or Durham, finds instead the littered remnants of unfulfilled visions and hopes. I tell her this is the real Irish story: potential never achieved, value never realized, happiness never shared in full measure.

Archaeologists have just finished some digs around the castle, the results of which I detail. I find it interesting that the excavations were concentrated on the latrine pit and garbage heap of the old knights. "In shit lies the key to knowledge," I intone professorially. But what better place to find out about diet, hygiene, life spans (lots of bones were found, for example), the domestic bric-a-brac of everyday existence, or to put it summarily, the real face of medieval life. Some of my group would prefer discussing heraldry, armor, and antiques, however, and when I get to the part I really like—the Normans used straw for toilet paper—Julie brightly asks me if Yeats didn't live near here. I take the hint and switch gears. We are now going to "do" literary Ireland.

We walk over to the present railroad station, a quaint Victorian assemblage of buildings with plenty of wrought-iron fences and ornamental flourish that remind me of toy train sets from the early twentieth century. This is the site, I explain, where an enormous battle was fought in 1316, when the de Burgos finally crushed the O'Connors for good and all. The great climactic charge of the Norman cavalry took place, it is thought, right at the present ticket counter, where Lady Gregory, six centuries later, used to have her weekend guests for Coole Park picked up in a horse and chaise—O'Casey, Yeats, Synge, Shaw, and all the rest. The group is impressed by my vast sum of local knowledge, but they collectively agree that Athenry is a bit on the grim side, especially when they find out that Yeats thought so too . . . a forlorn place, it dampened his spirit, or so he said. As the group discovers, it's pleasant to find oneself independently in tune with the great thoughts of great men. As usual, I'm on the outside looking in. I love Athenry.

Before boarding our bus to head off for dinner, I knock on the door of a friend of mine in town and introduce the group to him. Tim is a magnificent gardener but also a shameless horticultural thief. He can't go anywhere without snitching a slip of something here or a bit of something there, then getting it to propagate at home. His tiny front yard is a jungle of exotic plants ablaze with color along with plantings that are common enough in Ireland, if not to me. We're stopping because Timmy has pulled some bulbs for me of a dahlia I'd never seen before, Rothsey Reveller, which he, in turn, had dug up surreptitiously years before when he had been a laborer at Castle Forbes in County Longford, a famous baronial establishment well known for its gardens. "I don't know if I should be giving these to you in front of all these people," he half whispers to me.

"Why not?" asks an eavesdropping Susan.

"Well, his honor here, I know what he plans to do with them, see." Everyone looks at the brown package as though it was a brick of heroin.

"Relax everyone," I say, "I'm just planning a little smuggling. I'm going to take these home."

"What's the matter with that?" asks Alden.

"Well, they have all these stupid dogs at Boston and New York these days, sniffing your bags for sausages, cheese, oranges, seeds, or any sort of vegetation. Marijuana's okay, but dahlias, that's a crime."

"I'll take it in for you, darling," Carol volunteers. "No one would ever think of searching me."

Tell them about Castle Forbes, I ask Timmy, who rarely needs an invitation to talk, tell them what life at a place like Woodlawn must have once been.

"Oh it was incredibly grand, incredibly grand," says Timmy, who had worked there for eight years as a gardener in the 1960s. "It had two thousand acres in all, and the building was huge, a real castle all in stone with great walls and towers. Lord Granard, who held it, was a knight I think. He had a ceremonial duty for the king's household, I think it was called 'Horseman to the King' or some such thing, but he was in poor circumstances altogether until he met his future wife, who was an American heiress, tobacco if I'm right. He was a rigid, stately, army type. She was just, well, very loud. You could hear her voice a couple of fields away.

"There were twenty-two of us working the place. Five men alone in the kitchen garden, six men alone in the pleasure garden, and we never saw one another, there was a great wall between us, like two separate kingdoms. There were two men who did nothing but work on the herbaceous borders, and two men whose only job was to gather leaves. I tell you now, those grounds were magnificent. Lady Granard wouldn't allow anything to disturb the grounds, she even made our work horses wear boots so they wouldn't mark the lawns. Lord Granard didn't like that much, but he held his tongue. She had the money, after all.

"Lady Granard was all flowers, she really knew them very, very well. Twice each year, for six weeks at a time, she'd go to Paris; they had an apartment there. She'd take two chefs, two horsemen, two footmen, a maid, and a lady cook with her each time, and she'd have fresh carnations flown in twice a week from Castle Forbes. Ah, she had a thing for carnations. She'd say to me, 'Timmy, if ever you see a better carnation than mine, get it, just get it, no matter how you do it.' Amazing thing was, I never saw a better one than Lady Granard's. And that's where I got my first Rothsey Reveller, and that's why you see them now all over Athenry. I tell you, Jim, you'll be the only one in America with it!"

"Unless they catch me and throw me into jail."

"What a great idea, talking to him," Cynthia says as I cartload her into the bus. "Can you imagine people with money like that?" Since both Cynthia and her husband are doctors, I certainly can. I know how Tim must have felt as Lady Granard marched about hollering for carnations.

◆

We have dinner in a small hotel on the road. This is a "free choice" affair, no "prix fixe" menu, so we can order what we want. I have a pint of Guinness, which slides down well, and look forward to a second to go with my usual fare, lamb chops and chips. "Don't bother with anything else when you order," I say from my knowing perch as we examine the menu, "especially if they claim it's French or promise a sauce. They can't cook worth a damn in this country." Carol is not going to eat lamb for two straight weeks and says brightly to the waitress, a numb colleen straight from the farm, "Now tell me, my dear, what's divine in the kitchen tonight?"

The poor girl is stunned to incomprehension by this inquiry. She looks like an ox that someone has just hit square between the eyes with a cleaver. Moved to pity, I translate. "My guest means to say is there anything out back there that Paddy will not mangle, overcook, or burn to a cinder. You know, anything he's good at?"

"The chops, Sir, I always have the chops meself."

Who says I don't know Ireland?

12

Moyode Castle

 let the group sleep late this morning. All the battles, sieges, evictions, and murders have drained their strength. I am beginning to think they view me now as a marauding Celt myself, bent on vengeance for the indignities heaped upon me in my new found role as Big Brother.

I use the hour or so to brood in my room, where I kick myself for being so free and easy when I wrote the brochure for this tour, because today is the nadir. I am scheduled to host, according to my own petard, "a reception" at Moyode Castle. Oh brother, I pinch myself, I hope they're not expecting tea at Buckingham Palace. I also hope whatever collection of rodents that has been comfortably ensconced in the place since my departure a week ago will have moved out again just as quickly. The last thing I need is for someone to have a heart attack as a bat flies into her hair net, or a cute little field mouse nibbles on heel or ankle. The closest thing to a man with a degree in my neighborhood is the local vet. If anyone keels over at Moyode, that person will die.

The great yellow bus barely makes the gate into Moyode Demesne, in fact, with only inches to spare, Seamus Taylor helping John through with grimaces and shoulder shrugs as the enormous side mirrors clear the granite posts. Certainly I feel peculiar as we motor in along the dirt road toward the castle, perched up front with John, waving to my old friends below who stare up in near stupefaction. I had joked with Seamus the week before that I wanted him and his wife to be barefoot, dressed in black, and both peeling potatoes while sucking on corncob pipes as we came past. We had all laughed over that, but here he is, clutching his cap and looking at me as though I were Prince Charles in a royal coach surrounded by beefeaters. Hasn't he ever seen a bus before?

As we approach Moyode, everyone is on his feet. Incredible as it is for me to believe, this stop is considered by all the group to be the high point of the tour, "to beard the Douglas in his den" as Sir Walter Scott put it. Again, I am fearful of letdown. Moyode is not a museum full of fine furniture, suits of armor, or tapestries, any of which would disintegrate with rot or rust if I kept them here. The place is outfitted like a hunting camp; decor is nonexistent. I have bought a couple of bottles of sherry for the occasion, however, which I hope will blot out a good many visual sins.

The western gales are howling as we arrive, so I tell everyone to gather by the oak door in the lee of the wind, while I talk about the tower and its history, in the meantime unlocking the ponderous key mechanism and pushing forward on my primeval entryway to get it open. As I turn around, what a sight before me. Nine enraptured faces taking in the sight, and then Carol, suddenly faceless. A heavy gust of wind has caught the rear of her cape and pulled it over the top of her head. Suddenly blind, she thrusts two frail arms in the air as though in benediction or, worse, malediction, one of which waves her druidic gold-headed cane. It looks to me as though Banquo's ghost has descended on Moyode Castle and this innocent group of intruders. My look of astonishment causes everyone to look behind, whereupon Carol, in the swoon of a falling swan, silently falls to earth, the heavy sponge of ground enfolding her wraithlike body.

We are all so stunned that no one moves. Like some scene from *Wuthering Heights*, all I'm aware of is the moaning wind. If she expires, I say to myself, I'm swearing everyone to silence and carrying her to the other side of my little stone wall. I have no insurance for this sort of thing, and I don't feel like being sued. Carol, however, is not dead. I don't know whether that is a good thing or a bad thing, but I sense movement all wrapped up in that cloak, then a muffled cry. "Get me up, get me up this instant," and suddenly we are all galvanized into action. "Honestly, what's the matter with you people, haven't you ever seen a person fall before?"

"Only in football games," says Ted helpfully.

I half carry Carol up to the Great Hall and sit her down on one of the rickety chairs that I have, then pour everyone a sherry. Carol says she hates sherry and wants an Irish coffee. Not a propitious moment, I'd say, to begin my sermon on the far-from-glorious history of Moyode Castle, but time's a-wasting, as they say, and I begin.

The Dolphins who built Moyode came to Ireland at the turn of the thirteenth century as feudal retainers of William de Burgo, a typically intrepid warlord whom we previously encountered at some of our earlier stops. William had received for services rendered a "paper charter" from the infamous King John of England. A paper charter, in effect, granted its recipient certain tracts of land and many rights thereon by virtue of a monarch's pleasure. The fact that the Crown had no rights to the lands it granted, lands in fact occupied for centuries by people who had no intention of moving, bothered no one. De Burgo could have these domains if he was strong enough, persistent enough, and lucky enough to conquer them, which this particularly headstrong knight proceeded to attempt.

He was followed by four more de Burgo lords in lineaged progression, each as fearsome and loathsome as himself, and after one hundred fifty years this family found itself established as the premier marcher lordship in Connaught. The Dolphins, as faithful retainers, followed in the de Burgos' train, providing manpower for their armies, stewards for their manor farms, wise counsel when such was required, and their deaths when the ebb and flow of fortune resulted in periodic reversals. In 1270, for example, the annals record the murder of John Dolphin and his son, defending a de Burgo from a predictably nefarious attempt at treachery on the part of the Gaelic O'Connor.

Over time, as is well known, the Normans debased their stock through intermarriage with the native Gaels, becoming "more Irish than the Irish." The de Burgos degenerated into Burkes and became the bane of an English authority that intermittently attempted to impose order and control over the perennially chaotic territories of western Ireland. The kings of Great Britain sought to extract revenue from Connaught, but instead they received mayhem, slaughter, expense. For generations Connaught lay well beyond the strictures of imperial control, its internal wars of internecine greed and vengeance little different from those described in pre-Christian sagas such as the *Táin Bó Cuailgne*.

Like the de Burgos, the Dolphins too went native. Their allegiances were no longer feudal but tribal in nature. They abandoned their Norman French for Irish, adopted Gaelic mores, dressed as the wild kerns they had become, and attended their chieftain on all his petty hostings and squalid intrigues. In 1543, however, one of the Burkes in effect betrayed his patrimony and accepted an English title, becoming earl of Clanricard. In exchange for the backing of Henry VIII in various local feuds—in effect, use of the king's cannon—this particular individual, known in the annals as "the Beheader," promised to adopt English ways, promote the use of the English language throughout Connaught, assist the lord deputy on whatever campaigns were initiated for the "suppression of rebels," and eventually to pay rent for his lands, now to be passed in civilized fashion from father to son.

The Beheader, in fact, fulfilled none of these pledges. He didn't speak English himself, for example, so how was he to encourage its use in Connaught? He merely continued on much as before. But the linkage to London, however tenuous its beginnings, proved over time more durable than anyone involved could have imagined, and eventually the wild Burkes, now Clanricards, became unalterably attached to the English interest. "Clanrackrent," the fifteenth earl of Clanricard, was everything nationalist Ireland detests to this day: a rich Protestant, absentee, evicting, stingy, merciless landlord. When he died without issue in 1916, no one mourned for him in Ireland. By then, there were no Dolphins to speak of anywhere.

Religion, that dangerous and deadly subject, was to be the Dolphins' undoing. Descendants of the Beheader, when it came time to choose, finally sent their sons to Eton in faraway England to learn the rudiments of Protestantism, to remove them from the wiles of wandering popish friars. The Dolphins, petty underlings that they were, clung to Catholicism instead, out of a variety of motives, we may suppose: habit, familiarity, tradition, true faith, fear perhaps of what the neighbors might feel should they turn apostate. Whatever the reason, the fierce and destructive wars that all but destroyed portions of Ireland beginning in the reign of Good Queen Bess, and stretching almost three centuries on up to the revolution of 1798, saw the Dolphins rally to the Catholic standard each and every bugle call. They endured Elizabeth's bloody-handed lord deputies, from Grey to Sidney to Essex to Mountjoy; they suffered through the horrific seventeenth-century wars of religion and Cromwell; they died on the Boyne, at Aughrim, and beneath the walls of Limerick for James II. By the time of the Protestant Ascendancy, they had lost everything. There are records of dispossessed Irish Dolphins in the armies of Catholic Spain and France; there are records of Dolphins transported to the West Indies for treason; there are records of Dolphins hanging on in threadbare conditions in the neighborhood of this tower at the turn of the twentieth century. But aside from a burial crypt tucked away in the ruins of a Carmelite abbey in a nearby town, there is nothing much left of them except this tower.

It is a long story but I tell it well, for if anyone should have a passion for finding out about Moyode, obviously it's me. I've certainly spent enough wasted hours tracking down details, tidbits, and remnants of surviving fact, all of which coalesce to paint a very bare picture indeed. Unlike England or even Scotland, most of Ireland's source material for local history never existed in the first place or disappeared long ago. Local antiquarians hate to admit it, but the Irish have been a race of pyromaniacs. What few facts made it onto parchment, vellum, or paper often went up in flames during countless unrecorded instances of parochial mayhem. I'm amazed, though perhaps the tour isn't, that I have anything at all to say about Moyode.

Since I'm playing a starring role in *This Old Castle*, I theatrically point out for the group how derelict this keep was when I first saw it in 1969, what repairs were necessary, the location of my dungeon where I lock unruly children, and how I function in the place now. I show them my kitchen—"Cynthia, he has a refrigerator!"—and the bathroom, which utilizes the interior shaft down which medieval men and women disgorged their bodily wastes. Susan flushes the toilet and seems amazed that it works. Those who are able, climb up to the top for its magnificent view, and Ted's hat flies off three hundred feet or so to the east.

Later on, we walk across the great field to the ruins of Moyode House, built by the Protestant Persse family in 1823, and right on cue old Frank comes out with his photograph of the place in its heyday. Frank's father is pictured holding the reins of a regal coach horse by the front door. It was his job to hang around and mind this gear when visitors came, and when he wasn't doing that, to make certain all the fires were set and going during winter throughout the mansion. Frank says there were sixty fireplaces in Moyode House. I find this difficult to believe.

My capacity for improvisation is now called upon. I had planned next to visit Kilmacduagh, a fine Celtic monastery from the sixth century, complete with a perfect round tower and set in breathtaking countryside, but everyone is keyed up for more old mansions of decadent aristocrats, and more "terrible beauty" of the Yeatsian variety. So much for the old monks.

Happily, the East Galway countryside is the capital, so to speak, of the Yeats industry. True, Sligo is where the great man spent much of his early life, and indeed, he's buried there, and no one will deny that the "Lake Isle of Innisfree" is still around for poetry lovers everywhere to view. And Dublin has some hold of Yeats's cloak as well, though the original Abbey Theatre was demolished long ago and the great yellow-bricked monstrosity that replaced it does not warm the heart or kindle emotion. But Galway is, I think it fair to say, the hub. Here Yeats purchased his own Norman tower, Thoor Ballylee, and even more important, it was here that Lady Gregory nurtured his genius.

◆

Lady Gregory was born a Persse in 1852 on their great estate, Roxborough, which is only a few minutes drive from Moyode. On the way there I grandstand and show the tour where Hollywood director John Huston lived for years, Saint Clerans, a Georgian mansion that also has an old tower house on its grounds. The group loves this. The place is immaculate, precise, ornamented, restored, tasteful, and rich. I show them the stables and servants' quarters, all spruced up, and relate what a difficult man Huston was to his immediate family while he lived here like a feudal lord. There's a very sad photograph somewhere in the sea of biographies written about Huston showing his daughter, Anjelica, holding hands with him in the garden, the smile on her face a blend of sheer joy and nervous release. Apparently Huston had banished his children and Anjelica's mother, his fourth wife (the model Ricki Soma), to the guest cottage out back, while he entertained various mistresses in the Big House. "I didn't take marriage all that seriously," he is reputed to have said, an understatement gargantuan even by Irish standards. Frankly, this is enough to sour me on what is, in truth, a beautiful estate.

Roxborough no longer qualifies as "a beautiful estate," lying more or less in ruins. Like Moyode, it was burned to the ground in 1922. Major William Arthur Persse was having breakfast one fine June morning of that tumultuous year when a delegation of local peasants knocked on the front door, caps in hand. They apologized for interrupting, but quietly let him know they intended to torch the place. Several helped Squire Persse save one or two family heirlooms and paintings, which they piled on the lawn. Then he and his servants watched as flames consumed everything else that he owned. Persse left Ireland, never to return. The current scion of the family lives in California.

The following morning hundreds of Galway locals swarmed over the smoking heap of brick and slate. Rumor was about that the estate's original founder, Dean Dudley Persse, had purloined the communion chalice and assorted ecclesiastical treasure from one of his livings in the 1680s, allegedly walling it up in Roxborough, and this scavenger hunt was the result. No one today has much good to say of the Persses, but as some sort of redemption to their family honor, let the record reflect that nothing of value was found that day.

We walk through the imposing pair of front gates, reputedly for sale to any foreigner who would like them for his driveway, and walk down what was once the main avenue. The group's interest is high and full of cheer, not so much because anything here is grander than the decrepitude we've toured already, but because this place is tinged by its association with famous people. This is what amuses me about Lady Gregory. No one of my acquaintance, including anyone on this tour, has ever taken the time to read anything she ever wrote—and she wrote voluminously—but everyone knows something about her, no doubt because *she* knew everyone that we'd like to know: William Butler Yeats, George Bernard Shaw, Sean O'Casey, Edward Martyn, and many, many more, they are all in Lady Gregory's diaries and guest books.

The grounds of Roxborough are superb. Sloping pastures edge the little Owenshree River as it perks along merrily, spanned by what specialists (like myself) call the Volunteer Bridge, erected in 1783 by one William Persse.

The Volunteer Movement marks the apogee of the Protestant Ascendancy, that moment in the eighteenth century when Ireland was granted its own parliament and, in a way, the command of its own sovereignty. Those were the heady days of Henry Grattan's speakership, of "Independence" as the Anglo-Irish landowning class took the power that London granted, and Dublin all of a sudden became a real city of aristocratic pretension, with an architecture (Georgian) that suitably reflected and glorified this ascension to greatness. Catholics, of course, shared in none of this.

William Persse was among Connacht's most prominent Volunteers, and he had the money to flaunt that fact, as the construction of this "folly" bridge attests. He even ordered workman to install a memorial plaque in its wall (the Persses were fond of plaques) with a flowering inscription that proclaimed the end to "foreign domination." George Washington became William's hero, even though a Persse had been wounded at Bunker Hill. He corresponded with the famous general and even sent over gooseberry plants with detailed instructions for their husbandry (use plenty of fresh manure). I once wrote a letter to the Daughters of the American Revolution, who own Mount Vernon, to see if any descendants of these plantings still exist, but I never received a reply.

Persse was certainly a gadfly. He evidently harbored no malice toward those of his gentry neighbors who happened to be Catholic, and he forced a reluctant John Wesley to let Persse's coachman drive the preacher from crossroads to crossroads for proselytizing. Wesley, of course, wanted to walk. The Catholic Rising of 1798 ruined the Volunteer achievements, however, proving to extremists that you couldn't really make concessions to Catholicism, nor could you take the revolutionary principles of the American and French Revolutions too lightly. Property, after all, was property. When William Pitt bribed every Irish parliamentarian in sight to vote themselves out of existence as a sovereign legislative body and to acquiesce in governmental union with Westminster, Persse reluctantly went along. It broke his heart to do so.

As we meander through what's left of the Big House, Cynthia comments on how the living room, with its great windows, would have commanded lovely views of a perfect countryside. She assumes in her *Masterpiece Theatre* sort of way that the walls would have been covered with books, old leather-bound sets of Shakespeare and Dante, and oh what a glorious thing to have a cup of tea, a good book, and a cozy armchair by the fire, looking out the French doors to an immense panorama. I detest tea and say so, thinking instead that I'd be drinking port if I had the choice. Then, reminding myself to behave, to stop being so contrary, I continue right along and demolish her happy thoughts one by one. The Persses were, by and large, illiterate sloths who spent their time, energies, and wealth riding helter-skelter about the countryside chasing foxes. They were opportunistic scavengers when they first came to Ireland, and retrograde landlords by the time they quit the place. Unlearned, uncultivated, unsophisticated rural gentry, there were few books to be had in the entire house other than religious tracts, the contents of which they methodically ignored in everyday life. Given to the seduction of local girls, heavy drink, and rakish gambling, the Persses were an unmourned lot. Even Yeats, by God, had little good to say in their defense, and he got all the dirt straight from someone who would have known, Lady Gregory herself, who detested her family.

The vehemence of this oratorical display startles some of my people. They are on the edge, once again, of uneasiness, as their rogue guide appears to be losing it. With reluctance I restrain myself. They're here to have fun, after all, and why should I ruin their innocence any more than necessary? Chastened, I lead them back to the stables area, chatting away innocuously. In Big House terms, I tell them, the farm and service buildings are often all that remain of these aristocratic domains, but their comparative grandeur (considering what they are) still command awe and give a lesson. The pigs lived better on these places than the peasants did.

At Roxborough the yards are full of superb workmanship, with expensive cut-stone lintels and archways, beautifully carved drain catchments and manure troughs, ornate belfry and keeper's cottage. Some of the Gothic embellishments are particularly handsome, especially on what was once an elaborate gateway for horse and hounds that stands at the southeast corner of the walled enclosure. This crenellated, mock Arthurian enterprise, embellished with romantic clumps of ivy and wildflowers, is everything the "cult of antiquity" requires. Susan takes some pictures. She tells me to smile.

After lunch in a grubby pub, we stop at Thoor Ballylee, the de Burgo tower purchased by Yeats for £35, just a few miles walk away from where Sir William Gregory's Coole Park once stood, the country house to which he brought his much younger wife, Augusta, after their wedding in 1880. Thoor Ballylee, I must admit, had a profound impact on me when I first saw it in 1969. However jaded I may have become since those youthful days, there is certainly one body of work that I have never lost my affection or admiration for, and that is the poetry of this wildly erratic, contradictory, whimsical, perverse, and brilliant man, in my judgment the premier literary figure of the twentieth century. He transcends the entire galaxy of other famous Irish writers, even Joyce, who I fear will fall by the critical wayside as time and generations progress. The Irish identity, I foresee, will find itself pasteurized into a gelatin with all the rest of the

English-speaking world, and Joyce's intricate Hibernicisms will drift away into the dark cave of antiquarianism, thus unrecognizable to the mob. Not so with Yeats, who in his best work transcends an Irish parochialism to become, as it were, universal. Some of his poems stun me, and I cannot say that about anyone else.

Yeats lived here off and on for nine or so years. He prophesied that all would turn to ruin here once again, but Yeats never figured on the phenomenon of mass tourism that would alter his home more drastically than the rot and foul weather that he had in mind as the eventual despoiler. As he grew older, the place became too much for him to handle, a premonition I'm feeling myself about Moyode.

Thoor Ballylee is beautifully located in a slight dip between various meadows as they fall to the confluence of two streams. A lovely small arched bridge lies at the castle's base, and when I first came here, the property was walled, protecting a lovely garden of pear trees in which the poet and his family must have spent many delightful hours. This purity of atmosphere has since been unalterably ruined, and I know the tourist authorities who are to blame for it have no remorse whatsoever.

In a way, who can blame them? As the devouring hordes descend on Thoor Ballylee, whatever else could they do? Tourists need to park, they need to defecate, they need to have a Coke or a cup of tea, and last but not least, they need to be educated. Thus a greatly expanded car park, public toilets, and at least half the garden area were torn up to make way for, what else, a cafeteria, a bookstore, and space for the inevitable audiovisual program.

We sit through this movie, and it is dreadful. Just because Yeats is an icon does not mean the actor employed to intone his poetry must sound like Yahweh delivering the commandments to Moses on Mount Sinai—sententious, craggy, profound, and foolish all at once. The actor butchers some of my favorite poems, and I walk out. I've been through the tower many times before, but now something new has been installed, an electronic eye of some sort that triggers more wretched recordings as tourists enter the various rooms, and this same theatrical and utterly false imposter ends up chasing me without respite, slaughtering verse after verse until I finally run for the roof and its comparative silence. Carol thinks it's great. "Can you imagine having a dinner party with Yeats? I wonder if he recited poetry between courses."

I reply that when he visited my alma mater on a lecture tour in 1938, he instructed the president that no one was to talk to him or ask a question unless the poet himself initiated the conversation. "Sounds pretty boring to me." We pile into the bus and head for Coole Park.

"Coole is a real success story," a pretty young girl says to me as she hands over our tickets, entirely garbling the real message of this place, which is in fact that the Coole story is one of fiasco, shortsightedness, and blunder. But why make trouble for her?

Irish nationalists from the turn of the century, perhaps better described as Ersatz Celts, had conceptual difficulties with Yeats, Lady Gregory, and the whole renaissance in Irish literature that such literati embodied. These writers, poets, diarists, and dramatists were mostly, after all, Protestants. Even Sean O'Casey, the proletariat of them all, was damnably Protestant, and the slant they gave to both the Cú Chulainn sagas and the more up-to-date peasant tragedies and comedies such as Synge's *Playboy of the Western World* was altogether too intellectual on the one hand, yet too realistic (i.e., risqué) on the other, for popular taste. When Lady Gregory died in 1932, friends and family incised her stone with the words, "She Shall Be Remembered For Ever," which only applied, quite frankly, to those of her class and set. A good many Irish people would never have cared to recall her achievements.

Coole Park was built in 1770 by Robert Gregory, an Irishman who made a fortune through his employ at the East India Company. We would refer to someone like him today, anachronistically, as a "nabob." Sir William, Lady Gregory's husband, continued the family tradition of residing in far-off places, ending his career as the royal governor of Ceylon. Upon his retirement to Ireland he courted the much younger, though rather plain, Augusta, and their marriage produced a son, Robert, who died tragically in Italy during World War I (a pilot, he was mistakenly shot down by an Allied plane). Sir William died in 1892. Lady Gregory's long widowhood, during which she emerged from her husband's shadows, was the period when she grew most involved in the literary affairs of her country.

Her son's untimely death, however, skewered the family's finances. His wife, with three small children to support, resolved to sell Coole Park for the timber and pasturage, but Sir William had stipulated in his will that Lady Gregory be allowed to live in the Big House for the duration of her life. This deadlock was uneasily resolved in 1927. Coole Park was sold to the Irish State, but Lady Gregory remained in residence, paying rent. Nine years after she died, the government sold the actual house off to a contractor, who stripped it for building materials.

When I first saw Coole it had a hangdog air about it. Tinkers were camped all along the main avenue, their litter, camp fires, and laundry lines a sort of gauntlet through which the visitor had to negotiate. A few outbuildings still remained, mostly in ruinous condition; the footprint of the house could still be figured out; and of course, the famous autograph tree, an enormous copper beech, still lived. But the estate seemed a warren of muddy tractor paths that ran here and there through wretched plots of newly planted cheap pine, and the only aura still comparatively genuine was the lake that Yeats had so memorably described in "The Wild Swans of Coole." Lady Gregory's estate was deemed such a worthless destination in the opinion of the locals that there was never even a sign to the place.

The tourist boom of the 1960s was thus something of a national embarrassment, with rich foreigners wandering about the country with their paperback editions of Yeats, all asking about Lady Gregory and where on earth Coole Park could be found. The answer was not something that most officials or even members of the Gregory family wanted to discuss, that in fact its priceless memorabilia had mostly been auctioned or misplaced, the house itself abandoned and left to rot. Even at the last minute, when the choice had come down to spending a bit of money on the building or just letting it go, the decision was easily made. Bits and pieces of Coole Park now lie all around County Galway, its slate sheltering pigs and cattle in the back yards of local farms, its wood the floorboards and carrying beams of various houses here and there, the cut stone long utilized in local schools, municipal constructions, and the garish new cathedral in Galway City. All that was left went into county roads. A national treasure vandalized, in essence, by the nation itself.

I have a feeling that even now officialdom here does not intellectually regret the sequence of decisions it made those long years ago. Lady Gregory is as distant from them as she was to their 1940 compatriots, the benighted drones of Eamon De Valera, a Celt of the first order, who is said by his latest biographer to have "liked" books but never had the time to read any. No, what they regret is not the cultural choices they failed to make, merely the monetary ones.

Coole Park could have been a monstrous moneymaker. People pay a small entry fee today to see a meticulous and finely mowed grass platform where the house stood. We all walk by it, duly noting all the teenagers lying about, flirting and kissing. Visitors can also admire a few walls that still stand with neat little signs under them that say "The

All that remains of Coole House, County Galway

Dairy," "The Forge," "The Stables." They can wander along the grounds as though it was a battlefield from World War I, Ypres or Verdun, conspicuous for what has been destroyed, not for what has been preserved. Tourists are paying cash to have the point drilled into their heads that Ireland didn't care enough for its literary history to save anything important that might illuminate it. They'd pay more if there was anything to see, and that's the killer. More bed and breakfasts, more petrol stations, more restaurant business . . . who's to say what the potential might have been? Meanwhile, the custodians mow the lawns, sell vintage postcards of the old house, put up signs along the trails with snippets of descriptive poetry by Yeats, and direct the tour buses as to where they should park. The autograph tree where Lady Gregory's famous houseguests carved their initials is treated like the gold it is—the only thing left.

We walk down to the famous lake, but there are no swans. I am surprised the managers of this place haven't clipped the wings of a few to provide a tame menagerie for people with cameras. It might improve the ambience. All I see are bins full of trash.

As a specialist in the out of the way, I challenge my group: Who wants to follow me through wood and dale to see something interesting? I immediately regret having thrown the gauntlet down so impulsively—wrong group. But Ted, feeling his honor threatened, agrees, and off we go, hoofing along the shore and turning east, following a trail that eventually clears the forest and deposits us at the edge of several fields. We hike over walls and continue like a pair of hounds on the scent. A couple of times I think I'm lost, but recovering, I eventually see my goal, a small copse of trees and what appears to be an overgrown mound. Here we are, I announce. Ted is baffled and says so.

Most Ascendancy estates of this size had their own private burial plots, often elaborately decked out with mausoleums or vaults. Moyode has one, for instance, though it is quite simple, just an enclosure with a small arched gate, on either side of which sat a pair of angels, long since stolen. Because the Protestant landlord is not a revered archetype from the past, these cemeteries have largely been ignored or vandalized by local people. At Moyode, the Persse graveyard was used by Seamus Taylor as an animal pen. This at least kept the vegetation down, though most of the slabs were destroyed by cattle as they tried to scratch their backs. I wrote down all the information I could from the various inscriptions before raising hell with Seamus who, appropriately shamefaced at the desecration of people's remains, reformed his ways. The place is now so choked with brambles and rampaging undergrowth that I can't even get through the gate anymore.

Here at Coole you'd never recognize the burial plot if you weren't purposely looking for it. A small square raised earthen bed edged with a fitted stone wall, it is surrounded by a substantial ditch to keep the herds out. In Ascendancy terms it is rather modest. We hike ourselves up over the wall and I show Ted the grave of Sir William Gregory.

With my walking stick I clear off accumulated layers of moss and growth. The lettering beneath is incomplete, the metal picas once glued to the stone, giving out name, dates, positions held, citations received, and a biblical inscription of the usual mundane variety, having mostly fallen off and disappeared. "As Samuel Johnson said on Iona," I remark to Ted, "this is the grave of someone who did not expect to be so soon forgotten." At least the prospect that will greet the resurrected body of Sir William on the Day of Judgment remains noble, the long sweep of beautiful meadow ending with a brightly green tree line, beyond which lies the Burren. The curious thing about this grave, however, is the absence of his wife.

Lady Gregory died in 1932, but she is buried in Galway City next to her sister and brother-in-law. Actually, she is buried between them, which doubles my confusion. Wives and husbands generally lie together, and if one chooses to be interred separately, he or she is not likely to divide the mortal remains of another couple by being placed in the middle. Both Lady Gregory and her sister married men much older than they. Perhaps there is a story here for some matrimonial scholar to puzzle out and solve.

Just down the road from Coole is Tulira Castle, once the home of Edward Martyn, another famous literary friend of both Yeats and Lady Gregory. It is not on our itinerary, but I ask if anyone wants to see it, and at first they're predictably bashful. The place is privately owned and we'd be, in American terms, trespassing. But then I explain that Tulira represents what Coole and Roxborough and Moyode were like in their heyday, and their reluctance disappears. We drive down the long avenue surrounded on either side by thoroughbred horses and approach a Norman tower abutting a much larger building with a maze of turrets, crenellations, and princely decoration. In the words of architectural historians, what we have here is a "Gothic pile."

I, of course, have an additional incentive to see Tulira. The current Lord Hemphill is distantly related to my sister's first husband, who in the parlance of aristocratic privilege, once "held" Tulira. I had dropped in on Hemphill in the early 1970s, as a matter of fact, on the strength of this connection, and my wife and I, being scintillating company, had been spontaneously invited for the night by the lord himself. I recall that Lady Hemphill rolled her eyes and groaned aloud.

Hemphill's title is not an old one. If my memory serves, it originated about a century ago, the first lord being a solicitor general or some such thing. By the time the fifth lord had Tulira, the place was literally falling to pieces, the Hemphills clearly pressed for money. This is the problem of having a title and being Irish to boot. In the former instance, one must keep up appearances by at least the pretense of wealth, and by the latter, one must always be recklessly hospitable. Hemphill burned his candles from both ends in a valiant effort to fulfill these missions, and it eventually cost him the possession of this princely abode, which he duly sold.

I recall three highlights of that stay. The first, as we were having drinks in the enormous drawing room, was Hemphill's assertion that the ubiquitous Irish round towers were actually not monastic in origin, but were pagan temples predating Christ that served to worship that most awesome of gods, the almighty penis. I am glad to say that at one time this was a commonplace of nineteenth-century antiquarian speculation, so it is not as if his lordship was personally responsible for dreaming up this instance of scholastic lunacy. The second was my wife and I lying in bed that night in a blue guestroom, being pelted with falling plaster from the rotted ceiling. And the third was our elaborate breakfast, where the cutlery and plate seemed more appropriate for a state banquet than merely the entertainment of two kids from the States. Lady Hemphill went to great efforts disguising the fact that she could no longer afford an appropriate staff. Before every course was due she would say things like, "Oh dear, there's the telephone" or "Goodness, the mail so early?" then disappear out the hallway, running off to the kitchen, flipping the eggs or turning off the toaster, then reappearing with a tray and remarking, "Cook's ankle is turned and she can't walk, so I must serve you myself." The only thing hot was the tea.

We ring Tulira's enormous bell at the front door and greet the castle's new owner, a Dutchman. He is entertained by my stumbling, circular, deceitful explanation as to why I am disturbing his afternoon by stating, "You vish to see Martyn's study, is that right? Veel, vy don't you just say so and come in." The group is impressed.

Climbing a spiral staircase, we see where Martyn wrote his plays, where he read Virgil, where he prayed, where he slept, and where he died. Our host is very friendly and very rich, a businessman whose career has mostly been spent in the United States, working with a privately held company that makes dog food and candy bars. "This is the house Mars built," he says, an allusion everyone misses, but he is only now learning there are certain things in Ireland that money cannot buy. "I can't get a god-damned vindow fixed in this country."

He lists the various owners who have had Tulira since Lord Hemphill sold out. An American woman who put the place back in shape and then died of cancer, a syndicate of speculators who sold off most of the land, then another American of somewhat disreputable cast. This fellow evidently traded Tulira straight up for a yacht—"It's for sale in Miami right now for two million, I believe"—but the beneficiary of this exchange soon grew bored. "He loved it for three months. Then he hated it for three months. Then he sold it to me. I've heard he used to sit in the drawing room looking at television all day, with his feet up on the coffee table. Then he'd turn it off and go up to his bedroom, and turn another one on up there." Sprinkled all about the aura of these interim caretakers are tales of drugs and money laundering, rumors of which even Marie and Alphonsus had heard, repeating them to me in more or less lurid detail. The ghost of Edward Martyn, an enormously pious man, must often be seen prowling the battlements here in disgust.

Thank God, our day draws to an end. I am exhausted and talked out, as is most of the tour except Carol, who catches a second wind and keeps up a steady chatter, what I would describe essentially as a monologue. I keep partially attuned to her tone and pitch, the alteration of which in any form alerts me to the possibility that some response is required. I generally arch my eyebrows as though taken by her point, whatever it is, or shrug to indicate I have no idea without having to go through the effort of, in fact, saying so. My wife always says to me as I withdraw occasionally into a sullen silence that talk is cheap. I rarely argue with this assertion, though I heartily disagree. Talk is often expensive, given the time and effort it requires.

By the time we reach our hotel in Galway City it is dark. Once again the day's been far too long, but no one here is complaining. "I'm just struck by the dimensions of Ireland's story," Susan says to me. As I said before, Susan is by far the most reflective and serious of my charges, also the one most moved by its melancholy character. "To see and hear such heartbreak, it seems more than a single people can bear." With that she begs off from dinner and goes to her room.

13

"It's Getting Old She Is, and Broken"

oday is our big excursion, out to the Aran Islands. I come down to the breakfast room like a drill sergeant inspecting his troops and send everyone back for warmer clothing and whatever waterproof gear they may have brought. The day is crisp, clear, and blue, but Galway Bay is all whitecaps and froth, which means the wind is up.

For most visitors to Ireland adventurous enough to consider an off-shore excursion, Inishmore, the largest of the three Aran Islands, is the usual goal. In the old days one usually embarked from Galway City on the decrepit *Naomh Eanna*, an ancient steamer that departed twice a week, took five or so hours to get out, and was loaded with a hodge-podge cargo of livestock, food supplies, fishing gear, Guinness, and tac-iturn islanders traveling back and forth. That old tub is probably plying the Red Sea today, carrying dates, camels, or pilgrims bound for Mecca, because the Aran Islands trade is now high-tech and geared to speed. Get those tourists out there and get them back in as many round-trips as is humanly possible in the course of a day.

This effort has generated for the island a tidal wave of visitors, which has, in the process, generated an enormous volume of controversy. Many Irish people consider Inishmore a barometer as to the soul of their country. Yeats told Synge to go there in 1896, advising the young playwright to revel in the unblemished originality of Gaelic culture that

Curraghs

still existed then and there. Yeats said this to him in Paris, presumably over a glass of Beaujolais and a tray of cheese and crackers, none of which would be found on the hard, forlorn, and essentially barren specks of rock that lay far out in the Atlantic off the western shores of Ireland. But Synge went there all the same and found that Yeats had not deceived him. Boarding in an old peasant cottage, lying on the floor to eavesdrop on chitchat from the hearth below in the native tongue, he gathered material and jotted down all the oral gems, peasant wisdom, and bons mots that he could. *Riders to the Sea*, his finest play, summarized these discoveries, according the status of Greek tragedy to the rough and oftentimes noble struggle that malevolent nature put these poor and simple fisherfolk through. Every time I read that short, desperate, intensely focused work, I can hear the surf raging and see the curraghs founder within touching distance of the shore.

Many people like Synge have come to Inishmore to find themselves, whether culturally or personally it hardly matters. Writers have made the crossing, so too artists, photographers, linguists, historians, archaeologists, Irish students, teachers, poets—all manner of disparate individuals—but all in search for that something elusive, that inner certitude or calm measure, as though the people on Inishmore somehow had it themselves and could dispense the stuff when asked.

A great many people, not surprisingly, mistook simplicity for profundity. They felt that Inishmore possessed a kind of Celtic magic to bestow, some potion they could bottle and take home if they spent enough time rummaging about the old forts and early Christian monastic sites, located there in such desolation, or enough time to ask questions of the enigmatic islanders as they drove them about in jaunting cars. There was something inexplicable there, the only thing was to figure out what it was and divine the lesson.

I do not mean to belittle or mock this quest, being a prime offender myself. When I first came to Inishmore for a week back in 1969, I could almost feel the power of this place surging through my body. My wife and I tramped the whole island, all nine miles of it, visited every Iron Age enclosure, every church, every incised cross, every graveyard, and all the enormous headlands rising three hundred feet above the tempestuous Atlantic. At night we'd eat fresh mackerel dinners in our guest house, listening, as Synge had, to the idle conversation in Gaelic of our hosts sitting out in the kitchen. To me it was the equivalent of overhearing a Latinist or a Hebraist or some other exotic classical speaker, even though the matters being discussed were undoubtedly as prosaic as the weather or how pretty my wife was ("Cad é sa diabhal a fheiceann sí sa bhfear sin?"). Later on we'd walk into the town and see the 1934 film *Man of Aran*, then go sit around the real thing at the local pub, where islanders might be coaxed into a song or a joke in Irish. I was so dumbfounded I thought I was listening to Socrates, that I was somehow deeply reunited with something ancient and profound. The fact that I wasn't does not diminish my youthful desire to do so. Thus I feel a kinship and a nostalgia for people's deification of the Aran experience, and I sympathize with modern Ireland's anguish over the situation that has arisen there.

You read about it everyday and everywhere, and the questions people raise—how to preserve Irish, how to keep people who speak Irish on the land of their forefathers, how to sustain them spiritually and economically (two principles in opposition to each other)—I have discussed previously in this little book. I certainly will not accuse modern Irish people of ignoring these questions; indeed, the land is alive in debate. The *Irish Times* letter page, for instance, always an entertaining forum full of eccentricity, anguish, despair, and madness, is overrun with the subject, and once a month that paper's equivalent of an op-ed column, "The Irishman's Diary" (or "The Irishwoman's Diary," when appropriate), inevitably argues the subject. Contemporary books on Irish tourism or culture in general always refer to the matter, and even the *Wall Street Journal* and the *New York Times* will pay attention, often on their front pages. The question is the usual one: In order to save Aran, must we destroy it?

To me the question is moot. Mass tourism, of which my little tour is a part, has made too devastating an intrusion to the life of Inishmore for any one to reverse it now. The place has gone to the dogs and that's it. The dilemma now is to keep the disease from spreading.

I wouldn't dream of saying that to the group, of course, though I can't help regaling them with stories of the old *Naomh Eanna*. What a heap of junk that boat was. We, allegedly, will be traveling in style aboard a brand new conveyance that leaves from a little harbor called Rossaveal, which is the closest landfall to Inishmore. In the old days, islanders would row the eight or so miles across in their curraghs, picking the day carefully for weather, winds, and tide. Many islanders were lost when guesswork let them down, storms coming out of nowhere to catch these tiny craft out in the open. Our launch, however, can obviously handle anything. It has a gleam that only finely polished plastic can provide, a sense of confidence and elasticity of the sort moored all over the world in places like Miami and Monte Carlo. I can't help thinking that it seems rather out of place here in the west of Ireland.

The boat is mobbed with day-trippers like us. Our group assembles on the back deck, primarily in self-defense from these French, German, Dutch, and English hordes, and I proceed to give some orientation on the day ahead. The ship motors carefully out past a breakwater and into open ocean. Everything seems under control and moderate, the land breeze running with us, warm and comfortable. Susan takes off her nylon windbreaker, eyes me and rolls up her sleeves. I think she's doing this as a rebuke: "Our Leader tells us to wear winter clothing, well the hell with him, I'm going to sunbathe." Her comeuppance begins with a start.

I can imagine in retrospect the scene higher up on the bridge. Our captain, clearly a Celt of unbridled exuberance, grins maliciously as he grips the power control. "Let's see how the foreigners like this," he would say as he jams the lever full speed ahead.

For myself, I barely remember the next few seconds. One moment we're complacently bobbing our way over to Inishmore, the next we are inexplicably plunged into a Mach 1 surge that leaves my stomach back on the mainland. Without any warning the ship has lurched into a violent submarining maneuver straight through an ocean roller and emerges out the other side in a midair flight ready for more. The Punchestown race for Inishmore is on!

People are screaming in a nervous, high-pitched sort of way. Is this a roller-coaster or a ferry? Passengers lie scattered on the deck, many on their rear ends or clutching for something to hold as we violently lurch about. I find myself staring straight up to heaven, a unique camera angle achieved by sliding on my back toward the aft railing. This allows me an unparalleled view of the wrathful Atlantic Ocean as it cascades over the entire boat full force into Susan's face, who topples over my prostrate body. Luckily we're too overweight to slide under the life raft stanchion into water below. We both struggle up just in time to get whacked by a second wave, which sends her guidebook into Neptune's Locker. A human chain, initiated by John, manages to haul both us and some other flailing bodies back to comparative shelter. Susan doesn't know whether to laugh or cry. I wonder if she's in shock.

Julie, in the meantime, has turned completely green. She repairs to the WC for a good long vomit. My other septuagenarians I manage to seat in the lounge. I imagine that rocket travel to the moon has a rough sort of similarity to reaching our island nirvana, a comparison I never thought I'd be making. One thing is for certain, this trip won't take long.

We're a pretty sorry crew pulling into harbor. Susan gamely promises not to complain about being soaked through, which means I can't complain either, and that puts me out. Martyrdom is a suit I wear very well. Julie says she'll be fine after a few minutes on solid ground, and everyone else, though shaken, comments on their exhilaration at having survived the journey. I leave them with John and search out the pony drivers.

The quay is crawling with islanders in minivans and old VW buses, looking to drive people on up to the primary sight on Inishmore, the immense Iron Age fort of Dun Aengus. The jaunting cars are all lined up on the main road, however, so I head for them.

Ordinarily, need I say it, the idea of hiring one of these would be anathema to me, but given the choice between the internal combustion engine and pony power, especially here on Aran, I'll take the latter anytime, no matter how corny. Besides, the group will love it.

A teenager intercepts me, likely victim that I am, and we haggle over price. He's wearing a San Jose Sharks' cap, backward of course, and his general demeanor reminds me of a generic housing project, you name the city. We need three jaunting cars, his own and those of his father and uncle, who stand loitering over by the seawall, disdainful of approaching a stranger or discussing money. This kid is driving a hard bargain, so I go over to Da. "Whatever the boy decides is fine with us," he says, "and by the way, for the love of Jesus, did ye swim over or what?" If I wasn't so bedraggled and miserably wet, I'd probably laugh at his jest, but it pisses me off instead. I continue on and hire someone else. I'll be damned if I'm going to look at a Sharks' hat all day.

We pile onto the cars and head off. An entire stream of vehicles, pony-drawn and mechanical, turn off west for Dun Aengus, but I tell the driver to go east instead. I don't feel like following the crowd any more than I have to.

My mood improves as we leave the bustle of town and head out on the meandering little road, barely wide enough for two cars to pass abreast. The tour loves the pony traps, and why not? The drivers are chatty and responsive, the views are immense, we seem like the only people here, a throwback to times when the pace of life was slower and better. On the horizon, the Church of Saint Benan looms, and at the base of a high ridge, the traps can go no farther.

The principal saint of Inishmore was one Enda, whose monastery this may or may not have been. Certainly Aran was famous for its ecclesiastical schooling in sixth-century Ireland, and many of its patristic saints, men whose names are far more renowned in Ireland than Enda's (Brendan, Ciaran, Columcille, and so on) reputedly came here both to discipline the flesh and to study the ancient texts of Antony, Athanasius, Martin of Tours, and Cassian. The stump of a round tower survives, a few *clocháns* and some rough crosses. The old *termonn*, or sanctuary wall, can still be traced, and looking over the whole complex is the tiny and almost perfect chapel named after the elusive Benan, allegedly an early disciple of Saint Patrick, but about whom I know nothing. Again I throw down the gauntlet, "Who's going to the top with me?" and I am surprised to hear the eager affirmation that everyone's heading for the mountaintop. As time goes on, I'm noting, the group is shedding much of its timidity.

The pace is a snail's, but fine with me. John and I help people over walls, over slippery grass, on up over stones glassy with moisture. All are in good cheer, and we are rewarded for it when we reach the chapel with a view unparalleled in breadth and tumultuous beauty, an entire panorama full of ocean beating against rock, wind hurling spray hundreds of feet upward and inland after its impact, seabirds everywhere circling and diving. "This is paradise," someone says, and all I see are nods of agreement.

The little high-gabled chapel has presided over this scene for thirteen hundred years or so. Since it could hold only five or six people at a time, I am asked what its function could have been and how it was used, questions I cannot answer. Being in such an exposed position, it was certainly not lived in, nor was it a comfortable or even quiet place in which to pray, but then again comfort was not a quality that Celtic monks highly valued. My guess is that this minuscule church was used as a pilgrimage point for the monastery below, a metaphorical usage that featured in daily ritual and initiation, and most particularly on holy days, when its east-west orientation would have caught the first light of day. I can imagine all-night vigils in the building, fasts and mortifications, the entire assemblage gathered outside in the glare of an Easter moon. On the altar, again imagining, I visualize an illuminated gospel book, its gorgeous colorings reflecting the sputtering light of candles. But none of this can be proven. The details of life in a Celtic monastery can only be surmised, and no one can say with certainty how people lived here. All we can do is intelligently guess, guided by the hints we find here and there. I recall the little note a ninth-century monk scribbled in the margin of a manuscript he was copying, "How sweet the bell," referring to the divine office he was being called to sing.

"I'd rather stay in bed than climb up here in the dead of night," Cynthia says to her husband.

"Well, even the saints had their failings," I answer, with another old quote: "To go and say the office, great labor. The wind stings my two ears. Were it not dread of the blessed Lord, I would not go."

"I'm hungry," Carol chips in. "Is there anyplace to eat out here?" We come down from our Celtic Sinai and feast on Quiche Lorraine, of all things, at a little guest house below. My, how Inishmore has indeed changed. No more mackerel here.

◆

I had all sorts of things I wanted to show the group on Inishmore, but the pony traps are slow and there's our ferry to catch at 4:30, so it's off to Dun Aengus. You just can't come here and not see it.

Once again, I don't want to seem a snob, but my heart falls as we approach the site. Coffee shops, tea huts, Coke signs, and a makeshift parking lot full of carts and buggies and Land Rovers await us. Instead of a rough-and-tumble hike on up, a truly immense causeway has been built over the fields to haul us in. Trash and debris blow about us; pipes, hoses, rusted concrete buckets, and blobs of congealed cement lie about in chaotic, wind-driven scrub piles that litter the landscape. All the mess of building a house, but no house. I keep my thoughts to myself, take two old women by either arm, and start climbing.

Dun Aengus was once, in my estimation, one of the most exciting sights in the entire country, an immense Iron Age fortification with several rings of defensive walls perched dramatically atop a cliff overhanging the ocean. Other examples, not so big, lie in other parts of all three of the Aran Islands, and indeed the mainland features such structures as well. But Dun Aengus had been special. Its dramatic cliffside location, the height of wall and rampart, the desolation of its environs, all combined to make the place unique. That, unfortunately, is no longer so.

When my wife and I came here, we were alone to enjoy it. Today a couple of hundred people mill around, channeled by chain-link fencing and harried caretakers, whose sole responsibility, I am told, is to prevent people from hauling away a stone or two as souvenirs. Because the overhang is so potentially dangerous and the winds so powerful, visitors are now thwarted from going anywhere near the edge. This restriction has not prevented people from pulling up barriers and crawling to death's door anyway. I count eight kids cavorting within inches of going over. Their parents just stand there and look. I see other tourists idly throwing rocks over the side. Dun Aengus looks truly beaten up. We all feel a letdown from the euphoria of Benan's chapel, and after only a few wind-swept minutes I lead everyone down.

On the way back to the harbor we pass an open pub and grocery store, which sports Aran sweaters for sale on a clothes line outside. We have to stop, me for a quick nip of port, everyone else to haggle over prices. Susan is struck by all the piles of stone that stand haphazardly along the road and asks the woman here their function. "Those be markers to all the men lost at sea," she replies. We must have passed over sixty or seventy of them during the course of our day here.

Julie looks grim as we reboard the ferry. She takes a seat near the bathroom, which certainly has not been cleaned since last she was in it.

I'm warmed up by my little nip, so I stand on the deck again. As we venture into the Atlantic, I hold on tight, waiting for our mad captain to go full throttle. John joins me smiling. "Your man's chin is down in his socks. He blew an engine when we came out, we're only half speed for the return." That's the best news I've heard today. The only thing better would be if the thing sank.

"I hope we come in an hour late, and I hope it screws up everyone's plans."

"You're right there, Jim, everyone's in a mad rush these days. One of those things we've learned from you Yanks."

14

Israel

his morning's newspaper announces the approval of the biggest commercial development ever for Galway City, a £30 million hotel, apartment, shops, and parking garage complex that will dominate the picturesque, though decrepit, dock area and dwarf the so-called Spanish Arch, one of the few remnants left of the old medieval town walls. Every environmental, Green, neighborhood, and fisheries organization in Connaught opposed this scheme for the usual variety of good reasons, both aesthetic and pragmatic. All those happy tourists who stay at the new hotel, for instance, will be flushing their sewerage directly into the Corrib River and Galway Bay for at least five years, or until a hypothetical treatment plant of the future can be built. Is this Jakarta, I ask myself, or some cesspool in Bangladesh?

Needless to say, our prototypical flak of the month, some flunky hired by the developer, claims that the dramatic flow of river water at the point of discharge will generate so many tons of enzyme-eating oxygen that there will be no adverse effect on the community. I'd like him to take a swim one summer soon from the nearby beach at Salthill, and breaststroke his way into a floating piece of oxygenated human waste, then swim back and repeat his testimony. Ireland seems intent not to learn from other country's mistakes.

We leave these urban problems behind and bus northward into Mayo and Sligo, stopping here and there for abbeys and castles along our route. The Franciscan monasteries such as Ross are particularly stunning, most dating from a fifteenth-century building spurt that saw the development of a characteristically Irish architectural statement, the high and slender belfry towers that so grace whatever rural landscape they happen to overlook. The meticulous, albeit tiny, cloisters are also crowd pleasers. "This is so cozy," says Cynthia, who has toured extensively in Europe and seen many blockbuster abbeys whose cloisters take up as much space as a city square. But Julie is off-put. The Irish custom of burying their dead all over the monastic grounds offends her.

"You can't take a step here without walking over people's graves. I find this disrespectful and depressing."

"You have to remember," I reply, "that these buildings were ruins, burned down and despoiled by Protestants from Elizabeth to William of Orange. It was a sign of reverence, really, to put their people here, a connection to the old faith. You shouldn't feel badly about it." What I don't tell her is that the Irish, in fact, often have very short memories when it suits their purpose. The old Penal church near me at Moyode, where the forebears of my neighbors worshipped for over two centuries under a variety of proscriptions, was abandoned for a new building some years ago. A farmer moved right into the vacant structure and made it into a cattle pen, where he daily dehorns, castrates, or injects his beasts to their no doubt bellowing displeasure right about where the main altar once stood. Now there's disrespect.

We pull into Ballintubber around lunchtime, ostensibly to see "the abbey that refused to die," the church here having been in continuous use since 1216, despite being roofless for something like three centuries. The group eats lunch in a pub across the street; however, I go off on a separate errand.

The castle "fraternity" is a close-knit group. Anyone embarking on the restoration of an Irish tower will want the advice of someone who's been down the thorny path before him. Whom to hire or whom not to hire is one central topic of conversation, but ancillary issues arise all the time, usually of a conspiratorial nature in that one's objective is to pry information out of someone who may not necessarily want to share it. "Where did you get that stone? I'm desperate for some, is there any more where that came from?" (Who's to say I want to share my cache with you?) Or: "Where can I get some liscannor pavers? So and so died and his quarry is closed." (Yes, but so and so's son has reopened the

Ross Abbey

quarry, and I want him to concentrate, if such a thing is possible, on my order, so I don't want him talking to you.) Or: "I need six twenty-foot planks of oak, know of any?" (Well if I did, I'd be there first.) Some queries are positively bizarre, exposing Ireland for the Third World country it can often be. "I need some three-eighths-inch wood screws and Galway's out of them. Have you a handful I could borrow?"

I got a card from an acquaintance of mine living in New York who was having work done on his tower, which happens to be, coincidentally, about thirty minutes north of here. The contractor on the job, however, was avoiding him. When he called long distance, the man's wife said he was always in the bathroom or otherwise unavailable. Could I take a quick look at the place if I was in the vicinity for a situation report? Of course I can now, other people's misery being my food and drink, so while the group eats sandwiches and drinks hot toddies, John drives me a few miles away for the papal inquisition.

I walk down an avenue to the site, and sure enough I pick out his tower peeking over the head of some surrounding trees, a noble, though unfeasibly big, castle from the look of it. I'm encouraged to see a sign or two of activity. The wall facing me, I notice, is neatly scaffolded; an equipment hut full of wheelbarrows and cement mixers is obviously in use; and I even hear some voices from around the other side. Following these, I turn the corner and there I see it. Disaster.

Three men are daintily shifting through debris. Mangled bits of piping and planks, obviously components of another set of scaffolding, lie half buried and clearly ruined in a great pile of masonry. "What's going on here?" I innocently ask.

A short stocky fellow whirls around. "What's going on?" he almost yells. "What's it look like, bejesus? The whole bloody wall collapsed, that's what's going on. The whole thing to hell and gone. I go home one day and everything's fine, I come back the next morning and everything's a smoking heap. This job's the death of me, and who might you be?"

"I'm a friend of Jerry's. Are you Mr. McNamara?"

The poor man groans. "That's me, you're looking at him, and a more miserable son of a bitch you'll never see again on God's green planet." As Caesar and a few other people have noted, the Irish are a people easily sunk to the depths of morbid anguish, and here's as plain an example as I've ever seen. Mr. McNamara seems close to tears. I let a few minutes pass in mute consolation.

"Jerry's been trying to reach you, you know."

"Do I know? I'd have to be a dead man not to know. Every night my wife is standing at the door, 'Jerry's called,' she says, 'Jerry's called again. You'll have to tell him, John, you'll have to do it.' I says back to her I'd rather put my hand in the kitchen fire."

"When did this happen?"

"Three weeks ago today, and I haven't been back here but once since then, it was such a terrible sight. I cried when I saw it, God knows I did. This place is putting me in hospital, I wish I was dead."

"Can anything be done?"

"To be honest, our lives are in danger just standing here, the other walls could go any minute. In some ways I wouldn't mind being here when they did. I'll tell you, Sir, you're looking at a miserable man indeed, a man who's paying for his sins in life, yes he is."

That evening I write Jerry a letter. It's like telling a person that his spouse has cancer. I hold out no hope for him. Ireland has broken yet another bank account and another heart.

◆

Ballintubber Abbey is a melancholy place. Founded by an O'Connor king, Cathal Mor of the wine-red hand, it was a jumping-off point for the pilgrimage to Ireland's most holy mountain, Croagh Patrick, which looms fifteen or so miles to the west in dramatic profile. On Pattern Sunday, the third weekend of July, the peak is jammed with pilgrims, many of whom have made the trek in darkness and barefoot. This may seem, at first glance, a pretty tame mortification, but when I hiked Croagh Patrick some years ago I couldn't believe that anyone could do it without footgear of some sort, the final ascent in particular being nearly vertical and covered in loose, jagged, sharp stone.

Portions of the Pilgrims' Way, a raised walkway over field and bog, can still be traced from Ballintubber, and sometime before I die I plan to walk the route and then climb the holy mountain again. As I look at my elderly charges I remind myself, as all good Catholics should, that to delay much longer might put my intentions, and thus my soul, in jeopardy.

The abbey itself is a plain building, looted and despoiled on many occasions, finally in 1643 by Cromwell's troopers, who pretty well smashed the place to pieces. The cloister walk, for example, is a collection of remnants, and we are reminded by the little girl who leads us about that cavalry horses were once stalled in the chancel. But the site was never truly abandoned, and that's the selling point for Ballintubber.

No matter what the dangers, no matter the persecutions then ongoing, no matter the political and social disintegrations of the moment, friars and priests remained lurking in the neighborhood. When conditions allowed, they would return to the building, reinhabit it in some nook or cranny, and carry on with their pastoral duties. When authorities periodically energized themselves into clerical witch hunts, these beleaguered ministers of the old faith would scatter once again to their hideaways in wood or bog, ready to come out again when they could. Old photographs from the nineteenth century depict these Penal masses being said out of doors amidst the ruins of Ballintubber, attended by all the peasantry who could walk that far in a day.

The nobility of this devotion to Rome is amply praised in the triumphalist literature for sale in the abbey gift shop, and indeed, it would be hard for me to disparage it. But I find the story more sad than uplifting, particularly in light of the Church's fading role here in Irish life and the speed with which it has lost that primacy of place. The Great Famine is an event of key significance in this country's history, but it is not an emotional high point or anything to rejoice over. Ballintubber's story shares in the same sort of maudlin misery.

As we continue north, I am pleased to see the sky to our west turning gloomy. What I had intended to be the pinnacle of my achievement as a tour guide is on our schedule for tomorrow, a boat trip to the island monastery of Inishmurray in Sligo Bay, but I am praying for stormy weather. I need the crutch of gale-force conditions to justify canceling the whole thing; otherwise, a rebellion will ensue.

It hadn't taken me long to figure out that jaunting to Inishmurray was out of the question for this collection of senior citizens. If the journey to Aran had taxed them, wait until they see the plan for Inishmurray, a nine-mile trip over open water in a small lobster boat, no protection against wind or water, no landing pier, ladder, or hoist to get them on the tiny island. The only boarding procedure possible is a good-sized leap to boulders slick with weeds and spray, a catastrophe waiting to happen. I cannot envision Carol making it, and as for seasick-prone Julie, well, I don't think she'll fancy throwing up over the side in front of all her fellow travelers. And Alden, sorry old sport, no bathrooms available, and no toilet paper for the ladies. I'm pretty sure I can convince them of the folly we'd face trying to land, everyone, that is, except Susan.

Susan had told me straight up that the major reason she signed on for this tour was to see Inishmurray. She had read about it in my book *Islands of Storm* and was determined to go. In many ways I know exactly what she's talking about, the power of the printed word.

I am an inveterate armchair traveler myself. I enjoy books that describe places I'd love to see but never will. I like the degree of difficulties and dangers associated with such visits. I vicariously shudder at the horrible inconvenience that people will endure to experience a place they've spent hours in bed at night thinking about, relieved that such obstructions are theirs to cope with and not mine. Susan could never have gone to Inishmurray on her own, but I, through the mindless enthusiasm that poured from my pen into the deceitful brochure put out by Eire Tours, had sparked her, and she was not to be denied.

I go back to the rear of the bus and sit next to her. "Did you have a chance to think about what I said the other day about Inishmurray?"

"What's there to think about?"

"You know, how shaky some of these people are. Carol should be in a wheelchair all the time, Penelope can hardly walk because of her ankle, Alden and Cynthia are awfully frail, Julie gets seasick—I can't see them making it out to Inishmurray in a primitive old boat."

"Tough."

Susan is from Ohio. She's thoughtful, smart, well read, and considerate, but she has a will of steel. I had figured her out from the start and reminded myself not to cross her. Thus I remained respectful as she lectured me. "Inishmurray is on the itinerary. Presumably, everybody read the itinerary. Ergo, weather permitting, they go to Inishmurray or they stay home, the choice is theirs. It's very simple, really. We're going."

"I just can't leave the whole tour at the hotel for a day while you and I go alone."

"Why not? You know something, Jim, we're all adults here. You treat us like children, which is an awful lot of fun for us, but exasperating for you. You just lay down the law and we'll take it."

"What if I lay down the law and say we're not going to Inishmurray?"

"I'll sue you and I'll sue Eire Tours." I get up to retake my seat up front. "Only kidding, Jim," Susan says, but I get the feeling she means it, being from Ohio and all.

Raindrops patter on the windscreen, relieving my anxiety. This is the first time I have ever been in Ireland and wished for a downpour. With luck, everything will click into place and ruin tomorrow's agenda.

◆

Coming into Sligo I decide there's time enough to stop at Carrowmore, a Stone Age cemetery full of megalithic tombs and eerie mounds, all scattered about on several fields that lie at the base of Knocknarea, which has on its summit the great cairn of Maeve, the Amazon queen of Irish saga. Yeats, of course, wandered all these pastures during his youth and undoubtedly climbed Knocknarea on several occasions. Certainly the atmospherics are stupendous, all these primordial remnants wrapped up in the stories and sagas of pagan Ireland, themselves embellished in the plays and verse of this preeminent modern poet. There will be no dearth of things to talk about here.

Precipitation has turned the whole world into a panoply of greens and grays, everything fresh and glistening. Ireland at times presents the eye with such depth of feeling that it turns your head, and my enthusiasm encourages everyone not to look on the wet weather as a downer. Notice the density of texture in these views, I tell them. Visualize how a Monet or a Sisley or a Pissarro would have treated these gorgeous, variegated hues. I refrain from saying how Jack Yeats, William Butler's brother and a famous painter himself, generally trashed these vistas in paintings that I regard as crude and boorish, but why complicate things? The French Impressionists never came to Ireland, although I've often considered the wondrous things they could have done with such a subject. But a place with no wine, no baguettes, no creamy Camembert would never have tempted them, to say nothing of the repressed women and the rainy winter months.

Carrowmore now has an admission fee and a little museum and a guide. This place is not on the main touristic menu, however, and doesn't rate a movie, so we settle for slides. The girl who gives the talk is well informed and friendly, and we kill a lot of time in good-natured chitchat with her before touring the tombs.

In and of themselves, they are not complicated structures. If you compared a megalithic dolmen with the new engine of a Toyota, for example, the contrast in levels of sophistication would seem fairly obvious. The difference is that a Toyota is only a machine. It may be fast, it may be slick, it may even tap into some significant libidinous streak in our character, but it has no soul, it has no link that takes us to the other side, it has nothing to say about anything important.

Carrowmore is a deeply spiritual place and deeply superstitious too. Whatever people believed about death and the afterlife four thousand years ago is a realm we will never penetrate, though the tombs here are like a blueprint of sorts, if only we could decipher the language. What I personally feel wandering about here is that I'm in a spotlight, in the center of an amphitheater charged with enormous emotional current. Maeve's cairn up above me on Knocknarea, the peak of "bare Ben Bulben's head," an enigmatic, powerful, druidic mountain over to the east of us, all loom over this strange assemblage of cairns and offerings. Holy land, in other words, or as Yeats put it in 1893:

> *The host is riding from Knocknarea*
> *And over the grave of Clooth-na-Bare;*
> *Caoilte tossing his burning hair,*
> *And Niamh calling* Away, come away:

◆

Our hotel this evening is an ice chest. Even I'm cold, and there's no hot water either, which emboldens me to complain at the front desk, something I never do ordinarily. This hesitancy has always annoyed my wife, who considers it a sign of cowardice not to assert one's rights as a paying guest, but it is a deeply rooted piece of my inner being, a psychological holdover from memories I've repressed all my life, and primarily associated with my mother. "If you ever saw what she pulled on that concierge in Nuremberg," I once confessed, "you'd never raise your voice in anger again." But the tour business makes it easy, emboldens me, I can blame the group. *They're* the ones complaining, *they're* the ones who can't take a little lukewarm water—heaven knows, I'm happy here, and aren't tourists a bunch of whiners and complainers. The large woman at Reception winks and squeezes my arm, it's us against them, and certainly she'll turn on the heat.

Supper is abominable. The thing I really dislike about being on a tour is that I can't order anything from the menu, like the nice simple dinner of my aforementioned favorite, chops and chips. No, we must eat from the "table d'hôtel," which is always loaded with extravagantly described continental dishes that I know will be butchered by mad chefs in silly white hats. Honest to God, you can't even get them to give you a piece of meat that's medium rare.

For once, tonight's menu has a simple steak on it, which I foolishly order. "Please tell the cook, medium rare, pink on the inside," I say to the waitress.

"Of course, Sir."

"Could you do me a favor, please?"

"Of course, Sir."

"Can you repeat my order back to me?"

"That's one steak, medium rare, pink on the inside, with chips."

"Exactly. Now, one more thing. The plate."

"The plate, Sir?" I have her interest now. No one has ever talked to her about plates before. Why would they?

"Yes. I want my dinner served on a cold plate."

"A cold plate?" The waitress is getting nervous. So is the group.

"Right. A cold plate."

"As you wish, Sir."

"Thank you."

Everyone else orders. No one says anything about plates, hitherto a subject of no possible pertinence. They haven't the courage until Ted chimes in. "Could you share with us your secret, Oh Master? What is it with the plate?"

"Well, I'm testing a theory. Do you all recall from other dinners we've had how the girls usually serve the plates?"

"Yes I have, now that you mention it," says Julie. "They hold them with heavy towels."

"Exactly. That's because they preheat the china. Christ, you can get a third-degree burn if you touch the damn thing, and that's the point. Who ruins the meat, the chef in the kitchen or the plate, which is so hot it can fry an egg? My suspicion is that most chefs in this country ruin the meat twice, first when they fry it, and second when they put it on the plate for that extra, unforeseen sizzle. This way we'll find out, we'll put it to the test and have it served on a cold plate. Ingenious?"

The steak comes. I touch the plate, it's frigid. I cut the steak, and triumphantly display its dismal interior shading of dead brown. I call the girl over, forgetting my mother's temper tantrum of so long ago in Nuremberg. "What color is that meat?" I ask her cheerfully. She squints.

"It looks very well done Sir, very well done indeed, and exactly what you didn't order and I can't for the life of me understand what Seamus was thinking because I told him, Sir, I told him you were setting him an exacting standard indeed, what you wanted and all, it was as clear as the light of day and that's what I said and I know he was listening and that's why it's incredible to me, to tell you the truth, because Seamus is a very bright lad and generally does what I tell him and everyone knows he's a grand chef and he went to school for it, he graduated with honors just last year, and didn't I go to the ceremonies myself, and he should understand that when a person orders his dinner cooked a certain way that it's a responsibility to prepare that dinner exactly as ordered and I'll be speaking my mind to him immediately and telling him to cook another steak exactly as you ordered it, Sir, which was rare."

"No, it was medium rare, actually, but I admire your response and I'm completely satisfied with your desire to atone for it, but it isn't really necessary and I don't want to get Seamus in trouble. Let's just forget it."

"Ah, he's in trouble no matter what you do, Sir, and it's generous of you indeed to take it so well, but he'll be hearing it from me anyway, Sir,

I'll be telling him to pay me more mind right through the night and into the morning."

"You will?"

"Of course, Sir, he's my husband, and I won't let him forget and put me in trouble with the guests again. And can I get you a glass of wine, Sir, compliments of the hotel?"

"Two glasses and we'll consider the matter closed."

"Right you are, Sir, done and all." This satisfactorily concludes my experiment. The chips are excellent and so is dessert, an apple tart.

As we repair to the bar after dinner to watch some Irish hurling—the men of Meath in their green shorts and checked green and yellow jerseys, fighting (and that seems the appropriate word, looking at this rough-and-tumble sport) the men of County Tyrone attired in red and white, with the enigmatic bleeding hand of Ulster emblazoned on their uniforms—Carol provides high drama for the evening with another spectacular fall. I am the closest to her as she ascends a short rise of three steps. For some inexplicable reason she misses the second of these, teeters backward, throws her arms above her head, cane flying, and achieves levitation. I react slowly, as though mired in cement as one often is during a dream. "Jesus" slips out of my mouth, I reach an arm out that just misses her body, I turn to look as her head smacks the floor, bounces a foot, then hits the floor again, all in slow motion. This time she really is dead, I'm sure of it.

Consternation everywhere. The large lady from Reception gets a pillow, Alden our doctor takes her pulse, looks in her eyes, daubs water on her face, a crowd gathers silently. This will be a corker of a lawsuit, I think to myself. What do I do with the corpse? How will this affect our schedule? Whom do I even call back in the States? . . . "Hello, your adored mother, who came here to have a wonderful time, never survived Sligo." I'm at a loss.

Carol's eyelids start fluttering, a collective "whew" exudes from the crowd. Alden recommends an ambulance. "Better take her to the emergency room, Jim" he advises, "and good luck." A few minutes later, in a whirl of lights, we speed off to Sligo Hospital.

This is not what I would wish on anyone, friend or foe. I love Ireland and I love the Irish, but if I get sick, take me home. Just last week my old friend Tom Jenning told me his saga of woe: horrible stomach pains for over three months, sloughed off repeatedly by his doctor in Galway. "Ye've a sour tummy, Tom, take some antacids for the love of God, and stop complaining." His wife finally had enough of Tom doubling over in pain, and took him to Ballinasloe one morning. The verdict—stomach cancer—they cut him open that same day. Tom looked pretty good, I'm glad to report, but that was close, and I've heard a lot of stories just like his.

Carol is conscious and alert as we wheel into the emergency room. Once there, however, all our rights to an opinion, or even a conversation, evaporate. We are now in the grip of matriarchal authority, the kind even famous writers like Edna O'Brien or William Trevor dared not confront in their 1950s melodramas, fearful that perhaps their own mothers might read these descriptions and see ever so painfully on whom they were based.

At the end of a long blue-green room sits Buddha. Or is it Krishna? At any rate, he's immovable, the silent, enigmatic king, a bulbous Pakistani or Indian doctor who sits in revered isolation behind a desk, his hands folded in front of him, not a trace of emotion, warmth, vitality, or blood in his face. Ineffable calm, staring blankly straight ahead.

His minions, however, are all business, two nurses in starched armor whose main job, as I see it, is to shoo off the ambulance driver and EMTs, take full control of poor Carol, and to throw me out of the room, just as I'm trying to pass along the info Alden gave me that he felt any doctor would want to know. For instance, the medications that Carol was on, her pulse rate, the lump he found on the back of her head, those sorts of things. These fascists will have none of that.

"Sit outside, Sir, we'll let you know when you're wanted."

"I have her prescription pills here if you want to see them," I suggest helpfully.

"We'll take care of that."

"I have the name of her doctor in New York if you need it."

"We know what we're doing here, Sir. We'll have no need for him."

"I have her passport here with her drug interactions."

"Not to bother, Sir, not to bother," as they push me out in the hall.

"Would you like to know what happened to her?" I shout.

"And there's no need for temper, Sir, no need at all. Temper never opened a door." What a country.

Three hours later Carol, having been lectured, interrogated, x-rayed, probed, and diagnosed as fit, is pushed back into my care. I catch a glimpse of the Rajah, still sitting at his desk, hands immobile, body quiet, seemingly unremoved from his trance. Did he ever get up, I wonder, did he minister to Carol in some transcendental sort of way?

I call for a cab, and at 1:45 A.M. we go to the car park to wait for it. "It's good to be out of there," says Carol.

"That's for sure," I reply.

"But it's a curious thing, Fred."

"I'm Jim, Carol, not Fred. And what's curious?"

"I had no idea we were in Israel."

"You may be in Israel, Carol, but the rest of us are in Ireland."

"Well, that's what's curious, don't you see?" I let the cabdriver talk to Carol all the way back. She's talking about what a terrible cook her mother was, and he seems interested. I give him a good tip at the hotel.

15

PURGATORY

hat a glorious morning. It's raining hard, the wind is whistling, I am positively merry as I phone the Inishmurray lad with his lobster boat and commiserate over the foul weather. He is unconsoled at missing out on such a lavish payday and offers to give it a try despite the conditions. This behavior is typical, and I've been through it before on other occasions with other skippers. They like nothing better than to take you out, proclaim the impossibility of effecting a landing, then motor right on back home for a snug afternoon before the fire with a cup of tea. This is known as soft money. I thank him profusely for his enthusiasm, but blame it all on my charges: They're too old, too infirm, too prone to pneumonia. Better luck next year.

Having solved that dilemma, I face another. What am I to do with them? I go down to breakfast and explain our options. The captain, I say, refuses to go out due to the hurricane outside. Even Susan, though glowering, can accept that. So what better way to start a rainy day, I improvise, than to visit some graves. This doesn't exactly cheer these people up, given their own proximity to that inevitable date with mortality, but they acquiesce and file into the bus.

Our first stop is an enormous cliché, the mortal remains of W. B. Yeats, but the Drumcliff churchyard is so atmospheric that I never mind coming here whenever the occasion permits. Drumcliff is the site of an ancient Celtic monastery, said to have been founded in the sixth

century by Columcille, in my estimation the most interesting of the patristic Irish saints, a man whose colorful career included royal intrigues,
battles, banishments, sea voyages, druidic encounters, and, not least, the
establishment, by himself or his followers, of some ninety-six religious
settlements. The most famous of those was Iona, in the Scottish Heb-
rides, a destination even Dr. Johnson felt worthy of praise.

A magnificent high cross, more delicate and certainly more worn
than those of Clonmacnoise, and a broken round tower signify most of
what remains here from those far-lost days. Long after the monastery's
abandonment and the desecration in varied wars of religion that wasted
these territories, the Protestant Church of Ireland came along and im-
periously commandeered the site, building a house of worship where
the old Catholic *clocháns* must once have stood. Most of Ireland's sacred
places, especially those closest to towns and villages of any importance,
were appropriated in just this way. Cashel, Clonard, Kells, Clonfert—
the list is endless—all were occupied by Protestants, whose descendants
may or may not be there today. In Drumcliff's case, probably because of
the Yeats association, a working church with a pastor and services still
exists. Indeed, a brass plaque to Yeats's great-grandfather, rector here for
many years in the nineteenth century, is polished each week, but I wonder if the congregation numbers more than twenty or thirty people.
Certainly the fabric of the building shares a characteristic universal to
every other Church of Ireland edifice: It's falling down. The ubiquitous
sign soliciting funds for maintenance and repair is conspicuously displayed as near to Yeatsian memorabilia as possible.

Yeats died in France when he was seventy-three, but the war years
prevented his body from being interred here in Sligo, as he had stipulated, until 1948 (though there is some talk that the transfer was bun-
gled, and perhaps most, if not all, of WBY remains on the Continent).
His epitaph, contained in "Under Ben Bulben," which he wrote in 1938
just before he died, is among the most perfect ever written in the English language and bears repeating here:

> *Under bare Ben Bulben's head*
> *In Drumcliff churchyard Yeats is laid.*
> *An ancestor was rector there*
> *Long years ago, a church stands near,*
> *By the road an ancient cross.*

No marble, no conventional phrase;
On limestone quarried near the spot
By his command these words are cut:
    Cast a cold eye
    On life, on death.
    Horseman, pass by!

The last three lines, as "commanded," were carved on his stone, and they have mesmerized all who have come here since. As Frank O'Connor wrote, nowhere else could have been more appropriate than here. "It was part of the work of art as he saw it that he who took inspiration from the landscape and people of Sligo should return to them in the end."

After reciting the last lines of "Under Ben Bulben" for the group, I ask them what if any word or words stand out as perhaps most revealing of the great poet. "I love the 'Horseman, pass by,'" says Cynthia. "That is so romantic."

"Actually, I'd say 'Jacobean' instead of romantic," I reply. "I think romantic would be a word he'd reject."

"The economy of line impresses me," is Alden's opinion. "Instead of saying 'carve' these words in the stone, he says 'cut.' It's not what you'd expect in everyday conversation. It's more poetic."

"That's the point, I believe. The key phrase for me is the 'no conventional phrase.' Yeats said things in ways that we would never think to. He abbreviates the obvious and renders everyday thought in a stout, energized, tense sort of way. His lines are fraught with mystery. He reminds me of Mozart, Mahler, Sibelius."

"Seeing Yeats this way saddens me," Susan puts in.

"Whatever for?"

"Because we're standing around here like it's the Tomb of the Unknown Solder, Jefferson's grave, or the Holy Grail. The minute we deify people and put them on pedestals, academics come along and tear it all down. I read somewhere that in the States these days you can be an English major at any Ivy League school and never read a word of Chaucer, Shakespeare, or Milton. If Yeats becomes an icon, people will think he's a marble bust or something, not current, not important."

"As far as Yeats is concerned, I think that's a long way off in the future. So many professors' careers are wrapped up in Yeats that it would take a nuclear apocalypse to knock him out of fashion."

"That's what people used to say about Hemingway, and not so very long ago. Remember that."

Continuing on, we stop at an excavated court cairn along the main Donegal road. This is a good vantage point from which to see not only Inishmurray, if we could through the drizzle, but also Classiebawn Castle, the summer home of Lord Mountbatten. He was assassinated from near here by remote control in 1979. An IRA hit man planted explosives on Mountbatten's motor launch, then stood on the shore and watched his victim as he left harbor with a boat party of friends and crew. A flip of the button, and the whole craft was transformed into a hail of splinters. Ted is a somewhat doctrinaire Irish-American. He spits out words like "Brit" and "NorAid" when the occasion moves him, and now he snorts something along the lines of "good riddance." John semiwhispers to me as we return to the bus, "Let's keep Ted from talking too loudly when we go into the North, okay? There be lads there that won't take to that." I agree.

Going across the border is no longer the ordeal it once was: a few guards perhaps, but no cross zones or Checkpoint Charlies. As we lunch in Belleek, however, a helicopter passes overhead and a patrol of heavily armed British soldiers marches through the alley beside our pub. Ted is excited and wants to do some anti-British trash talk, but I pinch his elbow before he gets started. "Let's save it for later, Ted, discretion being the better part of valor, if you get my meaning." For all his bluster, he takes the point and confines himself to looking defiant. It deflates him later when I explain that for many rural Irish people, the goings-on in Ulster are as foreign a subject matter as civil war in Zaire. A great many just don't care.

"You'd never know that from reading the *New York Times*," he says.

"Nor from overhearing talk in a Dublin pub," adds John, "but Jim's right. The average farmer cares more about mad cow disease than he does about Ian Paisley. For him, troubles in the North are of a politician's making. Leave it to them to screw it up or to solve it, but leave it to them for good and all."

The shabby little town of Pettigo, straddling the border, sports an IRA memorial statue in the main square, a flying column irregular dressed in a trench coat and cap, holding an Enfield rifle. Ted has us stop and asks me to take his photo standing in front of this image of rebellion. We then follow a narrow track northward, out of politics, toward Loch Derg and Saint Patrick's Purgatory.

◆

It is raining steadily as John drives through barren country of moor and wasteland, "the whole country like a puddle," as Tristam Shandy would have it in one of his "Opinions." Though a newly built arrivals hall and car park greet us as we arrive at the lake, additions to the scene since I was last here in 1982, there is no denying that this place is unrelievedly gloomy.

The Purgatory, if you can believe it, was once the stuff of dreams and fantasy for all of Western and Central Europe, a fixture of the imagination that influenced not only the spiritual lives of countless pilgrims but also the artistic visions of several notable writers, from Shakespeare to Dante to Calderón de la Barca. Their imaginations were piqued by the vision litera-ture that originated here when knights-errant in search of both adventure and redemption came to seek their destiny in a tiny, dark, and fetid cave located on a small island situated in the lake. Monks stationed here in a monastery abjured these warriors to refrain from entering "Patrick's hole," but most ignored the warning, presumably "dyed with sin so deep" that a truly mortifying experience was all that could save them. Individually or in groups of two or three, they would fast, then be locked in the cave for a night, whereupon, if they were lucky, the afterworld would be revealed.

The knight Owen was the first to record his impressions, and those of his travels through hell and purgatory were suitably Breughelian. The torture and stench and punishment reserved for the damned was horrifically draconian and contrasted starkly with the delights of heaven, whose gates Owen approached, so sublime that he could hardly account for the snippet of bliss that he was privileged to experience. The next morning, monks discovered Owen back in the cave, more dead than alive, and though barely coherent, his babblings were eventu-ally recorded in writing by a monk. It was more than enough to stir the imagination of all who happened upon the story.

Owen was followed by others whose experiences generally mirrored his, though unique grotesqueries were often sufficient to relaunch fresh rumors throughout Europe, kindling men's desires to replicate the ex-perience. Streams of royal visitors followed the murky trail to this cave, one of the most desolate prospects in all the known world, considered by many to be the lair of dragons and horrible spirits.

Some observers, of course, wouldn't believe any of it. The astute chronicler Jean Froissart, for example, knew the difference between a vision and a nightmare and said so in 1274. That was not an exciting point of view, and few listened to him. The Purgatory gained in such repute that it rivaled Santiago in northern Spain as the premier destination for the absolution of sin. With Gutenberg's invention of printing from moveable type in 1455, moreover, the myth leaped from its status as amorphous folktale to one of self-evident fact, translated and transmitted in Latin, French, Italian, Spanish, English, German, and Czech renditions wherever men might roam and gossip. When Dante constructed his cosmological world of inferno and paradise in *The Divine Comedy*, he appropriated a structure everyone knew from the Purgatorial legends. In Dante's case, naturally enough, "Patrick's pit" was transformed into a work of art, whereas in reality the place gradually became mired in ridicule and then squalid suppression.

By the 1600s the pilgrimage was in disrepute. Rumors of bribery, the reformations (whereby religious credulity was mocked), and the skepticism of most educated observers, such as Erasmus, all contributed to a general decay in its appeal, a process the new Protestant overlords of Ireland took one step further when they sent parties of workmen with sledgehammers and crowbars to destroy the place. By the Penal times, Saint Patrick's Purgatory had become a peasant attraction, a ritualized experience akin to climbing Croagh Patrick barefoot, and that is pretty much the way it is today. Irish pilgrims are the exclusive visitors here. Mostly in the summer, they come for a one-, two-, or three-night stay of fasting and prayer to cleanse their souls in a metaphorical re-creation of burying themselves in a cave where they can reflect on their dark sin.

But it isn't all gloom and doom. Many visitors come here to achieve a wish, usually of mundane nature. I recall the old caretaker here telling me that many visitors have nothing serious on their minds at all: "Nothing more horrible than praying to pass an exam" is the way he put it. And the coach of a hurling team admitted coming to the Purgatory in the hopes of persuading God to grant his squad the victory in that year's All-Ireland finals. As a matter of fact, Wexford's captain, covered in blood, dirt, and mud, was photographed at the final gun on his knees, hands clasped in prayer, an image that made a lot of conservative Roman Catholics in this country very happy, as it took people's minds, if only for a few days, off the burning issue of philandering bishops. The group laughs at that, as they were intended to.

But it bothers me a bit to play to the crowd with a remark so slighting, so I amend my sarcasm. Standing in the drizzle, looking across to

Saint Patrick guards "the kennels," Lough Derg

the deserted Purgatorial island, overawed as it is by a dreary, concrete basilica and crowded with ugly dormitories (called "kennels" by the nineteenth-century Irish writer William Carleton), I mention that the entire panorama reminds me, for some reason, of growing up as a 1950s Irish-American Catholic. "Was there ever a worse time to be a member of the Church?" asks Julie with some vehemence.

"Was there ever a better time?"

I get Julie's point, of course, I'm not stupid. The 1950s was a period in Church history that many would deride today as a guilt-ridden morass of angst best forgotten, a psychiatrist's dream, a time in life as spiritually barren as any that may have gone before. And the blame for it all can be loaded by the cartful on principles invented, perfected, and proselytized by the ancient Celtic church. Penance and confession, after all, are uniquely Irish.

That is a long and complicated story and has much to do with Ireland's Indo-European roots whereby the sociolegal foundations of Gaelic society hailed not from the classical backgrounds of Greece and Rome, but from the more ancient seams of Indic and Brahmanic custom.

It is certainly true that both John the Baptist and Jesus decamped to the desert for fasting and mortification, as did the earliest hermits and holy men who hid themselves throughout the wastelands of Judaea and Egypt. But those were idiosyncratic gestures of self-examination and reproach, rarely standardized or codified as universal custom within the fledgling Church, a commandment that all had to obey. Jesus, for example, was vague on the subject. He spoke mostly in generalities when it came to sin, atonement, and forgiveness, and Scripture has nothing to offer on the sacramental status of penance. When the individual zealot, overcome with remorse, fled society to confront his demons alone and in solitude, it was pretty much a singular experience undertaken with no one else in mind. Hermits were notorious loners. They hated women and bishops in equal measure.

The Irish, of course, hate being alone. That is a simplistic explanation as to why they developed rules to govern, in a corporate sense, how society was to deal with punishing itself for sins against the City of God, but there may be something to it. The old Celtic monks were famous for contradiction. They enjoyed withdrawing from the presence of their fellowmen, but they couldn't do without company either. So as they went about regulating monastic behavior, they took it upon their officious selves to regulate the behavior of their mothers and fathers, brothers and sisters, friends and relatives as well. They codified various levels and degrees of sin, using the hierarchical legal system inherited from Brahmanic codes of law, mostly oral, which had formed the basis of their own civil dealings, and they assigned an "honor price" or appropriate fine for those who found themselves in spiritual violation. They also transformed and regularized the notion of confession as a precondition to punishment, confession being a variation on the monastic practice of monks seeking sound moral advice from a "soul friend" or *anmchara* (in the Brahmanic lexicon, *acharya*).

It did not take long to apply this rigor to the lay population, which previously had admitted wrongdoing in only generic fashion, standing in sackcloth and ashes at the rear of a church, beating breast and looking remorseful. The *anmchara* transformed the penitential experience into a more personalized exchange of embarrassing information, followed as always by the dispensation of a preordained penance that somehow fitted the trespass. The Celts left no moral failing untouched. An ancient penance reads, "He who fails to guard the host carefully, so that a mouse eats it, shall do cross vigil for forty days."

That is now all dead stuff, of course. Innovations desired by our New Age Church, for which the death of our current pope is required, will certainly include provisions for a generalized, all-inclusive absolution of sin during an opportune moment during mass, thus eliminating the dreaded "black box" with its anonymous priest seated inside, the approach to which gave me diarrhea as a kid.

The drift of religion today is toward accommodation, which was never the case in 1955 when Cardinal Richard Cushing ruled my roost in Boston with an iron fist. The nuns I grew up with never stopped talking about sin and its consequences, eternal damnation in the fire pit of hell. In many ways, the more upbeat aspects of our doctrine, the resurrection and our path to redemption, were hardly mentioned, the rot within all of us being a more entertaining subject to discuss. You sinned, you confessed, you paid the price with a penance. And remember, child, no sin is so petty or so "venial" that God will not notice. "He who neglects little things, falls little by little," as Saint Columbanus put it, and the nuns reemphasized that nugget of advice with a vengeance.

But I will not stoop to cliché here. I liked the nuns who taught me the catechism on Dartmouth Street; they never rapped my knuckles with a ruler. They were fine and principled people, and though I resented missing out on sports once a week to spend the afternoon with them in prayer and instruction, I never thought for a moment that they might be wrong, misguided, or deceived. Their message was too fraught with concern and anxiety. My life was in danger, they advised, beware the snares of Satan, a figure dressed in black satin who wanted nothing better than to be in my company. I was always a cautious sort of boy, so I kept my eye out for this ingratiating, sinister character.

This wariness continued into adolescence when I was sent away to a boarding school run by Benedictine monks. They were more subtle than the nuns, but they had wills of steel too. The high point of our liturgical year was not Christmas or Easter or Saint Benedict's feast day, but Holy Week, when the entire community shut down and went on retreat. We never went home to be with our families during Easter. We sat shivering late into the night in a darkened church up on a hill overlooking Narragansett Bay, heat off, the winds rushing up from the water and causing the steeple to groan in ominous, dramatic fashion, a vow of silence embraced by all except the retreat master, usually an imported Franciscan, whose job it was to put the fear of God in us.

This man was generally a master of rhetoric and manipulation, gifted in the art of spinning stories, keeping his audience in thrall, unlocking that secret chamber in all of us that quakes at the idea of life after death, forcing us to confront, and choose, our faith's demands for obedience. The high point, for the cynical and prurient at any rate, was the special hour-long harangue on sex from which the younger boys were excused. By the time he had finished lecturing two hundred or so habitual masturbators, the mere thought of an erection was anathema. It would fall off in our hands, he implied; save yourself for marriage. Those were the grand old days of fear and certainty, Irish specialties the two of them.

The Church, in my opinion, was the better for these harsh remedial ways. It was, and could still be, a last bastion for the word "No." I say to the group, "I'm as self-centered as the next person, and I believe, now that my mother is dead, that I need someone, something, to remind me of that fact, to tell me, Don't do that again. I need that little voice in my soul to rebel against misdeeds; I need that priest in the confessional to lecture me when I deserve it. When the Church loses that, I'll never go to another mass. The whole thing will seem like a ceremony at a Moose Lodge or a Chamber of Commerce. If you look at the Purgatory here, and the shades of guilt and redemption that it proposes, you see the historical Church, the Church of the Desert, the Church at its best. I think it's a fine thing that it's gray and ugly. It's dealing, after all, with the underside of our souls."

This confession results in a wild conversation as we debate the merits of Catholicism. Alden, who isn't of our persuasion, says we're all crazy.

16

The Work of Angels

ynthia is reciting Yeats's "The Lake Isle of Innisfree," easily that great poet's most popular lyric, as I report for duty at the breakfast room next morning. Certainly we are going to the little island with its "bee-loud glade," everyone clamors. It's nearby and how could we come so far and not stop, if only for a second? Why not, I reply, having never seen the place myself.

John is happy. He too knows the poem by heart; it's familiar territory to him, both geographically and touristically; we won't be getting lost. Innisfree, I gather, is Sligo's version of the Blarney Stone, and every driver in the country has a good spiel to unravel for those in his charge. "Be there or be square," says Carol, her sense of humor undiminished, it appears, from her operatic dive of the evening before last.

We arrive, with two other bus tours preceding us, at a dirt indentation in the bend of a road that gives us a most sublime view of the famous isle, famous, that is, only because Yeats made it so in a poem so lightweight that it seems to float. It sits in Lough Gill with other attractive islets, wooded down to the water's edge, an undoubtedly bucolic spot, but in no way that I can see remarkable to any extravagant degree. Yeats probably had no idea when he wrote "Innisfree" that in a few throw-away lines he would capture the imagination of a million or so new readers each year, or however many youngsters there are in the English-speaking world who enroll in freshman-level lit classes. Cynthia repeats the poem again with much greater fervor than this morning over her eggs and coffee, the mere sight of the place putting her in a trance. Though cynical, I manage to restrain myself and keep some saucy remarks to myself. There's no need to attack every icon in the world, and besides, there's lots of dirty linen ahead at our next stop.

We depart on the road for Dublin, traveling southeast. In ninety minutes we enter County Roscommon and the village of Strokestown. Passing along the main street, a boulevard really, we approach in regal fashion the mock-Gothic gateway leading into yet another of Ireland's Big Houses. Everyone groans when they see a large sign posted on the entry, "Closed on Mondays," but not to worry, I say, this is Ireland.

Can you imagine driving up to Mount Vernon and talking some stiff-necked employee of the Daughters of the American Revolution into opening the place up for an impromptu tour? Of course not, but after five minutes of tear-inducing pleadings with a sixteen-year-old gardener, this young colleen dutifully trots off to the Big House to see if some special accommodation can be arranged for this "cartful of cunts," the expression an old huntmaster of the Killing Kildares once used (in my presence) when he spotted a busload of Americans as they viewed the bloody dénouement of that day's sport from their plush and heated transport. And sure enough, in a few minutes she's back. "Cathleen will take you through now, given the fact you're here, but you'll have to wait a few minutes, she's just after getting out of bed."

"It's 11:30 in the morning!"

"'Tis to be sure, but you're a lucky man altogether, for often the nights she's never here." That sounds interesting, but I've made it a habit never to question authority, so I return to report our good luck to the tour, who break out in applause. "You really are our Fearless Leader," Alden says to me. "I never would have tried that."

From the outside, Strokestown House is a most attractive building. Unlike Moyode House, with its frilly Arthurian hyperbole, or Wood-lawn, with its fake Italianate stuccowork, Strokestown is a fairly pure example of Irish Palladian. From a central block mansion in the center (with later Georgian alterations), two slightly curving wings reach out in both directions to culminate on either side with two slightly smaller, though no less grand, versions of the primary structure. And unlike some of the monster Palladians in this country, places like Castletown or Powerscourt, both near Dublin, Strokestown, being in the uncivi-lized west, is a far more modest proposition and thereby more appealing and approachable. As Carol had said in reference to Woodlawn, it's the kind of place you could move right into. It is also the kind of place that inflates one's self-esteem. Strokestown radiates the sense of design and proportion that is reassuring and tasteful, a confirmation of good breeding. Sophistication exudes from its careful placement of doorways and windows, fanlights and porticoes, gateways and formal gardens. Its demeanor makes a person feel elegant and knowing, attributes that few members of the horsey Irish gentry have ever been able to boast.

We wait for Cathleen inside the front hallway, and there whatever illusion the glorious outer facade might have generated simply evaporates. We are crammed in the midst of a decrepit, falling down, and soon-to-be derelict interior. There is not much charm here.

The ceiling is woefully cracked, carpets worn and thin, windows broken, and paint peeling everywhere. The ancient cane stand is full of broken fly rods and splintered walking sticks; a bundle of oily keys lie on the scarred floor; the air is full of that distinctive, dank smell that immediately accelerates this battle-weary homeowner to one inevitable emergency reaction: leaks, and plenty of them. There is also the sense of oldness here, a musty body odor that I usually associate with people on the verge of death. I'm not too far off from the truth with that one, either. Cathleen informs us on her arrival that Strokestown is unique in Ireland, the present owner having purchased the place lock, stock, and barrel from the frail, aging, and declining inheritors of the Hales Pakenham Mahon family. "When the last of them moved out," according to Cathleen, "they took nothing with them but their clothes and a check. Even their hairpins are still here. Nothing's been moved; everything's been left exactly as it was." Which includes, though I do not say so to our guide, about six inches of regal dust and horsehair.

The library, though, is absolutely fascinating. Typically, there are few books, hardly a surprise to me. Cathleen tells us proudly that the wallpaper is original, the furniture as well. She plays a 78 rpm—"This is what we found right on the turntable"—and suddenly the room fills with John McCormack singing *The Star of County Down*, scratches and all. I jot down a note to myself to find a CD of his stuff when I get home. That man had an incredible voice. Cathleen drones on about this antique and that, referring to various pieces of junk and overstuffed easy chairs that are now, from the looks of them, retirement homes for mice. The precious wallpaper, I also notice, is peeling in long strips from the walls. Nonetheless, this is a very revealing room: Ascendancy Ireland, warts and all.

I go over to the fireplace mantle and pick up an invitation from Buckingham Palace for Major and Mrs. Wilfrid Stuart Altherstone Hales Pakenham Mahon, the pleasure of their company demanded for the evening of May 18, 1933, at 9:30 P.M. "Ladies: Court dress with feathers and train. Gentlemen: Full Court dress." I am amazed the Mahons could afford the journey.

This family is not an old one by Irish standards, despite what its remnants and *Burke's Peerage* might say. Captain Nicholas Mahon earned his foothold here—some 30,000 acres eventually, with over 8,000 tenants—during the English Civil Wars of the seventeenth century, which, as they spilled over into Ireland, produced some evil days indeed. The Mahons prospered as country gentry, serving in the Dublin parliament and advancing the agricultural interests of landlords such as themselves. Maurice Mahon was wealthy enough in 1800 that his interests turned away from the simple accumulation of wealth to the aspiration of something more noble, namely a title. For his vote on the Union, he accepted Pitt's bribe and became Baron Hartland. Deluded by grandeur, he then redesigned the town of Strokestown, which he owned, broadening the width of its main avenue and ennobling its various public buildings. It is said he based his various measurements on those of Vienna's Ringstrasse, thinking that whatever was good enough for the Hapsburgs was appropriate for the Mahons here in Connaught.

The Mahons intermarried, as was the norm, with other Ascendancy families, most notably the Pakenhams, who were barons of Longford and held an immense country seat at Castlepollard in County Westmeath. Portraits of two Pakenham generals, one of whom died while commanding British forces at the Battle of New Orleans in 1812 (a bullet through the spine), hang in Strokestown's hallway. A more impressive marital connection was provided by Arthur Wellesley, future duke of Wellington, who also married a Pakenham, a loveless liaison, as it turned out. "She has grown ugly, by Jove," Wellington is said to have remarked when he saw his fiancée after some years' absence at various army postings. This may explain his diffidence in furthering the careers of various relations as they importuned the famous soldier for favors. "Dear Arthur, Just one word from you and I will be made a Bishop," wrote a Pakenham to the Iron Duke. "Dear Cousin, Just one word—no," replied Wellington.

Certainly the nineteenth century was not a propitious time for this family. Major Denis Mahon, for instance, a cousin who inherited Strokestown in 1845 when the main line, now lunatic, died off without issue, was murdered just two years later by sectarian hoodlums in a famous outrage of the times. The major, appalled by the ravages of the Great Famine but also keen to be rid of his beggared tenantry, hired transports to ship 981 of these starving souls over the ocean to Canada. Unfortunate rumors began to circulate, however, that Mahon had instructed his agents to sabotage the vessels during the course of their voyage, and though such suspicions must certainly have been false, the fact remains that these craft were barely seaworthy and reached Quebec only after the greatest of difficulties. Added to that over twenty-five percent of the passengers died at sea from disease and benign neglect. The parish priest allegedly denounced the major from his pulpit as "being worse than Cromwell," and Mahon was hit in the chest by duck shot as he road his coach along the main Roscommon road. Bonfires celebrated the event from all the surrounding hilltops, though two men were eventually hanged for the murder.

Olive Hayes Pakenham Mahon, whose photographs are placed here and there in the library, married on July 4, 1914, a captain of the Irish Guards. Four months later he died at Ypres, along with many thousands of other Ascendancy sons. She married again in 1923, this time to an officer from some lesser English regiment, who must have gloried in his marital success, so much so that he assumed the additional surnames of Pakenham Mahon to his own. On October 19, 1929, he may well have regretted that choice, because in the course of just a few hours Olive lost every penny she had from investments on the New York Stock Exchange, a sum reputedly well over a million pounds sterling: from wealth to poverty in about as long as it took to read a telegram. Strokestown's decay set in that moment. The current owner of the place runs a garage in town that formerly abutted the estate. He bought it for the acre or so that he needed to expand his tire-changing facilities, and many people told him to tear the mansion down to its cellar hole for all the good it would do him. There are times, according to Cathleen, when he is still tempted to do so. Our tour proceeds to a modest ballroom, various bed chambers and nurseries, then to the formal dining room. Cathleen produces a huge ceramic pitcher and explains that when the ladies retired to the library after black tie dinners, the men folk would pass it one to the other and urinate in it, either at the table or standing by a window. I never saw that particular custom dramatized in *Upstairs, Downstairs*, and rather doubt her story, but she is adamant.* Our last stop is the kitchen, huge and full of black ovens with pulleys, spits, and culinary weapons unknown to me.

"That wasn't so very glamorous," Susan opines as we reboard the bus, "and that's why you brought us here. I think you're out to debunk every cliché there is about Ireland."

"I just want you to discern—and that's the real word I want to use here, discern—just what counts here, what's valuable to pick out."

"I know what you think is valuable, all the monastic sites and what they represent. You bring us here so that when we go back home and watch Merchant and Ivory films, we'll see them all as bankrupt and deceitful. You want us to feel 'had' when we come out of the movie theater, that we've been taken for granted as weak-kneed when people puff up royalty and aristocrats. You don't like these Ascendancy people at all."

"Quite the contrary, I find their degree of eccentricity charming. I remember an old Ascendancy battleship who sat on the sofa with a Jack Russell on her lap, reading the Sunday paper. She absentmindedly took off her glasses and cleaned them with her dog's ear, then put them on again. Only in Ireland."

"You can't fool me. You don't think these Ascendancy people were worth a damn."

"Draw your own conclusions, Madame. It's noon, time for me to read the office."

"Yes, it is noon," Carol interrupts, "time for a hot toddy." For once, Carol is right on target.

◆

We have a long drive this afternoon, our destination the multifaceted Boyne Valley. By this point I've rather lost the focus of our trip, Celtic and Norman Ireland, and I'm having John stop at a wide array of interesting spots. The countryside here, as we enter the Pale, is full of curiosities: neolithic cemeteries, plenty of Celtic raths and old religious settlements, Norman castles and a plethora of Ascendancy follies, man-

---

*An eighteenth-century French visitor to England noted in his journal that "the sideboard is furnished with a number of chamber pots and it is a common practice to relieve oneself while the rest are drinking; one has no kind of concealment and the practice strikes me as most indecent."

sions, gates, pillars, and obelisks. Our final stop is the ancient monastery of Kells.

Some people may wonder why I chose to put this site on our itinerary. Kells is a nondescript, busy market town, full of trash, debris, and dirt, nowadays overrun with noisy traffic. The famous monastery here has been tinkered with so often in the past that it too has lost much of its charm, presenting a rather disjointed picture of what the original community must have been like. Within the high walls surrounding it lie various buildings associated with the (of course) Protestant Church of Ireland, and the graveyard is full of memorial stones to various of its nineteenth-century worthies. The round tower has long since lost its conical roof, and the collection of high crosses, while certainly fine, is not preferable to those we've seen in the more atmospheric west. And the most interesting remain in the entire complex lies beyond the encircling wall, in among dreary little one-story houses of bare cement and plaster. That is Saint Columba's House.

As we walk up to this little building, a barrel-shaped oratory built in a corbeled fashion that is distinctively Celtic, my heart sinks a bit. The street is being torn up for sewer lines, and all manner of equipment and rubble lie strewn about. The little ninth-century church looks forlorn and shabby, and our guide, who appears unbeknownst and unbidden from nowhere, adds little to the karma of our visit. She does, however, have the key, and we enter.

The inside is dank and bare, as is the descriptive oration that our master of the gate launches into, no doubt prefatigued after three or four months of giving the same speech to any number of high-season visitors. I retain my manners and listen politely as she mangles various themes of Irish history, then thank her profusely, tip lavishly, and ask for the key, which I promise to return when we're finished. Happy as a lark, she leaves. "Do I smell whiskey in the air?" Ted asks.

I explain why we're here. In two days time, in the stunning library of Dublin's Trinity College, we will view Ireland's premier artistic treasure, the illuminated manuscript best known as the *Book of Kells*. It is the largest, most lavishly decorated, most pleasing such compilation left in this world, a sad thought in a way if you think about how many others must have been painted and bound, but then destroyed, through the course of Ireland's troubled history. Even those who denigrated the Celts whenever they could had nothing but praise for these glorious books. As a Norman cleric wrote in 1185:

If you look at them carelessly and casually and not too closely, you may judge them to be mere daubs rather than careful compositions. You will see nothing subtle where everything is subtle. But if you take the trouble to look very closely, and penetrate with your eyes to the secrets of the artistry, you will notice such intricacies, so delicate and subtle, so close together and well-knitted, so involved and bound together, and so fresh still in their colorings that you will not hesitate to declare that all these things must have been the result of the work, not of men, but of angels.

"Don't let the museum-like atmosphere of Trinity fool you, though," I admonish the group. "Remember this smelly little hole of a place when you look at the manuscript. Remember that the *Book of Kells* was an artifact of faith and belief long before it became an art treasure put in an atmospherically controlled and bullet-proof case. Remember that it was used here, in this building, on whatever altar may have stood by the eastern window. Remember its function; put it in proper context. It will mean all the more to you if you remember that the book came from a place like this. Remember its journey."

I then proceed to tell them the story of this amazing gospel book. How it was begun on the island of Iona in Scotland, founded by Saint Columcille in the sixth century, a barren, lonely outpost of Celtic custom and eremitic fervor. (I almost use the words "beacon of faith" but catch myself in time.) The Viking visitations hit Iona in catastrophic ways: the monastery looted and burned, monks slain in fields, on beaches, fleeing into the hills. In 807 Abbot Cellach removed the community to the Irish mainland and Kells; it is thought that Saint Columba's House was built to commemorate this deed. It is also thought, for a variety of reasons, that the gospel book was finished here, though certain unresolved and unfinished artistic problems within the manuscript have left some experts to believe that enthusiasm for the project waned as the view of Iona receded over the waves. That it was reputed the finest work of its kind is attested to by the annalists, for when a thief stole the book in 1007, it was remarked upon as "the chief relic of the western world." The book was recovered, miraculously, in a nearby field two months later, "a sod over it," though minus its bejeweled cover.

The monastery of Kells proved no sanctuary for the Columban monks. Vikings heard rumors of the place and revisited the community with mayhem and slaughter. They were followed by renegade Celts,

Saint Columba's House, Kells

greedy Normans, avaricious Englishmen, and finally the heretic Tudors, who took the keys and possession to the abbey on November 18, 1539, from the hands of one Richard Plunkett, the last abbot of Kells. As that sad man left the grounds, he packed the book in his luggage and sneaked it away.

Along with other artifacts of the ancient faith, the *Book of Kells* then took upon itself a clandestine, almost underground existence, produced at masses when safe and appropriate to do so, at death beds and funerals where required, as a totem for good health, good luck, or the exchange of oaths, promissory notes, the clinching of a business deal. The Plunketts assumed the role of hereditary custodians of the book and possibly charged a fee for its use. There is certainly evidence of commerce involving other manuscripts whereby owners rented out their scraps of tattered gospels to local farmers, who soaked them in buckets of water and then tied the pages round a sick cow's neck. That any vellum or brilliant ink survived such treatment is astonishing, despite the old belief that they were immune to watery abuse. "Whatever book Columcille would write," wrote one old scribe, "it might be ever so long under water and not even a single letter in it would be drowned," meaning, I would pre-sume, "washed away."

The ultimate savior of the *Book of Kells* was James Ussher, Protestant primate of Ireland in 1625. A serious bibliophile, he purchased the manuscript from one of the Plunketts, probably for £10 or £20, and added it to his collection of some ten thousand pieces. The career of Ussher, a relatively quiescent man of learning, was uncharacteristically dramatic, a prime example of Dame Fickle Fortune's promise that "I give by chance, not by reason." He stood on the execution platform when the controversial Thomas Wentworth, earl of Strafford, was be-headed, an event many consider the beginning of Charles I's precipitous decline. He also whispered final words to Archbishop Laud when he too lost his head to the ax, and watched the king's own execution four years later, which Ussher, as a Royalist, considered a disaster. In the re-bellion of 1641 he lost everything to Irish renegades save his books and a few pieces of plate and jewelry, and then the Puritans came along and confiscated those. A friend generously repurchased the library when it was put up for auction and returned it to him, but after his death in 1656 his daughter, in turn, auctioned the collection for £2,200. It then formed the nucleus of a library for Trinity College, where it was largely lost track of. A notation from 1705 reads, "The Library of Trinity Col-lege, Dublin, where the noble Study of Bishop Ussher was placed, is quite neglected and in no order, so 'tis perfectly useless, the Provost and Fellows of that college having no regard for books and learning."

"That is a lamentable story," is Susan's response. "How could they turn their backs on such beauty?"

"If an Indian scalped your daughter, I rather doubt you'd find much good to say about the beauty of a headpiece or a pot or a necklace. The *Book of Kells*, as you'll see, will never be mistaken for anything other than what it is—uniquely Irish—and a great many Scotsmen and English-men have nothing good to say about Ireland. Today, of course, it is be-yond value, and if Trinity put little stock in it three centuries ago, you can be sure they've reassessed the situation by now. According to a friend of mine on the faculty there, Trinity reaps over £200,000 a year from en-try fees and the sale of souvenirs."

"It all boils down to money," says Susan, shaking her head and light-ing a cigarette.

"Not really. In this case it boils down to racial animosity." As we drive out of Kells we pass the Market Cross downtown, a huge monolith with many carvings still recognizable, an interesting preservation, given that it lay pushed over as so much waste for two hundred years, since the Rising of 1798. British troops used the cross as a gibbet, hanging from one of the sacred arms peasants and United Irishmen whom they happened to catch. Then they shoved it off its pedestal into a ditch. "I see what you mean," Susan says.

◆

The River Boyne is a shallow, meandering stream for the most part, largely pristine and rural, nothing but farm fields edging its banks. We are late again today, and our hotel for the night is in Drogheda, but I have John head for our lodging by the slow road, a small farm lane that runs along the southern bank. I want the tour's first glimpse of Newgrange to be from this very special vantage point.

It is easy to become historically confused here on the Boyne. The Hills of Tara and Slane, Celtic Camelots if you will, are over the shoulder in one direction, and Drogheda with its Cromwellian massacre of 1649 lies toward the other. In between we are driving right through the famous battlefield of 1690 where James II, "that pile of shit" in the blind poet Raftery's elegant phraseology, halfheartedly fought for his crown. And yet we are here to see Newgrange and the other megalithic tombs for which the Boyne is equally famous. If I want to confuse everyone, including myself, I could attempt to interweave all of these strands into some sort of coherent form, but I quail and refrain. Carol doesn't care, after all. She's talking about Ronnie Reagan again.

As we turn a bend in the road I have John stop and everyone gets off. We walk up into a pasture, then turn and behold the pyramids of Celtic Ireland. As a matter of fact, what we're looking at predates the pharaohs' megalomania by over a thousand years.

No more incredible view in Ireland offers itself than this. High on the ridge facing us across the Boyne stands the immense tomb of Brugh na Boinne, anglicized as Newgrange. When I first saw the place forty years ago as a child it was a weathered old mound, tall and uneven, surrounded by a ring of trees. Smaller cairns dotted the farm field that sloped before it to the river's edge, and you could see here and there standing stones in the vista. Looking east you picked out the second great mound called Dowth, and around the river's bend to the west, larger than all of them but obscured by distance and foliage, stood Knowth. Built over five thousand years ago by people who were here well before the Celts, these structures were already long deserted by the time Christian missionaries landed with crosiers and sacred bells; they of course condemned these sites as heathen sanctuaries, which they certainly were. The unreflective Vikings were not afraid of the place, they figured that temples this big must certainly contain loot and treasure inside, so they simply dug up what they could to find out if any gold was about. And the Normans built a castle on Knowth. But only recently have archaeologists put together a reasonable analysis of what these structures originally meant.

One of these, my old acquaintance Michael O'Kelly, excavated Newgrange and restored it, which caused all manner of controversy. He cut down the druidic-looking trees, discovered a ring of decorated curbstones that originally had formed a collar around the mound, compressing and containing the tons of fill that made up this artificial hill, and discovered that Newgrange had originally been faced with a decorative outer layer of brilliant white quartz. He proceeded to put this entire edifice back together in much the same way its original builders had intended, inserting as well the highly decorated "window box," first described by Oscar Wilde's father in 1850, who had no idea as to its fabulous function.

As O'Kelly said to me in 1982, "There had been a tradition at Newgrange, the locals would tell you, and particularly a very nice old man called Bob Hickey, the official caretaker there but long since dead now, that on a certain day of the year the sun would shine into the tomb, and the time suggested, particularly by Bob, was midsummer. Now for me, I wondered if this slit—a deliberately made slit in the roof with this built structure around it and the ornamental lintel on top [the one discovered by Wilde]—wasn't the place where the sun would shine through.

"But for midsummer the sun is almost vertically overhead; there's no way it could shine either in the entrance to the tomb or through this slit, so the possibility then occurred to me that if we looked at this in midwinter, when the sun would be rising at its southernmost point on the local horizon, could it be then that sunlight would shine there?

"So I went, I think it was in 1969, to see for myself. I was there entirely alone, inside the tomb, looking down the passage towards the slit, gradually seeing the sky go from gray to pink, and finally the tip of the disk of the sun appeared above, over the horizon, which is a hill about three miles away, and then this shaft of light striking straight in, right the length of the passage, and into the center of the tomb. First as a thin pencil of light, which gradually widened to a band about seventeen centimeters wide, and that slowly swung across the floor and gradually was reduced as the ray began to be cut off. Fifteen minutes after this whole process begins, it just disappears."

I remember asking O'Kelly about his reaction at the time. Did he feel like he'd discovered a new continent? "I wondered, should I be here at all. Would I hear a voice saying, 'Get the hell out of here,' or feel a cold hand tapping me on the shoulder or whatever, you know? It was certainly a very dramatic experience, the most exciting discovery you could imagine."

Since the completion of O'Kelly's work, the entire panorama has been transformed to a scene of extraordinary garishness, proving, I suppose, that popular taste five thousand years ago was no better than it is today. The white quartz gleams and glitters in a dull, plastic sort of way, radiating an aura of cheap sensationalism that a Ferris wheel might elicit from far off on the horizon. Despite its historicity, which O'Kelly proved in meticulous fashion, the resulting megalithic mirage infuriated academic purists, while the general pubic just shook its head in disbelief. Most people wanted the grubby old green mound back; it had a kind of hoary friendliness about it that the high-tech restoration simply lacked.

But the group is certifiably impressed. No one expected a megalithic construction to look so very, well, modern. There is no doubt in anyone's mind that this is a one-of-a-kind apparition. "I find it incredible that people can write so much about Stonehenge and yet I've never heard of this place," says Cynthia.

"Well Stonehenge is astrologically a more complicated monument," I reply, "but essentially you're correct. Unless your primary interest is Ireland, chances are you've never heard of Newgrange. The same is true of France, and the field of standing stones at Carnac in Brittany. Unless you're a Francophile, it probably hasn't landed on your desk." Cameras click away as the sun sets.

17

Semen

e spend this morning conversing with spirits long, long dead, as we crawl through the cramped passageway to the interior of Newgrange, viewing the funereal basins hewn from solid rock where the ashes of those inhumed were placed. The beam of an electric light shows the dawn progression as it would unfold on the winter solstice of each year. Our guide tells us that reservations for that particular moment stretch well into the twenty-first century, and woe to those who happen to be here during a rainy morning on a December 21 of the future when there are no sunbeams.

Newgrange will be closed to the general public sometime in the next decade, he predicts as well. People squeezing through the entryway are inadvertently erasing the neolithic decoration of chevrons, diamonds, and zigzags that were carved on the load-bearing orthostats, thereby creating the usual preservationist dilemma that curators at the caves of Lascaux and Chauvet in France, as one example, have faced. There is ambitious talk of building an ersatz Newgrange nearby, full of plaster reproductions along the line of Clonmacnoise and its high crosses. You'll still be able to wiggle into a weird-looking chamber and view the artwork and burial vessels, the only difference being that everything will be a "virtual reality" fake.

I feel a little drooped as we progress from one tomb to another, joining other bus tours coming to and fro along the narrow country roads.

After a while I tune out of it all and let the guides in situ do the talking. At Knowth I ask John to accompany the group while I take a walk alone down a lane.

◆

These narrow byways, as is so typical of Ireland, regurgitate a tumble of allusions that run through my mind. The Hill of Tara, so close by to the south of us, redolent with its Celtic associations; this string of mega-lithic tombs, overlooking as they do the Boyne, even more famous in its own right for the momentous battle fought here in 1690 that so shaped Irish history; the manorial estates, ruined abbeys, abandoned castles—a chaos of historical litter. Even the pastoral perfection of fields and woods, river, and huge, open sky cannot go unremarked upon, for these were claimed by Ireland's most forgotten poet, Francis Ledwidge, who took them for his own.

Ledwidge was born a few hundred yards down this road at the village of Slane in 1887, yet another mouth to feed for his poor, soon-to-be-widowed mother, who labored, more than likely, in many of these same pastures that I walk by. A handsome plaque now graces what had been a typically squalid "cabin" of the times, and visitors—mostly Irish—occasionally stop and visit, sign the guest book and perhaps purchase one of Ledwidge's slim volumes of poetry. They will be familiar with some of it, naturally enough, being a people who do enjoy the fine turn of a phrase or a heartfelt description, and Ledwidge provided plenty of those, being a keen and fervent spectator to what Oliver St. John Gogarty called "the perennial and abounding Boyne." But most of all, as Seamus Heaney observed, Ledwidge was "safe." You could find him in the "convent library," or you could be awarded some of his poems at graduation time; he was "a charm against all that modernity which threatened the traditional values of a country battening down for independence." The fact that he was more than that requires a judgment more subtle, and that eludes most people, which is certainly not a crime. Ledwidge was a conventional man in most respects, but beneath the surface he was struggling, a turmoil World War I solved for him by adding his body to the charnel pit.

Ledwidge is often lumped with Rupert Brooke, Wilfred Owen, and

Siegfried Sassoon as a "war poet," if only because he died in 1917 near Ypres, a freak casualty, hit by a random artillery shell behind the lines as he worked on a road detail. His patron, Edward John Morton Drax Plunkett, eighteenth Lord Dunsany, took the blow in stride. So many people perished in that enormous carnage that one or two more, no matter how gifted and how bright their future, hardly mattered. "Here were the makings of a great poet," he wrote, "whom the world will not know now."

Ledwidge had begun his working life as he ended it, scraping, shoveling, picking, leveling, and straightening roads, mostly as the foreman on a County Council crew. Such employment, then as now, required little ambition and less effort. "The hardest thing about a County Council job," as John explained it to me, "is getting up in the morning." Ledwidge used the time well, however, honing his skills of observation, keenly noting all about him on his leisurely forays out in the countryside, mostly the smallest details:

> *And wondrous impudently sweet,*
> *Half of him passion, half conceit,*
> *The blackbird calls adown the street.*

One day, screwing up his courage, he sent his poems to Lord Dunsany, whose noble castle nearby, dating back to the thirteenth century, would fulfill most people's fantasies as to what being rich and titled must be like. And Dunsany, amazed at what he read, invited the lad to visit.

Dunsany, like Ledwidge, is largely forgotten today, though he died as late as 1957 and was well in the mix with everyone who mattered in literary Ireland for over half a century. His championing of Ledwidge could favorably be compared with Yeats's of John Millington Synge, but such cursory similarities do not intrigue most people, be they academics or otherwise, largely because the Dunsany-Ledwidge tandem ran counterthematically to the "Celtic" renaissance. Synge went to the Aran Islands, as Yeats told him to; Ledwidge went to Ypres, as Dunsany told him to. That pretty much summarizes the dilemma.

Dunsany, as few people recall, wrote some of the Abbey Theatre's early smash productions. He had a bent for the mystical in life, was a highly imaginative lyric poet, and worked indefatigably on all manner of intellectual projects throughout his life. Unlike Yeats and Lady Gregory, however, he did not find his inspiration in the Gaelic twilight, the spirit of which, as a Protestant landlord and staunch Unionist, he felt alien to. That caused him their animus. Despite his undeniable popularity—in 1916, Dunsany had five different plays in production along Broadway in New York City alone, still a record—he was slighted by the Abbey board time and again. St. John Gogarty, the wit of his day, claimed that Yeats was jealous of Dunsany's pedigree. Their rivalry was not literary, he wrote, "far from it. Yeats had no rival to fear among contemporary poets. On Yeats's part it was envy. Yeats, through his descent from parsons, innately loved a lord. He was at heart an aristocrat, and it must have always been a disappointment to him that he was not born one."

As for Lady Gregory, well meaning and friendly though she evidently was, certain writers went too far or against the grain to please her. "She had no room for playboys except on the stage," said Gogarty, who couldn't tolerate her "namby-pamby humor." After World War I, Dunsany refused to submit his work for their consideration. He joined a long list of famous writers who either broke with the Abbey or were never given the opportunity to shine there.

Dunsany's role in Ledwidge's development was stylistically minimal. He read the first poems, strove to tidy up their amateurism, and passed along fundamental advice to the largely self-educated laborer. Lending Ledwidge a volume of Keats produced instant results. Though Ledwidge "imitated nobody," according to Dunsany, a certain refinement and classical awareness spread through his work.

Dunsany's larger contribution was material. He settled a stipend on Ledwidge, which freed him from the road gang, then introduced the young man to all manner of fellow poets and literati and talked publishers into printing his verse, for which he wrote the introductions. Ledwidge was profoundly grateful. He didn't seem to mind it when Dunsany called him, however deaf to the nuance, "a peasant." That was better, after all, than Yeats, who considered protégés little better than "fleas" who annoyed their host, "the wild dog."

World War I, the Dublin Rising, and a failed romance changed everything. Ledwidge matured, as did his work. Still ostensibly a nature poet, a new dimension of melancholia and dark, subtle anguish began to permeate his always-striking lines. In "The Dream of Artemis," written from the trenches, he transforms a simple hunt through his native Meath with the goddess of chase into something else: an admixture of desire, youth, and fond memory of a sacred landscape, all threatened by death in a war far, far away:

We passed a garden where three maids in blue
Were talking of a queen a long time dead.
We caught a green glimpse of the sea: then through
A town all hills: now round a wood we sped
And killed our quarry in his native lair.
Then Artemis spun round to me and said,
"Whence come you?" and I took her long damp hair
And made a ball of it, and said, "Where you
Are midnight's dreams of love."

The Easter Rising of 1916 confused the loyalties of men like Ledwidge, whereas Dunsany had not hesitated. Although home from the Western Front on furlough, the eighteenth baron motored into Dublin to assist in the suppression of rebellion. For his trouble he was shot through the cheek and taken prisoner, his captors sincerely apologizing for trying to kill him. Ledwidge turned sullen. In the very barracks where he had enlisted in the British army, Thomas McDonagh, friend and patriot, was sentenced to death and later shot on execution hill, occasioning Ledwidge's finest poem:

He shall not hear the bittern cry
In the wild sky, where he is lain,
Nor voices of the sweeter birds
Above the wailing of the rain.

Nor shall he know when loud March blows
Thro' slanting snows her fanfare shrill,
Blowing to flame the golden cup
Of many an upset daffodil.

But when the Dark Cow leaves the moor,
And pastures poor with greedy weeds,
Perhaps he'll hear her low at morn
Lifting her horn in pleasant meads.

Though court-martialed for insubordination and insulting an officer, Ledwidge followed orders and returned to Flanders, there to die his useless death. In the end, as Seamus Heaney pointed out, he "solved nothing." Had he lived, that particular corner would have long since been turned.

There is no point, I think, in talking to the group about Ledwidge. Puff pastry is difficult to describe.

◆

We lunch early in Trim. The huge medieval castle is surrounded by chain-link fence—closed for repairs—so I'm left with little to do here, and recommend that we fill our bellies, an opportunity never refused by this ravenous assembly. As we walk through the town to find a suitable pub, we stumble across Talbot's Castle, and this sparks me into repartee.

"You see how extraordinary Ireland can be," I say, "here we are on an ordinary street in an ordinary town that could be ordinary anywhere in Ireland, yet we have the confluence of so many life strands right here in this building." Everyone looks at me blankly, their expectations for a nice bowl of Irish cream soup suddenly fading away as their captain goes off on another of his long-winded digressions.

Talbot Castle is a fifteenth-century private stronghold, a small tower house built right in town as some nobleman's urban residence. It bespeaks quite plainly Ireland's continuing unsettled state, the idea being that no one felt so very safe in this perilous land that he could afford to let his guard down. You always wanted a good strong stone tower with a stout oaken door between you and your enemies, be they Irish or half-breed Norman. Contemporaneously in England, the wives of barons and knights were beginning to insist on friendlier quarters, mansions built laterally with larger windows for light and air, and more inviting doorways from which to bid guests enter. The Irish would continue throwing up gloomy tower houses for another two centuries, behind the times as always.

The group finds this interesting but can see no reason here for a delay in luncheon. "This tower was used as a residence, of course, long past the days of knights and crossbows. In fact, Esther Johnson bought it in 1717 as a home." This statement is meet with uncomprehending stares, as I suppose it should be, so I helpfully add, "Esther Johnson being Swift's 'Stella.'" From the continuation of mental fog emanating from my entourage, I can tell further explanation is required, so I launch into a lengthy discourse on the career of Jonathan Swift, who held a living near here in Laracor, where he preached to a dozen or so parishioners each Sunday and entertained his women friends, Stella preeminently. Swift is a recognizable entity to all here, but I can see their familiarity with the great dean and his place in the Irish saga is close to nil—perhaps a smattering of *Gulliver's Travels*, but that would be about it—so I switch gears for further name recognition. "And a century after Stella sold the tower, to Swift incidentally, it evolved into a schoolhouse, and it was here that the duke of Wellington first received his education."

"Wellington?" repeats Ted incredulously. "You mean *the* Wellington?"

"I do." More murmurs of amazement ripple through my audience. "What was he doing in Ireland?"

"Well, he was Irish." This is earthshaking information. No one can fathom the fact that Arthur Wellesley, the man who beat Napoleon, the hero of the Peninsula Wars and the victor at Waterloo, could possibly have been a Gael. "I can't say he was proud of the fact, but Wellesley was Irish. But remember, *Ascendancy* Irish, and that makes a huge difference."

I enlighten my charges with Wellesley's early history, his alleged birth (though some say it was in his father's townhouse in Dublin) at the nearby estate of Dangan, where the family was so wealthy that it moored an ersatz man-of-war in its small lake, from which ceremonial cannonades were fired on birthdays and other moments of celebration. Wellington had been the last-born of five sons, and evidently of such little exception that few if any anecdotes survived of his youthful days in Ireland, other than that he was a fairly bright mathematician, or so the schoolmaster of Talbot's Castle believed. Certainly Wellington, like so many others, whether Celtic and Catholic or not, found the opportunities for gainful employment fairly thin on Irish soil, and he gladly forsook its shores early and often, especially as his family flirted with bankruptcy, in time-honored Ascendancy fashion, and was eventually consumed in collective debt. All he took with him into the wider world, as his prospective brother-in-law put it, was that "rubbish of character."

His political attitudes were certainly unremarkable. As an Ascendancy Protestant he disdained the native underclass, referring to Ireland as "that country of scoundrels." Though he sat for Trim in parliament, his interests were purely those of his class, and later in life he took pains to distance himself from the unpleasantness that most people associated with Ireland. "Just because you were born in a stable does not mean you are a horse," he is said to have remarked, referring to himself, presumably, and not Christ, though one can never tell. Wellington never suffered the pangs of humility.

"A typical Brit," snorts Ted. "Let's have lunch." In a couple of moments, as an afterthought, he adds, "Can we see his place?"

"There's nothing to see, unfortunately. Dangan is a ruin. The lake is there, and I think one or two follies, but that's it. When the family sold the place in the early nineteenth century, a famous United Irishman rented it for the year 1803, in other words, an Irish Catholic nationalist, and his name was Roger O'Connor. To show the cultural schizophrenia that traditionally splits this country apart, Roger is said to have taken Dangan because he wanted a place suitably grand in which to entertain Napoleon Bonaparte, when that great revolutionary general landed in Ireland to free it from the bonds of oppression and feudalism. O'Connor's brother was a British loyalist, however, and had a great iron cage made for the same purpose, to lock up that atheistic pig Napoleon when he was defeated in battle on Irish soil. That was prominently displayed in Cork. Political passions in Ireland are highly pitched and highly divisive, as you can see."

◆

Dublin is our final stop on this two-week jaunt, but we have a point on our itinerary to visit first, the fabled Hill of Tara. The afternoon has turned windy and wet, but the group is eager to walk up the gentle incline to Tara's summit. The old Protestant church, deserted long ago, is now home to the inevitable slide show, and there I park Carol in the care of a friendly caretaker. "I'll keep her amused for ye, not to worry," he says.

Usually, on a fine day, the view to the west over the vast central plain of Ireland is immense, surprisingly so, given that Tara is little more than an elevated plateau. But today the mist is heavy, with moisture-filled clouds streaming overhead full of glowering menace. I'll have to hurry.

But I can't. Tara is one of the most interesting sites in the whole country, despite the meager remains that are actually here to see. A royal seat of immense importance and contemporaneous with the Iron Age histrionics of Cú Chulainn as narrated in the Celtic equivalent to Homer's *Il-iad*, the saga *Táin Bó Cuailgne*, this place emits a palpable aura of what Sean O'Faolain, on a walking trip here in 1940, called "the spacious savagery of pre-Christian Ireland." The royal raths, the palaces so lavishly described in poetry and song, the huge banqueting hall where champions fought to the death in drunken duels over who would receive the hero's cut of pig, all we see of their splendor today is the earth, disturbed, roiled, and rumpled from all the digging, erecting, destroying, and rebuilding of wooden lodges covered with thatch that the Celts were so proficient at throwing up and burning down.

The most important rath is called Cormac's House, allegedly the site of a chieftain's palatial compound, Cormac being the name of Saint Patrick's pagan adversary on a sixth-century Easter Sunday. A mediocre statue of the saint used to sit on the top of this mound, signifying who won the struggle, but it no longer does. Off for the usual repairs, I suppose, we'll see him back in a decade or so, staring off at the Hill of Slane, where he kindled his paschal fire to the fury of heathendom. I have no intention of getting into a discussion here of Patrick, the legend of whose association with this site being largely that, legend. Instead I point out the slab put here by the IRA in 1938 to commemorate the slaughter of Catholic peasants on Tara during the Rising of 1798; and then I point to a long, thick standing stone about five feet high and three around. "This is the coronation stone of Tara, the Lia Fáil."

Julie boldly goes right up and puts her arms around it in a great hug, something I've seen I don't know how many colleens do on how many countless Sundays when I've been here at other times on a day's outing from Dublin. I even remember my mother doing it in 1953. "And it's also called, according to George Petrie, who wandered up here in 1836 interviewing Gaelic-speaking peasants for local lore, the *Bod Fhearghais*, which in English means 'the penis of Fergus.'"

At this Julie jumps in the air with her face pushed back in distaste, as though someone had just stuck a cattle prod with a million volts up her nose. "That is disgusting," she says with some emphasis. Everyone else giggles nervously.

"You are a wicked man," Susan laughs.

"Well, the Celts were an earthy people, and to be a king or a chieftain in this country back around the time of Christ, your role essentially was to maintain a pact with Mother Nature or Earth Mother or whatever goddess of fertility they happened to venerate. A king had to be brave and resourceful first; he was required to battle the clan's traditional enemies, to secure hostages from them and other signs of their deference, and he had to clear the stage of rivals, usually brothers and

Lia Fáil, the Hill of Tara

cousins, whom he either murdered or maimed. Then he 'married the kingdom,' as they put it. Lia Fáil is a representation of marital union, it was the stone that screamed approval when a man worthy of Tara's kingship stepped upon it. That's no different, really, than Arthur's Excalibur. Everyone tried to pull it from the rock, but only Arthur could do it; only he was the anointed one. Ditto for Lia Fáil."

"You're going to tell me this stone can yell?" asks Alden.

"Yes, and it could ejaculate."

"Oh really!" says Julie.

"Remember when I touched on this story before? The custom is Indo-European and the Irish tradition is Indo-European. It didn't originate from either Greece or Rome, but from a deeper, richer, more primeval lode, a Brahmanic-Indian source. In India, for example, we have many instances of newly crowned kings having intercourse with a surrogate of sovereignty, usually a horse, and Giraldus Cambrensis, a Welsh and Norman cleric who came here in the 1100s, records a similar custom, again with a horse. After the king copulates and ejaculates, the horse is decapitated with an ax, cut into pieces and boiled in a cauldron. There are illustrations in old manuscripts of the king sitting naked in the pot, eating and dispersing meat and broth to the clan. It's a binding rite of passage between a ruler and his people."

"A meal fit for a king," jokes Ted. Julie looks pale, or so I imagine. Being a good Catholic, she looks disapproving as well. If that isn't a mortal sin, she seems to be thinking, nothing else could be.

The whole notion of sexual union between warrior and sovereignty survived the advent of Christianity for centuries. When monks finally began writing down some of the oral stories and traditions still then common in Irish society, the sexual element was very high. There were the old "hag of Ireland" tales, for instance. Warriors on a quest would find themselves separated in the great primeval forest that covered most of the island, and each would stumble on the lair of an evil, haggard, repulsive-looking witch—"blackened, nose awry, wide nostriled, a wrinkled and freckled belly, variously unwholesome, smoke-bleared eyes had she," as the old tale would have it. To each lad she would offer herself, but none could muster up the will to climb into bed, all save one. And at the moment of truth, as he placed his penis in her vagina, the hag would suddenly be transformed into a gorgeous young woman. Who are you, the awestruck youth would ask? "Royal Rule am I."

"So in other words you had to be an ass man to be king," says Ted, to the annoyance of his wife.

"You had to be willing to do your manly duty," I reply, "because if you didn't, you would be cast aside. As Maeve, the Amazon queen of Connaught put it, and she was a representation of sovereignty, 'Never was I in bed with one man, than was not the shadow of another nearby.' Our image of a saintly, chaste, puritan Catholic Ireland, the Ireland of Eamon De Valera in the 1930s and '40s, should not obscure the fact that the Celtic temperament has traditionally been described as ribald, high-spirited, sensual, romantic, amoral, and pungent. It's a tribute to the power of the Catholic church that it's been so successful in repressing these elements for so long. But beneath the surface, I submit, all is turmoil."

"That's the role of priests and politicians, to quash people's individuality, to make them toe the line," says Susan. "It can make for a lot of unhappiness."

"But it also makes for order. If you don't have order, you have anarchy," Ted pipes in. He's run for political office twice, once in Vermont, clearly on the Republican ticket.

As we walk down the hill, Alden sidles up and remarks that the animal business amazes him. "How could anyone do that?"

"I'm told if you close your eyes it feels the same. That was the word from on high that ran through my prep school anyhow. And a vet I know says it's pretty common in the countryside even now, usually with cows."

"Oh dear."

"Saint Patrick thought it was a particularly Celtic vice, the Irish addicted to intercourse with cows. But more interesting to me is the controversy surrounding Lia Fáil. There are legends, some quite credible, that an Irish tribe emigrating to Scotland took the original Lia Fáil with them, as a symbol of legitimacy I suppose, and set it up in Argyll, and from there it somehow became the Stone of Scone, or the coronation stone of Scotland, which Edward I took to England after his Scottish victories of 1296."

"Meaning?"

"It was put under the coronation seat of Westminster Abbey, the idea being that when the English king or queen was crowned, sitting on the royal stone of Scotland, he or she was therefore the legitimate monarch of unruly Scotland as well. A nice touch."

"That's all poor Prince Charles needs. After all the trouble he's had with Diana and Camilla and his awful mother taking so long to die, so on and so forth, he finally gets crowned and the bloody stone starts screaming and ejaculating. That will be quite a sight."

"And right on live TV for the whole world to see."

"Exactly! I'd like to be in the front row for that, with earplugs and a bib."

18

"Dublin, O Dublin,
Fumbling And Tumbling"

hile in Dublin, I rely on John to provide the cattle fodder. He's a Dubliner, after all, and he knows every street corner, every public building, every church, and every event that ever happened here, plus the usual dose of double entendres, witticisms, and corny, lewd jokes that are to be milked from various geographical oddities. I have about reached my tolerance at being a gracious host; I'm counting the minutes until I can deposit my charges in the departures lounge of Dublin Airport, so I gratefully defer to his expertise.

The drive into Dublin had been suitably grim. Dublin, need it be said, is no longer the backward, grimy, provincial, and ultimately endearing chimney sweep of a town that it had been in the 1950s. Instead, it is bounded by suburban development of the usual sort, ringed by a variety of new highways, and absolutely jammed with people, cars, crime, drugs, students, foreigners, and all manner of the latest excess. Why bother to clutter these pages with repetitious description?

I do not interrupt John's patter. I don't tell everyone what I miss from the old days: Daly's Grill down on the waterfront, the old Guinness steamers that used to tie up on the lower quays, the decrepit Russell Hotel and its dowager cousin, The Royal Hibernian; Dublin Bay prawns served up at The Red Sail, my old solicitor's chambers on College Green, piled to the ceiling with Dickensian trunks full of scruffy, singed, and sooty legal documents that chronicled the declining fortunes of Ireland's great families; the no-frills Callaghan Tailors across the street, where you had the finest of tweeds to pick over for a splendid jacket, fitted by a half dozen fussy, demanding, utterly eccentric old men; the bookstalls on the Liffey where Joyce used to browse for Italian poetry, the courtyard of Kilmainham Hospital, a storage bin full of old Empire statues that a Free Ireland threw away—I loved the one of a plump and grandmotherly Queen Victoria; any number of genteel old boarding houses on Leeson Street, where I could rent a room for £25 a week and eat breakfast with some the heaviest knives and folks ever made, all monogrammed with coats of arms; the plethora of horses and carts that plied all manner of vocations; the old cattle mart off North Circular Road, an unfashionable neighborhood if there ever was one, with its clamoring herds driven through the streets; a glass of porter at room temperature, no refrigeration if you please; and above all, the great and acrid smell that used to pervade the whole city when Guinness brewed its magnificent drink and pumped that ineffable odor out of monstrous brick smokestacks to further foul Dublin's gritty air— those and a million other small details, all of which added up to make this city unique, all done and gone.

John is droning on. He's pointing out the new statues that Dublin has adorned its streets with since my last visit here, most of which are deplorably banal. One commemorates a famous prostitute, of all things, hawking cockles and whatever else on Lower Grafton Street. Another depicts James Larkin on O'Connell Street, and Joyce nearby over on North Earl Street, both copied more or less verbatim from period photographs. The only one remotely artistic is Anna Livia Plurabelle opposite the General Post Office, a sort of languid river maiden stretched out in a series of cascading pools, which I must visualize in my head since the water has been turned off and the various cavities lie full of trash. John refers to this as "the floozy in the Jacuzzi," which I imagine must be in the repertoire of every bus driver in town. It draws a laugh, as intended.

The various squares are dutifully reviewed in our "drive by," along with the duke of Leinster's magnificent mansion, Trinity College, row upon row of elegant townhouses. One thing is perfectly clear: The days of decrepit Georgian Dublin are over. Scaffolding and construction crews are hard at work restoring and refurbishing eighteenth-century Dublin, mainly for corporate headquarters and multinationals doing business here, but let's not quibble. In the bad days of 1950s depression, this was an architectural style detested by the Old Celts, it reeked of Ascendancy Protestantism, and if Georgian Dublin fell to ruin either from neglect or the bulldozer, so much the better.

Economic prosperity, or at least the desire for it, finally reversed this particular brand of ethnic cleansing, and thank goodness just in time. Dublin can be a handsome city if it wishes to be, and people in positions of governmental authority, no matter how provincial their backgrounds, have finally been convinced to stay the hand of mindless demolition. The preservationist battle has been hard fought, and it finally seems to have been won.

Our hotel, however, is a disaster, an American chain of some sort that makes a mockery of bothering to go anywhere in the world to see or experience something different. This could be downtown Anywhere, USA, except for the fact that all the computers are off-line and the receptionist has never heard of us. It takes a while to sort this out, but eventually I manage to check the group in, arrange their dinner plans, try to get Ted a last-minute invitation to meet the ambassador, Jean Kennedy (what a surprise, I can't, much to Ted's annoyance), before I manage to flee. Cook's night out, I tell everyone.

My Irish publisher, as it turns out, has invited me to dinner, despite having rejected my new book. I get the idea that a free meal is some sort of consolation prize; since your manuscript is no good, I'll buy you a steak. Needless to say, this is mildly irritating, especially as he tries to chisel me down on the quality of our projected tête-à-tête. "If you want a full dustup we can go to ——— or ———," he says, name-dropping a couple of Dublin's newest and most trendy restaurants, "but frankly I'm in a spot of hurry and I know a nice bistro that will do us just fine." Meaning, a cheap little dive just perfect for third-echelon writers, if indeed I haven't slipped even lower than that.

"I'll take the dustup, Tomás, if it's all the same to you."

"Well of course, Jim, that'll be fine." He's pissed and I know it. If he could get out of our date, he would, and frankly any old story would do, his dog is dying, his wife's water bag has broken, whatever. But he isn't quick enough to think one up. We arrange to meet at an old Dublin pub called The Stag's Head for a drink beforehand.

I arrive first, in fighting trim. An old drunk has just fallen flat on his face, upending three tables in succession, the last being mine. Guinness splatters all over my trousers. I look and smell dog-eared when Tomás arrives. The prim little prick pats himself down before condescending to order a brandy and soda . . . "spectacles, testicles, wallet, and watch," as the old saw goes. I'm glad to notice a slight grimace as he realizes his seat is wet. That makes two of us.

Throwing circumspection to the wind, Tomás gives me an insider's view of publishing these days, the need for interdisciplinary work, the requirement that scholars get a life, embrace varied subject matter to present a rounded integration of story line with popular taste, blend history with current observation, and so forth. "Sounds like my work," I say. "In fact, it sounds just like the book you rejected."

Tomás pauses. "If we're going to get personal here, Jim, there's no use in continuing. You're a fine writer, but you're lost in the past, if you don't mind my saying so. The old monks, well, let's just say the obvious. Who cares? Strongbow, the Normans, castles and battles, and who married whom? I'm sorry, Ireland is more than that these days."

"Is that why you're publishing Victorian love poems these days, on scented paper?"

"It sells, old chum, it sells. Which is the point. You do not sell. When you give me something that sells, I'll print it. There's a fair bargain." That evening, in between boasting about the Frankfurt Book Fair and all the incredibly huge book deals he's brokered there—none, of course, involving anything I ever wrote—Tomás tries to order a cheap Merlot for dinner, not the mark of a world-beating publisher I must say. I trump that by recommending a Burgundy I've never heard of, but the price is right, expensive. Tomás offers me a ride home in his new Mercedes, but I say no, I'll walk.

For some reason, I feel exhilarated. Trains pass me by, blowing their whistles, urging me to hit the road. I'll never see Tomás again in my life, and good riddance. I'm going to write whatever I want forever; a man's entitled to his hobbies. And come to think about it, I don't need Dublin anymore either. It's changed forever; it's a different place now, not in my league, as Tomás would say. I can't wait to ditch my tour and return to Connaught.

The next morning bright and early I get everyone up and out. We're going to be the first in line for the *Book of Kells* when the library opens up. This is important, I tell everyone, we'll have the place to ourselves.

How the plans of little men can be cast to the winds by those of the great. We arrive at the correct moment in time, but the library is closed

all morning to allow one individual the privilege of viewing the manuscript all by himself. German chancellor Helmut Kohl, it appears, is in
town for some European Union business, and we are herded off just as
the man himself careens into the inner quadrangle of Trinity College
for his private showing.

Kohl is so overweight that he prefers being driven in a van rather
than a limo, and as he emerges to a sparse crowd of some students and
us, I tell the tour to take advantage of fame and see for themselves what
a world figure looks like.

Well, not too impressive. Kohl is certainly, if not fat, let us say, large.
He and his wife recently compiled a cookbook of old family recipes, one
of which feeds four and calls for sixteen pounds of meat. I hope he enjoys the *Book of Kells* in the company of all the smiling sycophants who
surround him, the prime minister of Ireland included. I can't help won-
dering where Mary Robinson is.

No one in the tour thinks taking a picture of Herr Kohl is worth the
film, but Susan asks me to pose in front of the statue of the great Irish
historian William Lecky. "Two birds of a feather," she says, and I take
that as a compliment.

We proceed to larger fish. We view the exquisite Houses of Parliament
(now a bank) and the various statues of dignitaries overlooking College
Green: Henry Grattan, Edmund Burke, Oliver Goldsmith, and my old
friend Tom Moore, who casts his poetic gaze over a public toilet, in
Joyce's words, the truest meeting of the waters that he could recall. We
bus up to Dublin Castle only to find it closed as well—thank-you, Security Forces, here to protect the aforementioned German delegation—and
head for the twin cathedrals of Dublin City.

As my publisher Tomás so incisively put it, I give the group some
boring history as we proceed. Boring, of course, depends on your up-
bringing, genes, intellectual capacity, and brains, and I'm glad to report
that the tour doesn't find any of this boring at all. Perhaps it has something to do with my delivery, I wonder, but I slap myself for such con-
ceit. The story line deserves the credit. If you're interested in history,
these places have a great deal to say. It's that simple.

Dublin's first cathedral, Christ Church, was founded ca. 1035 by a
Viking, Sigtrygg of the Silken Beard, a unique happenstance in the
British Isles. When ragged Norman adventurers, led by the disgraced
and bankrupt earl of Pembroke, better known as Strongbow, stormed
the city in 1170 and took it, he favored this church with his patronage,

as did others of the freebooter barons in his entourage. Many Normans, deeply sinful men, frequently devoted great treasure from their lootings to the clergy, knowing full well that hell awaited them, in all likelihood, at the end of their mortal string. Endowing the religious was a sort of insurance option that many found attractive; it gave them a foot in the door of both spiritual camps.

The monarch of England, however, looked askance at the success of Strongbow and his cohorts. He had granted license to these motley scavengers to pursue their Irish adventure only because he considered them incompetent and certain to fail. The idea of an autonomous Norman kingdom in Ireland, ruled by the suddenly thrusting Pembroke, infuriated the Plantagenet Henry II, and he in turn launched a forbidding and hugely expensive enterprise to the island himself. He did that not only to frustrate Strongbow, whom he detested, but also to establish in Ireland a patrimony for his odious son, John Lackland, the only child for whom he held paternal feelings. It was also a convenient time in his career, given the Thomas à Becket fiasco, to be away from England and beyond the reach of censorious letters from the pope.

Henry proceeded to carve up the territories of Ireland, ceding many parcels to court favorites and men he thought powerful enough to frustrate Pembroke, to whom he grudgingly ceded Leinster. He also named as first royal justiciar Hugh de Lacy, a rough-and-tumble marcher lord to be sure, but not a member of Strongbow's circle or even one of the first adventurers. That, not unnaturally, created hard feelings all around, as Henry intended it should. One of Henry's preferred policies was to sow dissension, to encourage rivalry.

These newly favored Normans stood apart from Strongbow, and in time they established and endowed their own cathedral church, called Saint Patrick's, which was built just outside the city walls, a dangerous place in a time when Gaelic raiders often sallied out from neighboring hills to reeve and loot. Today, as there are no walls, the two buildings can almost be seen from each other and are a five-minute walk apart. They have always been in competition, until that moment when people no longer felt compelled to care, which happens to be the case today now that God has died.

Our favorite whipping boy, the established Church of Ireland, finds itself the custodian of both cathedrals. A century ago it managed with some success to set off a bidding war between two eminently wealthy Protestants. One, a distiller, poured several thousand pounds into the restoration of Christ Church, whereas the second, one of the Guinness magnates, did the same at Saint Patrick's. That sort of benefactor is hard to come by in a world no longer graced by noblesse oblige, however, and both cathedrals are now falling apart once more. It is rumored that the Church of Ireland offered one, free, back to the Catholic church, but papists delight in watching Protestant resources strained to the limit, and they declined. These great albatrosses are thus hanging from its neck. Weekly sermons stress financial woe as opposed to spiritual crisis, all to congregations that number in the dozens. Since Dublin has plenty of theaters, tourist centers, and amusement facilities all in place, I wonder for the future of these ecclesiastical behemoths.

I decide myself that two cathedrals are one too many for the tour, and opt for Saint Patrick's, mostly because of Dean Swift, who ran it for thirty-two years and is buried there alongside Stella. Christ Church has its treasures, though they are subtle. I particularly enjoy James II's traveling mass kit, consisting of candlesticks, portable altar, and a few other liturgical odds and ends, which he used on the day of the Boyne. These curios sit in the dirty crypt, covered in cobwebs, along with other strange items. There is also the heart of Saint Laurence O'Toole, a famous Norman bishop, hanging from the wall, and an enormous memorial sculpture to the earl of Kildare, who died in 1743, so lifelike that you half expect that august millionaire to step right off the pedestal and shake your hand (or ask for a maintenance donation, more appropriate, given the circumstances). But Saint Patrick's holds more, and John lets us off at the side entrance.

There are several features of great interest here, and one is a beat-up door with a rough hole carved through it, a mutilation of 1492. As the other tour operators haul their people about to the usual Swiftian memorabilia (a plaque the great dean put up in memory to the groveling servitude of his manservant, for instance, hardly worth a note), I take my people to the old door.

This relic reminds us of the Irish penchant of nursing a grudge. Descendants of those vagabond Geraldine Normans who backed Strongbow were the earls of Kildare here in County Meath and the Desmonds in Kerry. Their mortal enemies were the Ormondes (or Butlers, as in William Butler Yeats), relative newcomers to the Irish scene, and generally regarded as men who had won their great fortune through duplicity and diplomatic wheedling, as opposed to the more honorable course of martial arms. In the year Columbus discovered America (having visited Galway first to pick up navigational lore from Irish seamen), Kildare and Ormonde found themselves having an argument here in the cathedral. Tempers ran hot, and all of a sudden the animosities of several generations erupted in a brawl, swords and daggers drawn, men hacked and stabbed, blood flowing in the nave. I am reminded of how often in history the houses of God played witness to such ferocity, the occasion most memorable to my mind being the attempt on the life of Lorenzo the Magnificent in the Duomo of Florence, the assassin, dressed as a monk, making his lunge as the host was elevated at the moment of transubstantiation.

Kildare, driven into a corner, found himself trapped in the sacristy. After an hour or so of shouting to and fro, cooler heads prevailed and a truce was agreed to. Would Kildare come out? He would not. Would Ormonde come in? No, he would not. So Kildare carved a hole in the door with his knife, took a deep breath, and put his hand and arm through to the other side. There, though tempted to cut it off I'm sure, Ormonde instead shook it with his word of honor. Those were perilous times to be sure.

No less so a century later, my next stop being the garish Boyle memorial. Richard Boyle was the most famous Protestant scavenger ever to try his hand in Ireland. Born of a noble English family and well educated by standards of the day, Boyle arrived on these shores as an adventurer, with about £50 in hand to try for fortune, an enterprise he pursued with vigor, intelligence, and amorality for a course of fifty-five years. Enormously enterprising, Boyle mastered the ways of court intrigue as it applied in particular to business opportunities—in other words, he bribed often and well—and he mastered over time the development and administration of all that these opportunities had to offer. Whereas Sir Walter Raleigh, knight-gallant, poet, and dreamer that he was, frittered away the chance for wealth that his enormous land grants in Cork held in potential, selling 12,000 acres to Boyle for a paltry £1,000, the land turned to gold under its new owner's direction. By 1613 Boyle was both the richest and the most powerful man in Ireland, a thorn in the side of Catholic and Gael, a proselytizer of forward-thinking Protestantism and the bounty it promised.

Unfortunately for Boyle, now the earl of Cork, he had grown rich during the "expansive days of great Elizabeth." The Stuarts were a different breed, and during Charles I's disputes with parliament, as that monarch sought to finance his nation's affairs without recourse to calling the Houses to attendance, he looked to extract as much income as he could from Ireland. To do this dirty job he sent his dogged servant Wentworth, i.e., Lord Strafford, who took it upon himself to curb the grandees of this disorganized realm and to extract from their coffers the funds required by Charles. "No physic better than a vomit," as one of the king's advisers put it.

Strafford unnecessarily embarrassed these powerful men, however. When he went to pray in Saint Patrick's Cathedral, for example, he pointedly expressed horror that Boyle's elaborate tomb to his wife, one of the largest and most ostentatious in the British Isles, stood so near the high altar. To whom was he, the new lord deputy, to pray, his Lord Jesus Christ or Catherine Fenton, a person of no distinction other than having borne the earl of Cork eleven children? Strafford ordered it removed to some dark recess of the cathedral's cavernous interior, and by doing so earned Boyle's bitter enmity.

Many men rejoiced when Strafford's head was struck off by an executioner in 1641, no one more than the first earl of Cork, who had intrigued in many subtle ways for just this bloody dénouement. Why do churches have so many reminders of how hate governs behavior far more than love? "Someone should dust all these figures," Susan comments as we study Cork's multilayered monument. Strafford, no doubt, regretted the day he ever saw fit to mock it.

We continue on for the obligatory ramble through Swift's mementos: his pulpit, his death mask, some books from his library, his highly admired epitaph—"He lies where fierce indignation can lacerate his heart no more." This, of course, was written in Latin, so I translate for the group. Still smarting from my evening with Tomás, I tell them that I hope they will all buy my next book, a "History of Irish Toiletries and Bathroom Manners," to be published in the vernacular of Julius Caesar, Mark Antony, Emperor Octavian, and Dean Swift, a guaranteed bestseller. This is a joke no one understands.

We are in line behind a pompous tour guide, a woman in her sixties who is working herself up to a fever pitch about the inalienable right of satirists like Swift to intellectually maim, assault, defame, demystify, disassemble, and verbally castrate their opponents in any way they see fit. Swift is clearly being canonized right in front of us in this impassioned tirade against, I guess, censorship or government control of the media or restrictions to freedom of expression. It is very tiresome (Swift

Death mask of Jonathan Swift, Saint Patrick's Cathedral

would have agreed), so I bring a different slant to this wretched, tormented, unhappy man.

"Remember what I've been saying about Ireland. You look around this cathedral and you think, what a glorious job this must have been for Swift, the dean of this, one of the greatest buildings in the country. Wrong. For Swift, this was a hellish backwater, the back of beyond par excellence. Ireland has always been an exile, a place of last resort for soldiers of fortune, the last refuge for those who have failed in the greater arena of European affairs. Do you think Swift was happy to be here in Ireland? Of course not. His ambitions had been far loftier; he had a taste of it himself during years of some prominence in London. When he was awarded the deanery here it was virtually a sentence of death for him. 'My enemies,' he sadly said himself, 'are glad to see me here,' and no amount of cajoling, letter writing, or insinuations for advancement ever rescued him from this oblivion. What you see here in Saint Patrick's, and in his literary work, is bitterness, pure and simple. Ireland has broken more hearts than it has ever had the time to mend."

Sobering news for the group. Perhaps these people would have preferred something more upbeat, a harangue on Swift the Liberator, Champion of a Free Press. Come to think of it, that sounds pretty boring.

We end our day back at Trinity. The *Kells* exhibit is mobbed, so I direct the group in through the door and wait for them outside. I had hoped for a less distracting visit for them, but this will have to do. All are somber as they come out after an hour. "I am speechless," proclaims Susan emotionally. "I have never seen anything like that in my life. The guard up there was perfect. When the line behind us sort of pushed forward, he stepped right in and said, 'Give everyone their due now, let them have the time they need for the great *Book*.' I tell you, that's a religious experience." I visually check out the bags of Kells booty that the group has collectively purchased in the gift shop. Another grand day for the coffers of Trinity College.

This evening I host a "cocktail reception" at the wretched hotel, supposedly prepaid by Eire Tours. At the end of this gala affair I'm presented with the bill, Eire Tours having conveniently omitted sufficient funds to cover same. Disconcerting, to say the least. A fellow habitué at the bar, from New York City, consoles me when I've finished wrangling with the staff. "Does this usually happen to you guys?"

"Not generally. Very unprofessional."

"I can understand that. Do you really do this for a living?"

"Sometimes. What do you do for a living?"

"I'm in telecommunications."

"Then you should help these hotel people fix their computers."

"Oh, not that kind of communication," he laughs. "I do phone sales for Dial-A-Mattress." He gives me his card in case I need a bedroom ensemble when I get home.

Several tour members want to hear some traditional music, so I take them to a weird place out near Dun Laoghaire that puts on Irish step dancing, storytelling, and song, with a promise that after their performance these "real" Irish people will mingle with the crowd for a drink or two. The audience this evening consists of about fifty Korean, Japanese, and Chinese visitors, all here as computer trainers for some foreign company just setting up for business in Ireland. They must surely be confused as a half dozen teenagers go through a few frenetic step dances, an art form that has always reminded me of calisthenics. At the end of a joyless forty-five minutes or so, the troupe disappears, leaving us alone with a roomful of Asians, of whom none speak English. They all gather on the stage for a group photo op. Being a generous sort of person, I take their fifty cameras and snap fifty pictures. They never get tired of smiling.

Back in the hotel room I of course turn on the television and watch the Red Sox play baseball with the Yankees, live from Fenway Park in Boston. I've had so much to drink tonight that I find myself in a true cultural stupor. Where am I?

19

"Unnatural Insurrection!"

oday is the last day of the tour, and I am off until dinnertime. Because my group is incapable of making any independent choices, I plan out everyone's schedule. The National Museum is an easy choice and good for the whole morning. The day being sunny and warm, I heartily recommend a walk through Merrion Square, the most innovative example of horticultural design that I have ever seen. I trundle Ted off to the old Kilmainham Jail, where many heroes of 1916 were executed, and for Carol I hire a companion for three hours to accompany her on a shopping expedition. After that she can sit in the lobby and swap stories with other aged Americans. I have a pretty full day going too, but I hope to get a couple of hours in the afternoon to do a little touring on my own.

A Dublin friend of mine, a World War I historian, once asked me if I'd ever seen the memorial by Edwin Lutyens to the Irish who fell in that conflagration. I've seen most of what there is to see in Dublin over the years, but his question had mystified me. I am a great admirer of Lutyens's work, but I had never heard of such a place. Quickly jotting down the general location, I had promised that on this trip, if I had the time, I'd try to find it.

Easier said than done. I knew the memorial was on the Liffey opposite Phoenix Park and near Heuston Station. But Phoenix Park is over fifteen hundred acres and stretches on for an eternity, and as my wife has always complained, I hate to ask for directions. So starting at the train station at around three in the afternoon, I hike where I think it may be. After forty-five minutes or so, I'm nowhere.

My 1932 *Blue Guide*, a traveling companion more dear to me than life itself, is uncharacteristically vague, so I finally bite the bullet and inquire, quite appropriately it seems to me, at the Defense Headquarters of the Irish Army, located on the river's edge. The sergeant in charge of the main gate, however, has never heard of World War I and knows nothing of any memorial. As I find out thirty minutes after that, it's right across the street from his bunker.

This is not the place to discuss the career of Sir Edwin Lutyens, a landscape designer and architect who "flourished," as they like to say in old genealogical treatises, during a long career of over fifty years until his death in 1944. Known for country houses, enormous schemes of civic planning (he designed New Delhi, designated in 1912 as the new capital of India), and—at the other end of the spectrum—the incredible dollhouse commissioned for Queen Mary in 1921, his perception changed radically when he met, and then collaborated with, the famous gardener Gertrude Jekyll. He did some marvelous historical restorations, exemplified by his work on the Holy Island of Lindisfarne, and he was kept very busy after World War I doing memorials and cemeteries. He is probably best remembered for one of the greatest white elephants of all time, Liverpool's Roman Catholic cathedral, a gigantic conception that, thankfully, never got past the crypt stage. (Its hideous modern successor was finally completed in 1967.)

Lutyens's father was the well-known painter Charles Augustus Henry Lutyens, who specialized in hunt scenes and equestrian portraiture. His enormous painting of a famous (to me, that is) nineteenth-century Moyode Persse, amiably walking his stallion through a pack of hounds he led for the Galway Blazers, has been banished for some years now to the narrow servants' hallway of a lunch club in Galway City. I'm probably the only person in the world who knows its whereabouts, or for that matter even cares.

There is a small sign, probably eight by ten inch, to guide the prospective visitor into Dublin's War Memorial Garden, designed by Lutyens in 1930. Commemorative plaques lie scattered all over the city to various republican heroes of the Rising on Easter Sunday 1916, where they were wounded, where they were killed, where they surrendered; and of course the enormous General Post Office, where Patrick Pearse read his famous Proclamation of Independence ("In the name of God and of the dead generations from which she receives her old tradition of nationhood, Ireland, through us, summons her children to her flag and strikes for freedom"—stirring words), and where the rebels fought valiantly for seven days and six nights, is a featured stop on every bus tour, as it should be. Official Ireland will not forget the 450 men who died that week. But the 49,000 Irishmen who fell in the mud of Flanders, that's a different story. Eulogistically speaking, they might as well have never existed.

The Protestant officer class, Ascendancy Ireland's contribution to the war effort, is handsomely remembered in the great cathedrals here in Dublin, and certainly throughout Ulster, but men in the ranks are all but officially forgotten. In town and village squares, in Catholic parish churches, in municipal buildings anywhere in the Republic, these fallen are not remembered.

This was an article of faith in De Valera's Republic. The gullible lads were those who followed John Redmond's advice and those of his Home Rule Party, Irish parliamentarians seduced by the false promises of clever Westminster politicians, who foolishly urged their countrymen to enlist in the British army, to fight for Ireland's freedom in the trenches of faraway France. The IRA said to fight here in Ireland, while British blood was being sucked dry at Ypres and the Somme. What a horribly convoluted, bitter choice. Parents could only grieve when telegrams arrived announcing a son's death. What had he died for, well might they have asked, as British artillery leveled blocks of central Dublin in 1916?

To the victor go the spoils. With Ireland's final achievement of independence, the souls of its lost children who died in British uniforms entered a gray zone of semiofficial oblivion. They died, and we will forget their error.

The memorial garden, located where no one ever comes except to walk a dog, is stunning and typical of Lutyens's work, albeit cold in feeling. Something here disturbs the spirit on this suddenly chilly afternoon. The design is circular, with Georgian pediments and archways, obelisks and follies, surrounding a central space, with a fountain in the middle, all overlooked by a large cross. Suddenly, the obvious occurs to me. This is all Big House architecture, and not the ornate facade facing

British war dead, Bully's Acre

outward, but the domestic feel of the rear yard and stables. The archways here are reminiscent of Roxborough House, Moyode House, Woodlawn, and Strokestown, the avenues and gates and well-worn byways that stable boys, manual laborers, gardeners, and smithies all must have been familiar with as they labored for the master and his family in virtual serfdom. Inadvertently, Lutyens created here a monument to the back door, as it were, and reemphasized the role of so many Irish peasants during Ascendancy times as essentially that of servants, the underclass, the exploited, and yes, unfortunately, cannon fodder. For all Lutyens's stylistic genius, this memorial can only be regarded as a disaster. Britain pays homage to those it deceived, promising liberty but never fulfilling that pledge until people at home—traitors—fought for it on Easter Sunday 1916. No wonder De Valera shunned this place in his heart. No wonder David Lloyd George could refer to Ireland as "that sad, beautiful, bitch of a country." There is something here deeply disquieting.

Another memorial, though hardly meriting that name, lies several hundred meters up the riverbank. I inquire for Bully's Acre, one of Dublin's oldest (and seediest) graveyards, at the Royal Hospital of Kilmainham, established by Charles II as a nursing home for wounded soldiers and pensioners. The receptionist tells me where it is, but says I must write for permission to borrow the key. Absolutely, I say, please give me the appropriate person's name, address, and phone number. Ten minutes later I've hopped the wall, not a mean feat considering its height and my condition, and start searching. In about twenty minutes I find what I'm looking for, a row of stones marking the graves of British soldiers who fell here in Dublin during the Rising. These poor fellows have really been forgotten.

They lie in a garbage-strewn corner of Bully's Acre, the din of rush hour traffic and exhaust fumes pouring over from a new highway extension a few yards away. Certainly if I were a relative of CQMS J. Coyle, RFM C. Duggan, both of the Third Royal Irish Rifles, or Pvt. Leen (no first name) of the Fifth Royal Irish Lancers, I would be quite unhappy with this unkempt, miserable, overgrown lot of weeds that cover these bones of men who died so violently, it would appear, for nothing. "Death divides, but memory clings," reads one inscription. I rather question that particular sentiment. Nothing is clinging here except swirling trash and ice cream wrappers. This has been a most enlightening afternoon.

20

Saint MacDara

n our way to Dublin Airport. Last evening, courtesy of Eire Tours, I hosted our break-up dinner at a well-known institution here, Dobbin's Wine Bar. I will never forget the hostess who greeted us at the door. Originally, and by that I mean when she got out of bed that morning, she must have been one pretty colleen, but by evening her looks had been rearranged to obliterate most every natural detail of beauty. This was a face deformed by the cosmetic industry, hair frozen in place by the aerosol industry, and a figure rearranged by the undergarment industry. I've never seen an apparition quite like it. "Was that Christine Keeler?" Ted asked me, and I knew exactly what he meant.

Eire Tours, being quite lavish for a change, arranged for plenty of wine, but I feel no effects this morning. This is liberation day, both for myself and my extended family. Some of these troops are ready for home, but others are ready for more. Susan tells me that whatever I do next year, she's signing up. This is followed by a big hug and kiss. I take all this, again, as a real compliment. Maybe I do have a future in the industry.

John delivers an impassioned speech at the airport. Tell everyone you know, he says, that Ireland is the greatest place on earth. Come one, come all, come often. This is not exactly the message I would choose to give, but I stay quiet. We all shake hands, we say good-bye. Carol is wheeled off to immigration in a courtesy wheelchair. I feel exhilarated but also flat. What have I to look forward to, going home to my wife? She thinks I've been on vacation for two weeks, and having an affair with some wealthy septuagenarian to boot. John drives me to the bus station. I've a long ride ahead to Galway.

◆

I'm left off in Loughrea, a market town eight miles from Moyode. I have about a thirty-minute walk until I can get off the main Dublin-Galway road to a neighborhood boreen. My duffel bag "must be full of rocks," as John pointed out on more than one occasion (actually, it's full of books I picked up during the tour, mostly in Dublin), and I'm getting tired myself of lugging it. As soon as I'm on a back road, though, I get a ride straight to Moyode. Everyone knows me by now around here, I'm the King of the Castle.

I have a feverish hour or so closing up Moyode. Draining pipes, clearing out the ice chest, covering my few sticks of furniture with plastic, all take time and energy. I made a decision riding out here on that bus. With four days left before my own flight home to Boston, I'm off, like Brendan the Navigator, for the high seas of the Atlantic and the stolid pearls of rock that lie offshore.

I pull out next morning before dawn. Never could I have awakened on my own, so I had borrowed an enormous alarm clock from Marie, vintage 1940, I'm sure. "Lay it on the side," she tells me, "it doesn't go off if you stand it up."

"Like a normal clock, you mean?"

"Right you are, Jim, this is an Irish clock."

At 5:00 A.M., instead of rising from the sweet bliss of a dream to modulated Mozart or the low drone of an announcer telling me the weather, Marie's version of Big Ben broadcasts the ungodly hour with the equivalent of an air raid siren. I feel as though someone has battered my head with a hammer.

I drive through Galway City in a flash, not a soul awake. I drive non-stop through Connemara until I reach Clifden, and then Claddaghduff. I don't get out of the car until I reach Féichín's house, overlooking Omey Island. But I've missed him.

His father invites me in for a cup of tea. "Just sit ye here by the stove and look at the telly," he says, "something special today." In a new twist on the never-ending saga to preserve Irish, a new television station has been added to Ireland's roster. Based in a facility somewhere out here in the bogs, it broadcasts three or so hours a day, mostly cartoons, with Mickey Mouse and Goofy speaking Irish. "They want the children to watch this," the old man says, "to encourage them to use the Irish. Have you ever seen anything so silly? The poor deprived people of the west, ha! It costs £40 to get a special antenna for this, and what do we watch, cartoons! And to make matters worse, all the engineers are English. Och, the money people waste." Féichín, it seems, passed me coming out here. He's in Galway City for the day. "It will be very unlucky if you can't get out tomorrow, though."

I meander along the coast with another plan in mind, being reasonably resourceful. A photographer I admire, Paul Caponigro, had taken some magnificent shots of an old church on Saint MacDara's Island, and I had never been there. From the map it looks to be only a mile or so offshore. Maybe I can cadge a ride over if I find a fisherman loitering about.

By lunchtime I'm in a little hamlet called An Mas, which is Gaelic for "thigh," the approximate shape of this irregular protrusion into the sea. As far as I can tell, this is the closest inlet to MacDara, but a more desolate looking little harbor would be hard to find. A couple of curraghs lie tied to the crumbling concrete breakwater, their lines frayed and surely ready to snap. An old Galway hooker, or tramp sailor, lies beached on the field behind, its tarred hull cracking and peeling to the touch. Garbage and debris swirls everywhere; the few cottages seem deserted even though wisps of peat smoke curl out from their chimneys. Walking along the dock I can plainly see MacDara close by, and a curragh motoring in, whose captain I'll approach.

A middle-aged man walks over from a house right on the farthest tip into the Atlantic, and leans next to me against the seawall. He asks, and learns, my name, country of origin, profession, marital status, number of children, and the reason for my being in Ireland ("pleasure"). He introduces himself to me as Paddy.

"Well tell me, Paddy, will that man take me out to MacDara?"

He squints. "That man will not, no more contrary man could you find in all the parish. But Billie will, he'll be here this afternoon sometime, he'll gladly take ye for the company, and maybe a shilling for his petrol."

"Is the island worth seeing?"

"Oh it is, it is, there's fine grazing to be had on her. Not too many people come here anymore, and if they do it's on the saint's feast day. You know the old custom of the fishermen?"

"I do." Skippers of the old hookers used to circle the island diurnally, or sunwise, and dip their red sails in respect to the saint. There aren't any more hookers left, however, and the custom has pretty much died away.

"Well, they're going to revive it this afternoon and tomorrow," my man tells me. "The Tourist Board people have gathered up eight hookers, the last in the world if you ask me, and they're going to film them going round the island, dropping sails and so on."

"Whatever for?"

"Oh, a propaganda film of some sort, for the tourists in America. You know, come to Ireland of the Welcomes, look at the silly, primitive things we still do here, that sort of thing. They don't tell them hookers have all but disappeared.

"My father, I'll tell ye, he ran a goods and provisions shop out of our house for years and years, and all the hookers came to buy supplies here, that they'd go off and sell to the islanders. Ah, there were grand numbers of people living offshore in them days, and the hookers were their merchants. They'd bring them tea and food and coal and paraffin and whatever. There's no one left anymore out there; it's a lonesome place now, the old islands. There's nothing left, there's no surviving. The crowd here in An Mas is all gone too, mostly to Boston, and not a person in it had anything but the Irish when they left. I've heard there are parts of Boston now that all you can hear on the streets is Irish."

I let that one pass. "How's the state of Irish here?"

"Ah, the young crowd won't have a thing to do with Irish now. They view it as a dead language; you cannot go anywhere with it or do anything with it. They look at the telly and pick up their bad English there and never speak the Irish at home anymore, the shame of it there for you to see."

"What about their parents?"

"They don't care either."

"What about your kids?"

"I have no kids. I'm not married and, as they say, not living either."

MacDara's church

Billie comes by in an hour; he'll be glad to drop me off while he checks his lobster pots. We motor out into choppy water, he tosses me a soup can and I start to bail. His little boat is so corroded with salt and bait fish that my hands reek of brine from just touching the gunnel. In about twenty minutes I hop out onto the strand of Saint MacDara's Island, smelling like some castaway who's been out to sea for several years without respite. Billie shouts over to me to say hello to the hermit.

The island is small, sublime, stunning. The church is a perfect example of eighth- or ninth-century Celtic construction, small, but very high gabled, surrounded by several cross slabs with incised carvings. Aside from sheep, no one is here, but from the looks of things that will change. I can see a flotilla of small craft beating down along the coast from the direction of Galway City. I also notice helicopters flying about. Time to go.

Billie is bobbing up and down in his curragh, hauling up big cages and, by the looks of it, not taking anything out of them. In about three hours he comes back to pick me up. His catch, typically miserable, is four lobsters and five crabs. "I just do this to pass the time," he remarks. "There's not a lobster left in Galway Bay."

"What did you mean, by the way, to say hello to the hermit?"

"Ah, that was a joke, Jimmy, but I thought you might see his ghost."

"Whose ghost?"

"The hermit's, the lad who was out here two, maybe three years ago now. He was a young lad, really, I took him out, it was winter, February or March, and I thought he just wanted to stay the afternoon like you, but no, he says don't come back for him. I couldn't believe it for sure, so I came back, but he wouldn't come aboard, he said to go away. He brought nothing with him, he had no food, no bedroll, no cooking stuff, only a heavy jacket. He must have lived on winkles, barnacles, and fishermen sometimes dropped a cake on the shore. He ate that and whatever else God gave him. He slept in the old church, on the dirt floor, and you know how bad that must have been. Och, he was a crazy man. So after a week one of the women on shore called the police and they sent a sergeant out to see if he was right in the head. The sergeant said the young lad told him he was fine and to leave him be.

"He stayed out there forty days and forty nights, in the winter, then he left. 'Twas some great sin surely that drove him out there, and redemption that drove him back."

An Mas, as we return, is now a riot of activity, an invasion from Dublin. Tractor trailers full of movie cameras, lights, tripods, generators, and a flood of production assistants with walkie-talkies have taken over the entire hamlet. Gangs of muscular men with earrings, beards, tattoos, and a steady barrage of foul-mouthed language haul equipment about helter-skelter. Chez Simone Catering has set up a kitchen, surely the best food An Mas has ever seen in four thousand years of human habitation. The hookers parade in front of the harbor, heading for Saint MacDara Island, and Paddy joins me in staring out to sea.

"I suppose I should be thrilled," I blurt out, "watching all these old timers sailing down the bay, but I'm not."

"And why should you be?" he nods. "It's all a fake."

21

Loca Sancta

oday is Wednesday. Last night Féichín had told me that we could go to Ardoileán on Friday, weather permitting, because Thursday was booked. He was taking a Board of Works crew, some of his friends, and the old parish priest on a cruise to some of the farther offshore islands on his trawler. "Official business," he called it.

"What's that mean?"

Féichín has a reputation. He considers himself not only an expert on these islands, but their guardian as well, and the Board of Works people are coming at his behest to look at monastic sites that he deems worthy of state protection. He won't take just any riffraff out when he visits such special places, hence the priest. I am pretty disappointed—it's not everyday I'm dismissed as riffraff—but I can accept it.

No moon tonight. I stand by the car and look west into darkness the consistency of ink. There isn't a light to be seen anywhere out to sea, except the flashing beacon of Slyne Head, about eleven miles south of us. I hear Féichín's door open and see him walk out. "You're still here then. I knew I didn't hear your car."

"I'm going, I'm going."

"Not at all," he laughs, "but tell me, can you keep a secret?"

"An American secret or an Irish one?"

He laughs again, "You know the difference then."

"I do. An Irish secret is something you tell one person at a time, an American secret is the real thing. You take it to the grave."

"Meet me at the quay at eight in the morning. You're welcome to come along."

Thursday is my hors d'oeuvre to Friday. The god of weather has granted us a perfect day, the sun shining, the sea a deep blue, the heathery mountains of Connemara a subtle blend of greens and browns, a battalion of heavy white clouds streaming eastward. We motor on out to open water, passing first Ardoileán, a great hulk of an island that reminds me of a battleship, then Inishshark, Inishbofin, and Inishturk, where we stop for a half hour. This isolated bastion is home to about sixty people, all struggling to survive, because Inishturk is not a tourist destination. No ancient remains to speak of, no picturesque fishing village, no association with famous literati like Yeats or Synge. It's a rough-hewn place, primitive and stark. The priest, retired from a lifetime of missionary endeavor in Nigeria, visits the local church. An old, gnarled man guides us to the door, which he opens, cap in hand. "Go in and see God, and say a prayer for me." We do both.

Motoring off again, we approach our goal, the name of which eludes me (a lie, of course, but I have a promise to keep). The ocean is dead calm; Féichín anchors the trawler and ferries us in with his curragh. The priest slips on a wet rock and almost goes over, but we collectively manage his safe debarkation. Climbing up from the shore we wade through sea grass and then pasturage until we come to a brow in the hill. Prepared now, we step back in time, into the desert.

I have seen many churches in Ireland, visited all the great abbeys, priories, and monasteries, but I have never seen anything like this. A small roofless oratory sits in the hollow of the meadow, surrounded by a small cashel, or wall, of dry, unmortared stone. Clearly, from the decorated slabs within this enclosure, graves of hermits and monks lie beneath. A circuit of station crosses, many among the finest of their kind, lie on the perimeter, a complete set of fourteen. "In the modern Church," according to the priest, "you sometimes had a fifteenth station added, Saint Helena finding the True Cross. You have to have a happy ending after all." As we go from slab to slab the quality of decoration staggers us all, particularly the Board of Works people. They know this is special.

One particular cross slab is immense, well over five feet high, and it stands on a small projection or hillock that overlooks the tiny complex,

Incised cross, offshore island, County Galway

as well as affording immense views to both the Twelve Bens and the open Atlantic beyond. I am taken by how fresh and new everything looks; if you closed your eyes you could see the monks of seventh-century Ireland doing their rounds or going about the day's business of work and prayer, prayer and work. This is a genuine time warp.

The priest says very little. Of all the people here I would have expected him to be the most excited. But perhaps a long life of dealing himself with spiritual certitude has immunized him from the excess of emotion that we all feel. A mind reader, he knows what I'm thinking. "There's nothing here I don't know already," he says.

After everyone has snapped away their rolls of film, and the Board of Works crew have taken some rough measures, we tramp the island. Féichín has an old map, and we find the Saint's Well on the other side, first crossing row upon row of nineteenth-century potato beds. The water tastes slightly brackish, but it is definitely fresh; it wouldn't take much to clean out and restore to purity. One of the board fellows picks up a decorative piece of driftwood, and the priest shows fire. "Take nothing from the island!" he commands, and the wood is dropped. Returning after our circuit to the hermitage, the priest says a prayer at one of the crosses. "You," he says in my direction, "do you know what a saint is?"

"A holy man, father, one who follows the Way of the Cross."

"Yes, but he's more than that. Saints were generous men, the best of them shared the secret. They let the light in."

I mentally disagree with this. Many hermits were willful, crotchety, disagreeable people who had one thing only in mind, their own salvation. "Do not lose yourself in order to save another," says an old maxim of the desert fathers. I keep that to myself.

As we motor back to Claddaghduff, a baroque sunset blinds our vision. We have a good two hours to go when night descends. According to Féichín, we have covered almost seventy nautical miles today. It starts getting cold, then really cold; soon we are all shivering on the open deck. Like every other Irish fishing boat I've ever been on, there are no running lights on board, and the navigational equipment, what there is of it, is either broken or strictly for show. We travel in complete darkness. Aside from staggered blinks from the lighthouse at Slyne Head, there are no signs that I can see to guide us. I ask Féichín how he plans to get us safely ashore. "It's like the road home, I know it in here," he says tapping his head. For some reason, I believe in him completely.

22

The Holy Land

I go to mass the next morning. Being a weekday, there are only five of us in attendance, four old women and me. The priest comes out slowly, he says the mass in a thoroughly unhurried fashion, lingering at all the right places. Practice, in this case, makes perfect. The epistle has a perfect line that summons the Catholic right out of me in a prideful way: "And Jesus said, 'I know my flock, and my flock knows me.'" The only aesthetic discord here is the microphone on the altar. As the priest drinks the Blood of Christ, we hear every rasping gurgle.

"Are you off to America, then?" he asks me afterward.

"Tomorrow. Today I'm going there." Ardoileán.

"I've not been. I'm too old, Féichín says, to manage the landing. I'm too old to manage much of anything, really. But you're right to go there. That's the last of old Ireland."

Féichín meets me at the crumbling quay again, we set off in his battered curragh. The day is overcast, the seas a bit on the dirty side. I'm getting wet.

Féichín has a busy day's work ahead. He plans to leave me on Ardoileán and will return at dusk. This suits me perfectly, the whole place to myself.

We reach Ardoileán in about forty minutes. There is no natural landing place here, so he angles the curragh carefully into a fissure between some high cliffs. Seals, detested by all fishermen, raise their heads in the little cove. "There's your welcome then," says Féichín.

I clumsily reach for some sort of handhold on the rock, but there's nary a one. "Watch yourself now," warns Féichín, just as a roller rushes in. The curragh jumps several feet up against the rock, lurching me upward, and then falls several feet back, leaving me hanging. I pull up my legs, a lucky reflex, because the heavy curragh bobs up again a few seconds later in the foamy turmoil of waves surging back and forth, and might have knocked me in the water or broken my feet. Féichín gives me a complimentary smile, not so bad for a fat old man. He'll see me later, I scramble ashore.

I start climbing. Ardoileán is called "High," quite obviously, because its fertile plateau is reached only after several dozen meters of rough ascent. When I get to the top a standing stone with incised cross meets me.

I purposely brought no map with me, and I purposely read nothing about Ardoileán before my trip. Only a single monograph on this place has been written in recent times, and it is undoubtedly full of interesting detail, but although I have it in my duffel bag, I will not study it yet. That means I may miss something, but I don't care. I want Ardoileán to unfold itself to me. I don't wish to discover it like some explorer to the New World. This is the Old World, after all, there's nothing new here.

I wander the eastern end first, several small fields of coarse pasture and plenty of rabbit skeletons. Rabbits have been the bane of these offshore islands, especially now that no one lives here to hunt them and keep the population under control. They dig and tunnel, undermine the soil, often damaging the old ruins still standing. A plague of some sort periodically ravages these communities, as it may be doing now, given the abundance of carcasses that lie scattered about. This is a Beatrix Potter nightmare.

I turn around and head for even higher elevation, toward the western edge of the island, often generically nicknamed on places like this, "the nearest parish to America." Some landlord from the turn of the century tried to set up a mining operation here, looking for God knows what, and the little hut he built for his workmen contains stonework jobbed from the ancient monastery further up. Such casual spoliation amazes me.

Wind blowing harder, seabirds swirling around this stranger's head, I continue up a narrow ravine. To my right I see another carved stone, then steps leading down into the ground—the monastic well. A shower breaks overhead, I nestle under a stone outcropping. In a minute it's teeming, visibility down to just a few feet. Like Knight Owen at Saint Patrick's Purgatory, I am suddenly overwhelmed with fatigue and nod off. It's hard to tell how long I sleep, ten minutes, an hour? No dreams or visions, however, and my right leg, which I had straightened involuntarily during my nap, is soaked from the thigh down. I eat a candy bar, not exactly the appropriate, salted fare of a saint, and start climbing again. A few more yards to the head of this pathway.

A *termonn*, or sanctuary cross, signals the monastic precinct, the center of which is plainly visible down in an exposed hollow next to a bog tarn, or tiny lake. I can see the ruins of beehive *clocháns*, an oratory, the cashel, and many standing stones. Archaeologists have done some digging here; they uncovered four graves and there are certainly more. They want to remove these bones to mainland laboratories to investigate for ages, general health, diet, DNA, and so forth. Traditionalists are deeply upset over this, as well as with talk about the removal of crosses and decorated slabs to the alleged security of the mainland.

In former times, the locals usually twisted their caps in their hands and just rolled over when academics or officious government people came to the outback to take away whatever artifacts they wanted. When Inishmurray was deserted in 1948, museum officials simply took the fourteenth-century wooden statue of the patron, Saint Muirdeach, that islanders had worshiped for several centuries, to a Dublin storeroom. In return they left a plastic reproduction. It doesn't work that way these days. There will be a fight about taking anything away from Ardoileán.

The day has turned steel gray. The sky is gray, the water is gray, the wind feels gray. Sunlight, also gray, breaks through some of the overcast and emblazons long strips of ocean at my feet below, ocean that stretches on forever to an unobstructed horizon. The water so illuminated twinkles like a prism. There is no landscape in the world as beautiful as this.

I walk down and explore the monastery. I look for a message in its ruins, something profound I can personalize. But as the priest said yesterday, you can take nothing from the island. He meant souvenirs or mementos, but I think the message is plainer. I'm not a hermit, I'm not a monk, I'm not even a faithful Catholic. I wouldn't have the discipline to stay here; it's not for me. Oh, maybe a week, perhaps a month, but

Ardoileán

unlike that crazy boy on MacDara, the boatman will be coming back
for me, and thank heavens for that. Suddenly depressed, I realize the
whole experience of Ardoileán involves worthiness. The saints had it,
that blind faith and certainty. Many people trivialize their strength by
calling it superstition, but that misses the point by a very wide margin.
They looked inward, I look outward. I may certainly claim an interest
in the place, may congratulate myself on having the resolution to come,
as many fainthearted people would not, and I may be one of the few
people around to appreciate what is here, but that doesn't mean I be-
long.

Walking around the pond, I come to a curious sight: a rectangular
rock with a neatly carved hole in the middle; sitting in the hole, a rough
piece of stone shaped like a headless cross, in other words a capital T. I
take the stone with both hands—it's heavy—and pull it out of its
holder, and intuitively I know what it is . . . a tool of mortification.

Old Saints' Lives are full of stories depicting monks in cross vigils,
where they stood or kneeled with their arms outstretched as though
nailed in crucifixion. They often stood this way for hours, sometimes in

streams or wells, up to their necks in cold water, sometimes for so long that birds, it was written, built their nests in the open palms of the monk. This cross I envision in just such a fashion, with monks, on their rounds, approaching the station, perhaps on their knees, then stretching their arms to hold this cross outward for who knows how long a period of time. One can imagine, taken to extremes, that this could be a very wearying, even painful exercise.

I take the cross and put it on my shoulder. I do not mean to parody the old monks, but I see something good for me here. I tramp off to a *termonn* cross, look for another and head for it. I circle the entire perimeter of the monastic precinct. I make a very hard effort to clear my brain of the accumulated rubbish of Guinness, candy bars, marital strain, writerly complaints, intellectual ostentation, and personal esteem, the "burning city of vanity." I try to be a blank, I concentrate on the wind, the wet, the heavy rustle of long reeds bending backward to and fro in formless turmoil. I say a special prayer, the only one I can remember from the many I've read or used in my books, to the memory of my dead parents, especially my mother, an O'Brien, and more Irish than she ever cared to admit. Then I replace the cross in its socket and leave this place behind. I have come, and more important, gone. A pilgrim, my feet "cymbal shod," it's time now to find my way back.

◆

I pull into Moyode Demesne around 9 P.M. that evening. My ride will pick me up at 5:50 next morning for the trip to Shannon. I stop first at the gate cottage to say good-bye to Seamus and Nancy Taylor. Nancy has a porter cake for me to take to Boston, full of currents, raisins, orange peel, Guinness, and heavy as a brick. "That's the last of those for ye, Jim."

"What?"

"I'm giving up the baking. These children of mine have had the last of me slaving at the stove. They can go to the market and buy what they want; it's just as good as what I can do." I'm appalled. No more soda bread, no more apple tarts, no more spotted dick? Store-bought bakery goods as opposed to home cooking?

"I'm finished with all that, Jim. And don't ye complain about it, the end of old tradition and all that, I'll not hear those words from you in my house." She pauses, knowing that despite the banter, I'm a disappointed man. "Will we still be friends, then, Jim? Will you still stop and visit?"

"As long as you've roses to share, dahlias to clip, and tea to serve, I'll be here, Nancy."

I go on to Marie and Alphonsus. Their dogs go crazy, they nip my heels, the TV is on, kids racing all over the place, but what do I care? These are my friends; this is my small Irish world, the place I can hide away from everything that spoils the country beyond the confines of these few dozen acres. By the time ruination finds its way into Moyode Demesne, I'll be dead and gone, I hope. If I've learned anything from the miles I've traveled, it's to enjoy what you still have when and where you can. From the top of Moyode Castle I'll maintain my vigilant and cynical watch, but as the Dolphins who built this place took as their motto, *Nihil in Vita Firmum*, "Nothing in Life is Permanent." Everything else is beyond my control.

My last stop is old Frank's. I walk over the rubble of what used to be the main foyer of Moyode House. I cross the back stable yard and pull in my paunch to pass through a stile to the old dairy. And there I see, and hear, an Ireland I hope will never die but I know to be doomed.

Frank's door, as usual, is open. The man himself, well over eighty, sits in the tiny parlor where years ago the cans of milk were stored, his face bright pink, reflecting now the luminescence of open flames in the ancient, sooted fireplace. A traditional, mournful tune, accordion and fiddle, plays from the enormous wireless set that stands out of sight around the corner. Frank is perfectly still, holding a cigarette, staring at the glowing peat, intent to the strains of this familiar lament as old as time. I kick a pebble to make my presence known. "Jim, for the love of God, ye came unknown to me, sit ye by the fire, ye must be damp, we've been lonesome for ye." He gets up and pours us both a thimble of Irish. It tastes like fire going down. Though I'm flying away tomorrow, it's good to be home.

Acknowledgments

To Alix Cochran, who laughed out loud at all the right places.

To Dana Blennerhassett, who swept the castle clean while I took a nap.

To Beth, who told me I'd written a tear jerker.

To James, for telling me to lighten up.

To Diarmuid, for the Irish.

To Féichín, for taking me out.

To those who traveled on the Big Yellow Tub, for putting up with me in mostly good humor.